Latin American
STREET FOOD

Latin American STREET FOOD

THE BEST FLAVORS OF Markets, Beaches, &
Roadside Stands from Mexico to Argentina

Sandra A. Gutierrez

The University of North Carolina Press CHAPEL HILL

Designed by Kim Bryant and set in Merlo and Museo types by Rebecca Evans.
Photographs by Fred Thompson unless otherwise credited on page 335. Props
and food styling by Sandra A. Gutierrez and Fred Thompson. Set design by
Kim Bryant. The paper in this book meets the guidelines for permanence and
durability of the Committee on Production Guidelines for Book Longevity of
the Council on Library Resources. The University of North Carolina Press has
been a member of the Green Press Initiative since 2003.

Some of the recipes in this book include raw seafood or shellfish, which, consumed raw, can pose a risk from bacteria that are killed by proper cooking and
should not be consumed by pregnant women, infants, small children, the elderly, or people with autoimmune conditions. Please purchase all ingredients
from trusted sources and read and follow recipe instructions carefully. The
author and publisher disclaim liability for illness or injury that may be suffered
while cooking and consuming foods described in this book.

Library of Congress Cataloging-in-Publication Data
Gutierrez, Sandra A.
Latin American street food : the best flavors of markets, beaches, and roadside
stands from Mexico to Argentina / Sandra A. Gutierrez.
pages cm
Includes bibliographical references and index.
ISBN 978-1-4696-0870-9 (cloth : alk. paper)
1. Cooking, Latin American. 2. Street food—Latin America. I. Title.
TX716.A1G884 2013
641.598—dc23   2013008285

17 16 15   5 4

To all of the street food vendors
*who get up each morning and trek to their outdoor kitchens
so they can feed the world*

Contents

Acknowledgments

The writer's journey can sometimes be a lonely one, but I am lucky to have a slate of wonderful folks who have cheered, helped, and joined me on mine. It has been such a joy to be able to work with everyone at the University of North Carolina Press again, especially with editor, wordsmith, and dear friend Elaine Maisner. I'm so indebted to her for her careful nurturing of my writer's voice, enthusiastic support for the theme of this book, and tremendous creative force. I'm also honored to work with and owe so much to publicists Gina Mahalek and Jennifer Hergenroeder, for their expertise and dedication.

Thanks also to Dino Battista, Michael Donatelli, and their entire team. Special thanks to David Perry—to whom I owe plenty of acarajés—for your enthusiasm, support, and friendship. Editors protect us writers from ourselves, and I'm indebted to copyeditor Mary Caviness for having my back in this project and for helping me polish my words.

An eye for detail is key to a beautiful cookbook, and my profound gratitude goes to Kim Bryant, the amazingly creative design director for UNC Press for expertly designing a book that captures the fun that this subject matter warrants. Photographs are an important part of this book, and my deep appreciation goes to Fred Thompson, my colleague and good friend, who translated a whole world of street foods into vibrant photographs. Working with both Kim and Fred was a highlight of this project. Thanks also to Kyle Wilkerson for his help. Photo shoots mean long days of planning, shopping, prepping, cooking, and washing, and I wish to thank my friends Tracey Shea, Sally Fry Scruggs, and Denise Noonan for their invaluable help and generosity of time and for hours of camaraderie that made these days go by quickly.

An agent is an author's best advocate, and mine happens to be an amazing one, as well as a treasured friend and a valued mentor. Thank you, Lisa Ekus, for recognizing the epiphany it was when I came up with the idea to write this book years ago in Portland, Oregon. My deepest thanks also to Sally Ekus. She fell in love with this subject matter as hard as I did and sold my proposal with indomitable enthusiasm and incredible speed. I owe much gratitude to you both, and to the entire team at The Lisa Ekus Group.

A street sign for ceviches, smoothies, and sandwiches.

For almost three decades, my husband, Luis, has provided me the opportunity to do what I love, given me a safe place to grow, and embraced me with his staunch support of my work. His generosity of heart and encouragement move me. We are blessed with two amazing daughters. Alessandra tasted each and every recipe with joy in her heart that kept me smiling. Niccolle was my cheerleader throughout this project as she patiently and meticulously helped to measure and weigh ingredients and transcribe and edit recipes during months of recipe-testing. I love you all so much.

I owe special thanks to my friends Norman Van Aken and Nancie McDermott, who recommended the publication of this book and gave it an enthusiastic thumbs up—your friendship and mentorship mean the world to me, and I'm indebted to both of you for your kindness and for inspiring me to continue to write about what I love.

Great recipe testers are hard to come by, and my sincere gratitude goes to my dear friend and recipe tester extraordinaire, Liz Tarpy, for her devotion to exactitude. I wish to thank my colleagues and friends Elissa Altman, Jean Anderson, Virginia Willis, Cheryl Sternman-Rule, Jill O'Connor, Kim O'Donnell, Tara Mataraza Desmond, and Robin Asbell for the advice, the laughter, and the friendship that has enriched my life.

Many thanks to my Latin American friends and relatives who so generously shared insight into the modern street food scene of their countries, or who offered corroboration as I developed many of the recipes in this book: Irene de Alfaro, Maria Esther "Tey" de Alfaro, Victor Quesada, Luisa Fernanda Ríos, Vivian S. de Solís, Georgina Zúñiga, Irma Barco, and Maria del Pilar S. de Fernandez, and to my Facebook friends around Latin America who answered my queries every time I had a question. Special gratitude goes to my sweet friends Elena and Francisco Fumagalli for years of friendship and for sharing their special family recipe with me.

A teacher is only as good as her students, and mine are fabulous folks who keep on inspiring me to learn more each day. My most sincere thanks go to all of the booksellers and culinary directors of cooking schools who have so kindly welcomed me so I can continue to spread the gospel of Latin American food.

I thank God infinitely for blessings received.

Latin American
STREET FOOD

A Peruvian schoolgirl waits for her orange juice.

ASOC. AMEDIL PERU
DISCAPACITADOS

Construyendo

MUNICIPALIDAD D

Introduction

My first memory of street food involves eating hot, sweet churros directly from a paper bag while strolling alongside my mother as she ran her errands through the streets of downtown Guatemala City, known as El Centro. I distinctly remember the grainy texture of the sugar surrounding the curls of fried dough, how my sticky fingers felt right before I licked the sweet goodness away every now and again, and how the crispy exterior of the pastry gave way to a spongy softness whenever my teeth sank into it. I can't recall what errands got completed that day, but the taste of hot, sugary fried dough is etched clearly in my mind.

I have many such fond memories: the first time I ate a hot dog with sauerkraut and avocados wrapped in a soft flour tortilla; or the millionth time I stood in line waiting for my turn to savor a cream-laden ear of corn on the cob, topped with salty cheese and spicy chiles. I remember racing with schoolmates to see who could buy the first bag of citrusy mango salad from the street vendor around the corner, as clearly as I do competing with my brothers for the slice of orange that had the most *pepitoria* (pumpkin seed powder) sprinkled on top. The memories are many, and the feeling elicited by them is always the same one: nostalgia for moments of pure joy.

There is much to love about the festival-like atmosphere that goes along with eating delicious food *al fresco* on a sidewalk, surrounded by other food lovers. Standing in line at a food truck or waiting to make a decision about what to order from the menus of food stands that boast today's specials doesn't get old. Here in the United States, street food is a relatively new phenomenon, but for millions of people in other countries, it's always been a way of life. In streets all over the world, each day offers flavorful, colorful, and texturally explosive dishes that restore the gastronomic spirit one bite at a time. In Latin America, the scope of street food offerings is enormous. This book will give you a good glimpse of what you would find if you were to eat your way along Latin American streets.

What people see when they think of street food can differ from person to person and from place to place. Some picture a crispy taco, deliciously filled with spicy chicken and topped with refreshingly addictive tomatillo sauce; for others, an image of freshly sliced raw fruit simply sprinkled with spiced-up salt comes to mind. But no matter how one imagines street food, it always evokes a celebratory feeling.

Street food's popularity continues to grow in cities all across the world. From Sydney to Santiago, from Lima to Bangkok, street food enlivens busy cities and large metropolises. Here in the United States, cities like Portland, San Francisco, Los Angeles, Chicago, Miami, Austin, and Manhattan are at the vanguard of what has now become a trendy movement. In the last few years, a food truck revolution has taken smaller cities and towns across America by storm.

These days, foods like tacos, *arepas*, *pupusas*, and *tlayudas* garner tweet-ups and Facebook posts as food truck owners announce their daily locations over social networks. Every day, loyal patrons are picking up e-mails and tweets, creating fan pages, and spreading the word so that hungry new followers can dash out and grab a quick, handcrafted meal from the latest mobile locations. Street food gives an entirely new meaning to the words "fast food." With this book, you can prepare delicious Latin favorites in your own kitchen and serve them up at your own family table.

A POPULAR AFFAIR

Why is street food so popular today? To begin with, it's inexpensive, which, given today's economy, is very attractive regardless of one's financial situation. Add to this that it's also fast and flavorful, and you've got a winning combination. There is no question that street food is hip, convenient, informal, and entertaining. In my opinion, though, the biggest reason that people can't get enough of street food is that it's *fun*.

Not surprisingly, food enthusiasts all over the country are foregoing meals packed in paper bags or lunch boxes and replacing them with street food offerings. More and more foodies are choosing to escape their workplaces—albeit just for a few minutes—to grab a flavor-packed, Latin American lunch out on the street at taco trucks, churros kiosks, and empanada stalls. And the enthusiasm has not been lost on the owners of the hot dog stands that have long been fixtures on city street corners. Today, they offer the classic toppings like chili and onions alongside jalapeños and *chimichurri*.

A TASTE OF HISTORY

For centuries in the more than twenty countries that make up the Latin American territories, street foods have been a way of life for millions of people who depend on inexpensive and flavorful meals to get through their daily routines.

Records date street food in Latin America back to colonial times (the 1600s to the 1800s), but from earlier writings by travelers, we know that tortillas and other masa-based foods were already sold in Aztec markets by the time Spanish conquistadors arrived in Mexico. In her book *A Taste of Latin America: Recipes and Stories*, Elisabeth Lambert Ortiz recounts how Bernal Diaz del Castillo, a Spanish captain during La Conquista and author of *La Verdadera Historia de la Conquista de la Nueva España* (*The True History of the Conquest of New Spain*) described the food sold in the outdoor markets of Mexico City, including tomatoes, corn, and chiles. And in his well-known work *Tradiciones Peruanas*, published in 1883, author Ricardo Palma described the street food found in Lima at that time and included a careful timeline outlining what kinds of foods were likely to be served depending on the time of day. For instance, tamales were sold in the midmorning and early evening hours and *empanadas de picadillo* were sold at noon. He also mentions other foods sold on the streets at the time, including cookies, ice cream, beans, rice, kabobs, peanuts, and candies known as *turrones*.

Toward the middle of the twentieth century, street food's popularity surged in Latin America. What was once a few food vendors here and there—mostly catering to laborers, construction workers, and hungry patrons visiting religious festivals—became a tsunami wave that today provides breakfast, lunch, and dinner—and midmorning and late-night snacks in between—to millions of customers.

Food has always been an integral aspect of society in Latin America, where gathering to share meals with friends and family is still a daily ritual. Modern-day Latin American cities hustle and bustle with great activity as people across the social strata go to work each day. In the past hundred years, Latin metropolitan areas have grown exponentially, becoming heavily urbanized. A direct result was the mind-boggling traffic that began to make it hard to get from one place to another efficiently, no matter how short the distance. More and more people joined the workforce—including scores of women—and many were finally able to afford a car or two, which added to the cities' congestion. Today, most workers in Latin America don't have time to go home for lunch as they used to when I was a little girl growing up in Guatemala. Street food, then, offers a good option in lieu of a home-cooked meal.

As late as the 1970s, businesses, government offices, banks, and schools in many Latin American countries (such as Guatemala, where I grew up) shut down for a two-hour period every day so that most everyone could go home to a warm meal around a family table—a practice dating back centuries. I have clear recollections of riding the bus to school in the morning, climbing back on to head back home for lunch in the afternoon, riding it back to school, and once again riding it back home in the evening. This coming and going, back and forth, made for long days that started before dawn and ended near dusk.

By the time I was ten years old, my school was already serving lunches, and school hours had been shortened. Traffic made it impossible for us to go home for lunch on the bus, and the subsequent gasoline shortages that hit the world in that era also made public transportation prices soar. People had to stretch their money, and busier times demanded shorter commutes and new options. This was not lost on savvy food vendors, who soon began setting up mobile businesses near schools and universities that were not equipped with cafeterias. Vendors also began to set up food stations outside office buildings, offering up-and-coming office

workers meals that were quicker and less expensive than those served in cafés and sit-down eateries.

Though urban growth occurred at different times throughout the Latin continent, the same thing happened in every major Latin American metropolis, and as cities burgeoned and traffic swelled, food vendors expanded their businesses as well, giving patrons new alternatives to long commutes. The restaurant business soared to new heights, but not everyone could afford the high prices. On the streets, the food was good, the was service prompt, and the custom to tip was forgone.

Today, as fixtures in Latin American city life, street food vendors not only offer a much-needed service to the public; they also provide a place for impromptu social gatherings, an opportunity for people to socialize, where they can exchange gossip, learn of new job opportunities, network, or organize politically. In Latin America, a food stand takes the place of the proverbial water cooler.

NUANCES AND DEFINITIONS

When people in the United States think of street food, most envision the trucks that are showing up on the streets as of late, what Latin Americans refer to as *carritos*. These are the vehicles that feature tacos, sandwiches, salads, and stews that drive to construction sites and park wherever prime space can be found during the lunch hour, when workers look for a quick bite to eat.

In Latin America, however, street food can come from many different places: from makeshift kitchens and market stalls called *puestos*; from carts or *carretillas*; from stand-alone kiosks that go by various names, like *ranchos*, *casetas*, or *casitas*; or from stands set up on city streets, whether on a busy corner or in a quiet alley. Street food can also be food served in rustic outdoor kitchens in front of small houses in tiny villages; sold on the side of a dirt road; provided on tables set up next to bustling bus stations; sold from take-out counters; and peddled by walking vendors through the streets or on crowded beachfronts.

Whether you are visiting Quito, Buenos Aires, Managua, Rio de Janeiro, or Bogota, you will find food vendors at kiosks, trucks, and stands brimming with edible offerings of all kinds at the exits of stadiums during sports events, in parks, in city markets, near churches, and near the entrances of libraries, museums, schools, and universities.

Food vendors are also a fixture at religious festivals, for example during Easter Week, when Catholic processions through the streets of Antigua, Guatemala, highlighted by giant floats carrying religious depictions of Christ's Calvary, attract thousands of hungry celebrants each year.

The *melcochas* (taffies), *algodones* (cotton candy), *rosarios* (sugar rosaries), and *cocadas* (coconut macaroons) you'll eat at an outdoor festival or during a *feria* (fair) are also common street foods, as are the innumerable permutations of *batidos* (fruit smoothies), *bombones* (candy confections), and *croquetas* (fritters) that you can purchase from food posts during carnivals and *kermeses* (school festivals).

Street food in Latin America can mean a mango, sliced and dusted with ground chile, that you eat while strolling through a market in Guatemala, or it can mean a carefully crafted sweet potato doughnut bought in the central plaza of a town in Chile. It can be citrus-marinated meat threaded on a stick that you can purchase as you exit a soccer game in Panama, or it can be a black-eyed pea fritter that you can grab for lunch on a busy street corner in Brazil. It can be corn, stewed and topped with cream and chile served near a bus station in Mexico, and it can be a yuca and pork rind salad served at beaches on the coast of Nicaragua.

In Latin America, if you can't go out into the streets to get your food, the street food will come to you. Such is the case with the tortillas delivered to people's homes by *tortilleras* who carry them in large baskets on top of their heads, or the sweet desserts on makeshift carts that men push through the streets of Central America, yelling "Corbatas!" (which literally means "men's neckties" but also refers to the fried dough slathered with honey). It's also the case with the colorful candy cones (*pirulís* or *chupetes*) sold to children all over Latin America, and the ice cream that arrives in neighborhoods each day in trucks that beckon customers with calliope music to enjoy beguilingly frozen flavors.

Most of us think of street food as fast food, and in a way, it is. However, some distinctions must be made. Fast food as we know it in this country is the highly processed stuff that's made on assembly lines and that we eat because it's convenient. It's food that is quickly assembled but that sacrifices craftsmanship in the name of speed. In other words, it has no soul. In contrast, a vast majority of the dishes you'll find on the streets of Latin America are made with fresh ingredients and have been prepared as lovingly and with as much attention as those made in the kitchens of the finest four-star restaurants.

A movable farmers' market in Trinidad, Cuba.

(opposite, from top) A hard-working vendor sells gastronomic creations in Trinidad, Cuba.

A food vendor selling steamed corn stops to talk on Ipanema Beach in Brazil.

PRIDE AND PERCEPTION

It is true that as Latin American countries become more developed, fast food restaurants have permeated the scene, but most of the street food still remains true to its handcrafted tradition. For the most part, street foods are not standardized or homogeneous; most are prepared by individuals or small business owners—many of whom still use their own recipes, most of which have been passed down through the generations.

Food vendors' livelihoods depend on their ability to sell quality products so that, in turn, they can feed their own families. On the streets, word of mouth can build or destroy a business, so the competition is fierce. There is always an incentive to produce the best food possible. Vendors in close proximity who offer the same dish vie for the same customers, which inspires them to give recipes their own spin. Some vendors develop a reputation for their outstanding food, so it's not rare for people to walk more than one or two more blocks in order to get to the best empanada or sope stand. On the streets, competitors don't win customers by packaging little toys in pretty bags; they do so solely based on flavor and quality of their offerings.

NOT ONE BUT MANY

From Mexico all the way to the Patagonia, each Latin American country has developed its own special kind of street food using local ingredients. That's what makes Latin American street fare so exciting. There are over twenty different cuisines represented in Latin America, and each one boasts a wide array of foods that when put together offer a bounty of unique flavors.

The variety of street foods in Latin America begs comparison with that found on the streets of Asia, where you can eat for days without ever eating the same thing twice. Since Latin streets offer everything from sandwiches, refreshing salads, steamy stews, deep-fried morsels, and raw fish to sweet candies and cooling drinks, there is something for everyone.

Latin cuisines feature an explosion of fused flavors from all over the world that through time have resulted in some of the most colorful and appetizing dishes imaginable. If you wonder what real Latinos eat, head out to the streets. You'll discover the Italian roots of many Argentinean dishes, the African influences on the food of Brazil, the Asian intonations in the cuisine of Peru, and the many other world cultures that have shaped (and continue to shape) modern-day Latin American food.

The fact is, no two Latin American countries have identical cuisines. Each cuisine is a quilt made up of its own cultural blend. For example, Peruvian cuisine combines the culinary traditions of Asia, Africa, the Middle East, Spain, and the indigenous cultures of both ancient and present-day Peru. That's a lot of different culinary cultures! If you want to experience a true melting pot, eat on the streets of Latin America.

But Latin American street food also has a very local and even regional character. What a Mexican customer eats in Sinaloa, say, is not the same as what another will eat in Acapulco. And although you'll find similar dishes in a number of countries, each country will have its own variations that reflect the particular cultures represented in each place. For example, ceviches are prepared all over Latin America, but you'll find Japanese *Nikkei*-style ceviches—featuring a touch of soy sauce, ginger, garlic, and green onions—only on the streets of Peru, where Asian culinary influences dominate.

Even while the cuisines of some Latin American countries have been influenced by similar world cultures—as is the case with neighboring Venezuela and Colombia, which have African, Spanish, and some indigenous similarities—they manifest themselves differently in the regional street foods of each nation. As hard as you may try, you simply can't box Latin American cuisines together because each cuisine has its own characteristics.

Another intriguing aspect of the food sold on Latin American streets is that sometimes, even countries in completely different parts of the continent will share the same global culinary influences, but will have incorporated them in completely different ways. For instance, in the street food of both Mexico and Brazil you'll find Lebanese-inspired elements, but in Mexico, you'll find *tacos árabes*, while in Brazil, where you won't find tacos, you'll find spicy Lebanese meat-and-bulgur fritters known as *quibe*.

Even within the same cities, though, the flavors of similar dishes will vary from cart to cart, and from vendor to vendor. Think then of the profusion of flavors that are available on the streets! If you can count the number of towns, cities, and regions that make up each Latin American country, and then multiply that by the number of countries in Latin America, and again by the number of cooks who are constantly spinning off new recipe innovations, you can begin to understand the true scope of Latin street food—it's a virtual horn of plenty.

FUN ON THE STREETS WHERE EVERY DAY IS A PARTY

One of the best things about street food is that a lot of it is portable, making it easy to enjoy on the go without too much fanfare. Empanadas are a great example of moveable, handheld morsels; so are the icy-cold *paletas* (popsicles), the carefully threaded *chuzos* (kabobs), and bite-size croquetas found all over the Latin American street food menu. On the streets, even stews and soups are offered in take-away containers. In some countries, in lieu of disposable dishes, ingenious vendors wrap foods in banana leaves, corn husks, or brown paper.

Some street foods are messy to eat, which I think is part of the fun. (If you ask me, the messier they are, the better!) These are the kinds of food that demand just a bit more time for their proper enjoyment, and eating them standing up often requires a certain, let's say, *technique*. If you've ever eaten a Philly sandwich or a gyro hurriedly, while standing, you know what I mean. There is a particular way to stand so that you won't wear the delicious juices that invariably drip down your elbows each time you bite into one. The drill goes like this: you hold your arms straight out in front of you and then bend them at the elbows; bend over a bit, then bring your mouth toward the sandwich, or *elote*, or taco—not the other way around—and bite! See? On any given day in Latin America you'll see plenty of suited-up executives with their sleeves rolled back and their ties tucked into their shirts, standing in line, ready to tackle their favorite food.

Of course, at home, you can serve all of the recipes in this book without the sloppiness. Or do as I do: have plenty of napkins to go around. As long as you are having fun and enjoying your food, anything goes!

Another fun part of Latin American street foods is the vast assortment of toppings and condiments available to garnish them with: salsas, slaws, and side dishes are all there for the taking. I don't know about you, but I happen to love add-ons, and to me, nothing compares to a sandwich, or a hot dog, or a taco piled high with toppings. There is so much to add:

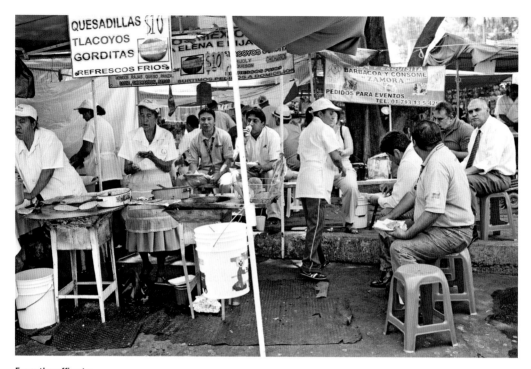

From the office to the street: a break for lunch on a Mexico City street.

a little bit of heat, a touch of tanginess, and a dollop of creaminess. The more I can pile up, the happier I am. Many of the dishes I've included here are ideal for serving buffet style or "bar style" so that all of the meal's components can be lined up on a table, making it easy for you and your family to relax and have a great time.

Get ready to assemble tacos to order, to top sandwiches Dagwood-style, and to dress *huaraches* as extravagantly as your palate desires. Equipped with this book, you will be able to throw street food parties any time you wish.

STRETCHING THE DOLLAR OR PESO OR QUETZAL OR BOLIVAR

Street foods are inarguably inexpensive. They're easy on the wallet when you buy them on the streets, and they're not expensive to prepare at home, either. What makes street food so affordable is that the basic ingredients used to craft them are inexpensive to begin with. Street offerings are simple, unassuming, and humble foods, but they pack a lot of flavor—as long as they're good quality and fresh. When paired with the

Introduction

best cooking techniques, fresh ingredients yield some of the most addictive and comforting dishes imaginable. On the streets of Latin America, vendors transform humble ingredients with able hands into tasty morsels every day. Whether it's pork cooked slowly for a *butifarra* sandwich, local fish sliced to order for a *tiradito*, or an avocado transformed into salsa, each ingredient is treated with respect and served with a sense of pride. And, thankfully, affordability has stayed part of the equation, and street foods allow everyday folks to eat wonderfully each day without breaking the bank. For the home cook, this makes cooking from this book an affordable option.

TASTING A KALEIDOSCOPE OF FLAVOR

Latin street foods are filled with fun contrasts, offering truly remarkable juxtapositions of flavors: salty, sour, sweet, and spicy. Others join items of different temperatures expertly, and still others offer a combination of textures—crunchy and creamy, smooth and chunky—in every bite. A tostada, for example, can be built on a crispy tortilla, topped with warm chicken and crunchy slaw, and finally drizzled with cold, velvety *crema*. Separately, these elements aren't very exciting on their own, but in combination, they make the palate sing!

Latin American street foods are also as colorful as Latin American people. There is a saying in Spanish that "food is first tasted by the eyes," but the other senses are also involved—whether it's the thunder of waves crashing in the background or horns honking on the streets; the aromas of sausages grilling or the essence of simmering stews; or the taste of a sour marinade or the flavor of sugar and spice. With the visual explosion of colors all occurring in a single dish, the flavors that collide on the streets of Latin America offer a gustatory quilt stitched together with infinite sensorial possibilities.

BRINGING THE STREETS INSIDE

For all of these reasons, I think street food makes great party food. As you'll see in the chapter "The Raw Bar," many of the recipes in this book can be made ahead of time and assembled quickly when it comes time to eat. I like to call street food "happy food," not only because it's so pretty to look at but also because it makes people happy to eat it.

In addition, Latin street food offers plenty of dishes that translate into everyday food. It's not intimidating food but familiar food. Given all of the subcultures present in Latin cuisines, there are many recipes that successfully cross cultural boundaries, helping to make it food that is relatable to any palate.

Take the hot dog, for example, which is perhaps the most recognizable street food in America, and you'll picture a frankfurter set in a bun, dressed with condiments. But imagine a hot dog the myriad ways you'll find it on the streets of Latin America: wrapped in yeasty bread and generously slathered with mashed avocado and mayonnaise, stuffed in a sweet bun and topped with strawlike fried potatoes and cheese, or nestled inside crusty bread simply dressed with herbed chimichurri. It is still the recognizable meat in a bun—but with a succulent twist each time.

Of course, there are many Latin street food recipes that did not make it into this book, mostly because it would be impossible to put them all in one book. In particular, I left out recipes for the more exotic foods that are sold in some Latin American countries, such as the *chapulines* (grasshoppers) that are deep-fried, wrapped in corn tortillas, and drizzled liberally with lime juice and chile; or tropical smoothies made with the juice of the fleshy and astringently luscious fruit of the cashew tree, sometimes called *marañón*. Delicious as they may be, I want you to have recipes that you'll actually make at home, with ingredients that are conveniently found.

So what you will find in this book are recipes for favorites like tacos and churros, but they only scratch the surface of the amazingly colorful and flavorful spectrum of mouthwatering street food recipes here, including *choripán*, South American sausage in a bun; *papas rellenas*, Cuban potato balls stuffed with picadillo; *salteñas*, Bolivian chicken hand-pies; *acarajés*, Brazilian black-eye pea fritters; and *alfajores*, Argentinean dulce de leche sandwiches.

Now, there is no need to travel south of the border each time you want to enjoy these delicacies. See this book as your passport to flavor and a key to informal, fun, and fantastic food. It's my hope that you'll taste the spirit of Latin America in every bite you take, that you'll experience every bit of fun packed into every single recipe, so you, too, can say, "Stop the truck! I want to eat it up!"

Getting Organized

Preparing street food at home is a lot of fun, and with a little bit of planning, delicious tacos, empanadas, tamales, pupusas, and arepas are only a few steps away. Street food is pretty food. It's also jam-packed with flavor, dressed to the hilt with color, and topped to the limit with explosive textures. People find it easy to become enamored with the festive aura that surrounds street foods—I know I have loved it all my life. In my home, whenever I prepare a recipe like the ones in this book, whether it is for a casual supper with my small family or for a large and casual gathering with friends, every meal becomes a party!

Many of the foods you find on the streets of Latin America are healthy, but let's face it, some are not. If you look throughout the pages of this book, you'll find plenty of healthful options such as salads, fruit smoothies, soups, and even tacos. I also offer you plenty of vegan and vegetarian options. I'm not suggesting that you base your diet solely on the recipes in this book, but you will find that in moderation, you will be able to enjoy these dishes often and without guilt.

Because Latin street food, for the most part, makes great use of relatively inexpensive ingredients, you'll find many recipes that will give you a big bang for your buck. Here, tough cuts of meat are tenderized through easy cooking methods that allow them to yield fork-tender bites. Dried beans are transformed into yummy side dishes and main entrées, as are other grains, fruits, and vegetables. Cooking from this book will open up a lot of very good and economical meals for your entire family.

This book is divided into many exciting categories that will give you an idea of how varied Latin American street food really is. I grouped the recipes in such a way that will allow you to plan entire menus so that you can balance the flavors, textures, and temperatures that street foods are famous for. You'll find recipes that are ideal for breakfast, brunch, lunch, or dinner, as well as great options for fabulous snacks, jazzy appetizers, comforting soups, and scrumptious desserts. All of these recipes have the potential to transform a regular meal into a memorable one.

Latin street food is filled with tons of thrilling and quick options for every palate and satisfying choices for every taste. Here you'll find recipes for easy sandwiches, healthy salads, funky salsas, meaty kabobs, and refreshing drinks that will require merely a few minutes to create. These are the ones to reach for whenever time is of the essence and energy is low. These dishes will lift you up in no time at all, and they'll taste sensational.

Many of these recipes were developed to feed a small family, but since street food makes such magnificent party fare, some are suitable to feed a small crowd. You'll find precise instructions on which recipes can easily be divided and which can be multiplied without problem so that you can cater them to your needs. All of the recipes have been written in a way that I hope will make you feel as if I'm standing next to you in your kitchen, so that even if you're a novice cook, you'll find comfort in precise instructions, filled with plenty of visuals to help you achieve success.

If you like to grill, you'll enjoy the vast recipes for grilling here; if you love desserts, you'll find great choices from baked goods to chilled concoctions; if you like salads, you'll find plenty of new ideas; if you're in a sandwich rut, you'll find exciting, new renditions; if you need meals that take only minutes to prepare, you'll find plenty of suggestions; if you fancy spending lazy afternoons crafting food, you'll love the selections I've provided here; and if you just enjoy food in general, then this book is definitely for you!

Whether you're cooking for your family or for a larger crowd, street food makes it easy to place flavorful and exciting dishes on the table. Street food is perfect for everyday cooking, and that always makes me happy, because I know that I can reach for one of these recipes and serve my family fun and economical dishes that pack on the flavor every day of the week. When all you want is a sandwich and you don't feel like having the same-old, same-old, reach for this book and make a new interpretation. How about a Mexican torta stuffed with beans, chicken, and zesty avocado sauce; or a crusty roll filled with sliced beef tenderloin, topped with melting cheese and with an assortment of condiments that includes flavored mayonnaise?

If you're anything like me, you've experienced times when all you'll want to do is stay in and make a comforting meal. For times such as these, the Latin Bowls chapter, featuring filling stews and soothing soups will fit the bill. Make yourself a steaming pot of hot pozole, slip into your favorite pair of pajamas, and sit in front of the fireplace and enjoy a relaxing meal.

Getting Organized

On those days when you have to take your kids to a gazillion different activities and you don't have time to sit for dinner, pack a few portable handheld empanadas and take them along with you. The empanadas in this book are truly spectacular, and many of them are satisfying enough to carry you through a game of soccer or a ballet class without missing a single beat.

Before you start any cooking, you need to do some planning ahead. Part of that includes understanding the logistics that go into crafting most of these street foods. The best place to start is at the beginning so you, too, can re-create all of your favorites at home. So let's get started. Think of it this way: street food vendors must assemble their creations in miniature kitchens, on the move, every day. Most importantly, they must serve food quickly to hoards of hungry patrons standing in line. Talk about pressure! Thankfully, we don't have to deal with this kind of pressure. So ask yourself a question: if we take away these variables, then street food shouldn't be too difficult to make, right? Well, it isn't, especially when you're armed with the recipes in this book and with a few of my tips. Get ready to cook like a pro.

There are some street foods that are so easy to make that they only require a simple toss—almost no effort at all. Salads, seafood cocktails, smoothies—these are just some of the delicacies that are usually made right on the premises before the hungry eyes of awaiting customers. In Peru and in Ecuador, for example, vendors mix ceviches—seafood dishes marinated in citrus juices—using the freshest catch of the day and only a couple of other ingredients.

The long and the short of it is that quick and easy cooking can be done successfully only if the ingredients in question are fresh and of top quality. In the streets, the customers who shop for what I like to call "toss and eat food" need to trust that their fish is fresh, that bright fruits are clean, and the salads are at their prime. It will be no different for you at home. Trust me: if you start with good basic ingredients, the flavor of the finished dishes will not only be authentic; they'll also be vibrant. Before you even start cooking, promise yourself to use only the best ingredients you can get. Only then will you be guaranteed clean and bright flavors each time you cook.

The secret to the success of many of these quick-to-make street foods is that they carry a lot of flavor. I don't know about you, but when I cook something quickly, I want to make sure it tastes as if it took a long time to prepare. Latin American street food is filled with multifaceted flavors that juxtapose contrasting elements. Every bite tastes complex even if the recipe is not. To me, complex flavors matter because I want the food you prepare from this book to be authentically Latin American. Every bite should be a cultural experience—and a delicious one. If your ingredients are subpar, and the resulting dishes are just okay, then the expediency of the dish really won't matter. Keep it fresh.

Having said this, when it comes to truly wonderful street food, *easy* does not always mean *fast*. I repeat: easy does not always mean fast. I like to make that distinction clear: it's true that street food is always quick to assemble, but it's not always quick to make. There are many recipes here that require long cooking periods, like the braised meats for tacos, sandwiches, and stews that must cook low and slow so they can truly develop extraordinary flavor. Skimp with your time on this step and you destroy their taste. However, where's the difficulty in covering a piece of meat with liquid, putting a lid on it, and then letting it cook at its leisure on the stove until it's ready to eat? There really isn't any. Mr. Time does all the work. The perception that only fast food is easy to make, in my opinion, should be thrown out the drive-through window!

What I'm saying here is that while some of these recipes may require hours of waiting, you can rest assured that they won't require hours of active work. I love cooking this way because I can whip a recipe together and then forget about it while I go about my other daily activities. Go ahead, make one of the soups or stews in this book, braise carnitas to make tacos, or boil a hunk of meat until it shreds so you can stir it into a sauce. And while you're at it, fold a load or two of laundry, read a book, or talk to a friend on the telephone. Let the food do all the work, pass go, and then collect the reward. Every time you taste a dish made from these kinds of recipes, you'll be rewarded with the pleasure of deeply flavorful food. Slow food delivers.

I always like to compare crafting street food to one of my favorite cooking techniques: stir-frying. This technique requires careful preparation of all of the components ahead of time. Before you can stir-fry, you must first chop the ingredients, mix the elements that will complete the sauces, and place them at the ready. Once the actual cooking begins, the process moves very quickly. Street food works in exactly the same way.

The French refer to the prepping of ingredients as *mise en place* (everything in its place). The ingredients that go into the assembly of delicious street food must also be prepared ahead of time, long before they make it to the taco truck, or food stand, or empanada kiosk. Ingredients need to be chopped, divided, and measured before you even turn the stove on. First you prepare and then you assemble.

The good news is that once you've organized the different components that go into the recipes in this book, the assembly will be expedient. That's why these recipes are a lot of fun to cook. And of course, the recipes in this book have been developed to feed small groups, and not the hundreds of customers that vendors must supply for. Prepping ahead always saves time, and once you get used to cooking this way, you may never go back to old habits again.

There are many examples of ingredients that will require further preparation in advance of the actual cooking: the beef that must be roasted and sliced for sandwiches, the corn that must be boiled so it can be grilled and sprinkled with toppings, the dried cod that must be desalted overnight and mixed with the béchamel before it can be shaped into fritters, and the sauces that must be blended and cooked a second time before they can be used are all examples of recipes that will fall under this category. But, again, none of them is difficult to prepare.

I'd be lying if I didn't tell you that there won't be at least a handful of street foods represented in this book that will be a bit more complex to make. Of all of the foods that are served on the streets of Latin America each day, tamales require the most time and effort to prepare. As you will see, though, my recipes are practical, and with them as your guide, you'll be able to make them with success. Not only that, but I will teach you how to freeze and reheat the dishes here so that if you work one day, you can enjoy their delicious flavors for many more, long after.

Throughout the instructions that make up the body of my recipes I will tell you how early a dish can be started, which recipes can be made ahead, and what steps can wait for the last minute. I'll share with you the secrets for bringing out the flavor in inexpensive ingredients, and I will offer you the storing, freezing, and reheating tips that my cooking students have found helpful over my two decades as a cooking teacher. I'll even offer you shortcuts and offer substitutions for ingredients so that you can always find flavors that you'll love.

You will also find helpful advice such as suggested instances when you should purchase store-bought tortillas or use canned refried beans if you don't have time to make them from scratch. I'll offer you ideas that will help you cut corners without sacrificing flavor, such as substituting rotisserie chicken in recipes that call for shredded chicken, so that even on the busiest of nights, you may reach for this book and cook a meal with the most ease possible.

This is the advice the I give to my cooking students: read each recipe thoroughly to make sure that you understand what you're making, check to see that you have all of the ingredients before you start cooking, review what parts of the recipes can be made ahead of time versus what you'll need to do at the last minute, and taste often. This will guarantee success in the kitchen every time.

Set up a Latin street food pantry so you can make any of these recipes on a whim. Make sure to stock it with dried and canned beans, chicken broth or stock, long-grain white rice, canned chipotle peppers, jars of gooey dulce de leche, an assortment of flours, hearts of palm, raisins, olives, dried and preserved chiles, canned fire-roasted tomatoes, and a nice variety of assorted vinegars. Don't ignore your spice rack; include granulated garlic, ground cumin, ground and whole coriander seeds, annatto (or achiote) paste, Mexican cinnamon (canela), nutmeg, allspice, thyme, and bay leaves.

We don't often think of our refrigerator or freezer as part of our pantry, but they're actually very key components. Make sure to have them well stocked with limes and oranges, cilantro, lettuces, milk, cream, eggs, and an assortment of fruits and vegetables represented in this book. I often store masa harina and flours, including the one to make arepas, in my freezer if I know I won't use them up quickly. Stored that way, they'll keep for up to one year.

Your freezer can also hold all of the ready-made empanada disks you can purchase or the pastry that you will be able to prepare ahead of time with my recipes. It will hold any leftover tortillas, selected cuts of meat, sashimi-style fish, and frozen squid and shrimp. Your freezer is also the place to store all of the finished empanadas, salteñas, and cookies you'll lovingly craft ahead of time with my recipes so that you can simply slide them into the oven and bake them to order. The same goes for the dozens of beautiful tamales you'll make with this book. Instead of filling your refrigerator or freezer with store-bought casseroles and TV dinners, do like I do: make some of these recipes ahead and freeze them for those nights when all the energy you can muster is to reheat a meal and put it on the table!

INGREDIENTS TO HAVE ON HAND

The recipes in this book will expose you to many new ingredients. You'll undoubtedly be familiar with most of them, and they're easy to find in grocery stores; others may not be familiar and may require a trip to a Latin American tienda or a specialty food store. The following are basic ingredients you'll want to become familiar with (if you aren't already) before you embark on your Latin American street food adventure.

Masa harina. You'll use this corn flour to make tortillas, pupusas, sopes, and tamales. The corn has gone through a process in which it is first soaked in lime (calcium hydroxide), slipped off its hull, and dried. The dried corn, also known as hominy, is then ground to a meal that requires the addition of water to become masa. There are many brands of masa harina out there, but I recommend using the two most popular brands available: Maseca or Tortimasa.

Masarepa or harina pan. You'll use this precooked corn flour to make arepas, tamales, and empanadas. It's reconstituted with a warm liquid, for example, water, milk, or broth. Two popular brands are Goya and P.A.N.

Yuca or cassava flour. This is a very powdery, sticky flour, similar to cornstarch, that is used for many of the breads made in South America. You'll need it to make the Colombian rolls in this book, and you'll find it only in Latin American markets. To keep it fresh, store it in your freezer for up to one year.

Lard. This is pork fat, which has loads of flavor, and many of the recipes on the streets of Latin America will use lard. Of course, you can always substitute a good-quality vegetable oil. Lard is available in both natural and hydrogenated forms. Stay away from the latter, which is really not good for you. If fresh lard is not available in your area's Latin markets, then render your own. To render lard, simply heat chunks of fatback or pieces of streak o' lean in a clean pot over medium heat; cook, stirring, until the fat has melted. Discard the solids and refrigerate the lard. If kept well sealed in the refrigerator, it should last for about six months. It keeps frozen for up to a year.

Dried chiles. You can find a variety of these in the international aisle of your grocery stores. To reconstitute them, simply soak them in hot water for up to 15 minutes. Then follow the instructions in the recipes to remove their spicy veins and seeds.

Fresh chiles. You'll use all sort of chiles in this book, such as jalapeños and serranos, among others. I suggest that you use rubber gloves whenever you work with chiles. If you don't want to wear gloves, do the following: Hold the chile with kitchen tongs (smaller ones can be held with your fingers from their stems). With a sharp knife, slice off the flesh from one of the sides of the pepper, exposing the seed pod. Turn the chile and continue slicing the sides away from the seed pod. You should end up with an intact seed pod and four slices of perfectly seeded and deveined chile. Then proceed with the recipe.

Poblano peppers. These large, green—almost purplish—peppers are widely available in supermarkets. Poblanos are always roasted, seeded, and deveined. To roast poblanos (or any pepper or chile) on a gas stove, place them directly over the flame, rotating them until their skins have blackened (about six minutes). Place them in a bowl and cover with plastic wrap, letting them steam for 20 minutes. Use a sharp knife to scrape off the skins; remove the seeds and veins. You can also roast peppers in a hot oven or outdoor grill, turning them until nicely charred. Continue as directed above. Roasted, peeled, and deveined poblanos can be wrapped in plastic and frozen for up to two months; to use them, thaw at room temperature for a few minutes and proceed with the recipe.

Chipotle chile peppers. Chipotles are jalapeño peppers that have been ripened on the vine, dried, and then smoked. These reddish-brown chiles are canned whole in a tomato, onion, and garlic sauce called adobo, and you'll find them in most grocery stores. To freeze leftovers, place each chile with a dollop of the sauce on a parchment paper–lined pan; freeze until solid and then transfer to freezer bags. You can also purée the contents of a can of chipotles and freeze the purée in ice-cube trays. One teaspoon of this paste equals one-half of a small chile. Use chipotles cautiously, adding small amounts first and then putting in more for additional heat. It's better to have to add more heat to a recipe than to find out that you've added too much—there isn't much you can do to fix the latter.

Peruvian peppers. These include the long, yellow ají amarillo or ají marisol, the long, brownish-red ají panca, and the rocoto, a spicy red pepper with black seeds. They are available in Latin tiendas and in some gourmet markets, as they're becoming quite trendy to use. You'll find them dried, preserved in jars, canned, frozen, or transformed into paste.

Tomatillos. These look like miniature green tomatoes. They are members of the gooseberry family and are enveloped in a papery, inedible husk. Peel the husk and rinse the tomatillos under running water to remove the gluey residue. Big tomatillos tend to be bitter. For the recipes in this book, use medium-size tomatillos. Four to five medium tomatillos will yield 1 cup chopped.

Tamarind. This is a fruit that comes enveloped in a brown pod. It's got a very pungent and acidic flavor, but when it's combined with a bit of sugar it becomes nectarous. The seeds of fresh tamarind are very large and the pulp of the fruit must be strained from the seeds. You'll find it in its natural state or transformed into extract and paste in both Latin and Indian markets.

Piloncillo, panela, or papelón. This is the unrefined sugar Latin Americans use to sweeten many of their drinks and desserts. You'll find it in Latin markets, shaped like cones or flat disks. You can always substitute it with equal amounts of the darkest organic brown sugar you can find.

Canela. Also known as Mexican or Ceylon cinnamon, this kind is sweeter and more brittle than the cinnamon we're accustomed to using in the United States, which is from the cassia tree. You'll need the Mexican kind for all of the recipes that call for cinnamon in this book. Find it in Latin American stores.

Annatto (or achiote) paste and powder. Annatto is for Latin cuisine what turmeric is for Indian cuisine. It's a seed used to color foods from a bright yellow to a vibrant orange color. Many of the recipes in this book use annatto in paste form, which is dissolved in warm water before it's used to tint foods. You'll find it in Latin stores.

Hibiscus flowers (flor de Jamaica). These tiny, red buds of the hibiscus tree are steeped in hot water to release their vibrant red color and acidic flavor. It's used to make some of the beverages and popsicles in this book. Find it in stores that specialize in Mexican cooking.

Dulce de leche and cajeta. These are the caramel sauces of Latin America, made with milk and sugar. They're used in some of the recipes in this book but are also delicious spooned over ice cream or stirred into custard. Dulce de leche is made with cow's milk, while cajeta is made with goat's milk.

Crema. Mexicans and Central Americans use a thick and tangy cream, similar to crème fraîche, to top many of the streets foods in this book. Mexican crema is the easiest to find in grocery stores. If you go to Latin markets, you'll also find other types of cremas, which, depending on which country they're from, will vary in thickness, color, and tanginess.

To make one cup of your own crema: In a glass bowl, combine one-half cup of sour cream or buttermilk with one-half cup of heavy whipping cream; cover and let it sit at room temperature for eight hours. Stir once more, cover, and place it in the refrigerator for twelve hours (or overnight). It will now be ready to eat and will keep in your refrigerator for up to four days.

Dried beans. Pinto and black beans are frequently called for in this book. You can always use canned beans for the recipes, but nothing tastes better than beans made from scratch. Dried beans must be presoaked overnight to soften before they're used in recipes. But you can always use the quick-soak method as follows: place the beans in a large pot and cover with water by at least two inches; bring the water to a boil and cook the beans at a rolling boil for two minutes. Turn off the heat, cover the pot, and let them soak for 1 hour; drain the beans and continue with the recipe as directed.

Yuca and ñame. You can usually find these tubers, which taste like potatoes, in Latin stores, but if you can't, you can substitute firm potatoes for them in any of the recipes in this book. The flavor of the dishes won't suffer. The root vegetables called for in these recipes are harder than potatoes, so if you do use potatoes, cooking times will have to be reduced.

Banana leaves and dried corn husks. These are both required for the recipes in the tamale chapter and will likely be hard to come by in regular supermarkets. I suggest you familiarize yourself with the nearest Latin American market in your region, where they are readily available. My recipes distinguish between dried corn husks and fresh ones; use the kind specified in the recipe. Banana leaves can be found fresh or frozen.

EQUIPMENT

You won't need a lot of special equipment or gadgets to cook the recipes in this book. In fact, most of what you'll need you probably already own. Here is a good check list of the equipment you will be reaching for the most:

Baking pans. You'll need a set of good-quality ones.

Metal cooling racks. You'll need a least a couple of these that will fit snugly into your baking pans.

Large, high-sided skillet or enamel-coated pot. You'll need at least one of these for deep frying. You'd make good use of a deep fryer as well, but it isn't necessary.

Tortilla press. I recommend that you invest in a good tortilla press because it'll save you quite a bit of time making tortillas, arepas, huaraches, and empanadas. You can find tortilla presses online and in many Latin stores. For the most part, they're inexpensive; on average they cost around twenty dollars. Some are made out of wood, but the majority of them are made out of cast iron. The shape or material they're made of won't make a difference in a recipe, but you will need one that is at least 6½ inches wide. If you don't want to invest in one, use a heavy skillet or plate to press down balls of dough. As long as the dough is centered between two pieces of plastic wrap (a plastic sandwich bag that has been cut open down the sides works best), you shouldn't have trouble forming thin rounds. You'll have to gage how much pressure is required to get the thickness that recipes call for, but that will also be the case if you use a tortilla press.

Panini press. Although it's not necessary, it will help you press and heat sandwiches as well as some kinds of arepas.

Bench scraper. You'll want one of these to scrape off the flour on your work surface as you shape empanadas and other goodies.

Ruler. Have a good, sturdy one on hand when you want to get precise measurements (for example, the diameter and thickness of dough).

Measuring cups and spoons. It's imperative that you have a reliable set of these. Purchase them at a high-end cooking supply store—they're totally worth the investment if it means that your recipes will work every time. You should use metal cups for measuring solid ingredients and glass cups to measure liquids. And use metal measuring spoons. These can all go into the dishwasher for easy clean up.

Citrus juicer or squeezer. I keep one of each in my kitchen, but you can select one or the other. My electric juicer comes in handy when I need a lot of juice for ceviches or lemonade. There are some pretty cool enamel-coated citrus squeezers in the market, too. Select the one that works best for you.

Blender. This is the most important small appliance in the Latin American kitchen, bar none. You'll use it to blend sauces, purée chiles, and blend beans and peas. It's not necessary to get one of the most expensive models. Mine cost around forty dollars and has lasted me over ten years.

Food processor. The handy appliance will help you make dough and pastry that must be mixed thoroughly and quickly. I offer you instructions on how to make them by hand, but a food processor cuts down the work and keeps cold pastry cold, especially if you have warm fingers, like me.

Wire pastry cutter. Use this to cut lard or other fat into dry ingredients when you're making pastry or some of the masa-based recipes in this book.

Wire mesh or splatter guard. You'll need one of these when you are cooking sauces in oil, as many of the recipes call for.

Pots and pans. You'll need good-quality heavy-bottomed pans of different sizes. Find some with tight-fitting lids. Good ones will last you for decades.

Dutch oven. I own several of these in different sizes, but I suggest that you purchase one with a 5- to 6-quart capacity to make the recipes in this book. I use mine for everything from braising stews to frying tortilla chips. It's perhaps the most important pot in my kitchen. Buying a good-quality one will be money well spent. Make sure it's heavy and that it can go from stove, to oven, to table.

Nonstick skillet or griddle. Either of these will be essential when cooking tortillas, quesadillas, and arepas.

Outdoor grill or indoor grill pan. These will come in very handy when you're cooking meats that will become the filling for tacos and the foods that are cooked on sticks. If you don't have either, however, a good panini press or a griddle will also work well.

Ice cream maker. You'll need one of these to make the ice cream in this book.

Other than that, and purely for fun, I suggest you purchase some nifty popsicle makers and a few squeeze bottles to put your toppings in, as well as pretty napkins and colorful plates (real or paper) to serve your food. With street food, there is no need to get fancy, but if you're up to it, get some martini glasses, pretty goblets, and large pitchers. Don't forget to pick up some disposable, earth-friendly utensils. Choose a varied menu from this book by selecting a few recipes from three or four of the chapters. Or plan themed parties inspired by the flavors of Latin America. Let your imagination run wild.

SIMPLIFY YOUR COOKING

Street food vendors generally start their workday long before their dishes make it into the hands of hungry customers. In fact, as a rule, taco trucks and street stalls are equipped with small kitchens—many of them built in a rustic and spartan fashion. For this reason, vendors must make sure that some of the food components are primed ahead of time and often in separate locations: meats require adequate marinating periods, yeasted dough needs to rise for a certain time, vegetables must be chopped, sauces constructed, etc.

With this in mind, I suggest that when it comes to the recipes in this book, you tackle them in stages. In order to make the best pork tacos, for example, marinate the meat a day in advance, make the tortillas and finish the toppings early in the day. That way assembling your tacos will not only be fast; it'll also be fun. When you're ready to eat, simply cook the pork, reheat the tortillas, and *Ya está*! (There it is!).

You can make many of these recipes from start to finish in one go, but for those dishes that have components that must be made in advance, my method of staging different parts of the recipes works quite well. When recipes are broken down into separate steps, they don't take a lot of effort to complete. This advice will come in handy, particularly when you're entertaining with street food right from your kitchen.

TAKE IT OUTSIDE

By nature, street food is casual food, and, not surprisingly, it's meant to be eaten outdoors. When the weather permits, decks and backyards can easily become extensions of our kitchens. Food tastes different when we're outside. Fresh air seems to awaken the taste buds, making the palate more receptive to flavor, and stimulates the appetite, making us more susceptible to the lure of street food fare. Without a doubt, eating outdoors puts me in a more relaxed state of mind, so whenever I can, I take pleasure in dining outdoors. Take advantage of good weather while it lasts; it's ephemeral and should be enjoyed whenever possible.

Latin street foods are so much fun for entertaining. With this book, you're only a recipe away from a party. The fact that most of these recipes can be prepared ahead of time is exactly what makes them so ideal for entertaining. Many of the sauces, condiments, side dishes, and salads can be completely made ahead and will sit pretty in the refrigerator while you wait for your guests to arrive.

Organize a taco party—what Latin Americans call a *taquiza*—and feature three or four of your favorite recipes in this book. A couple of days ahead, make dozens of homemade corn tortillas; seal them in plastic bags and keep them in the refrigerator, ready to reheat. Marinate meats; prepare a couple of chopped salsas and one or two of your favorite condiments to drizzle on top. On the morning of the party, make one or two of the cool beverages in this book and keep them well chilled. When your guests arrive, simply put on the finishing touches, cook the filling, and let everyone assemble their tacos, piling them up with as many toppings as their hearts desire.

Or select a few of the recipes that you'd find at a fair or a Latin festival and plan a menu around them: a couple of different kabobs, my mango salad, some of my colorful tostadas, amazing grilled corn with toppings, a bowl of guacamole, and loads of plantain chips. Do as I do and decorate your deck with colored paper wreaths, put on some happy music—think marimba or sambas—and fill a metal tub with drinks. For dessert, well, there's always room for ice cream, of course.

Plan a "vamos a la playa" or beach party and include at least one kind of ceviche, a shrimp cocktail, a delicious *mofongo*, and some fun fritters. Create a smoothie bar on the corner of your deck or backyard, and have all the ingredients well chilled so you can blend them to order. You can add a splash of rum to many of my beverages to make them more exciting if you wish. For dessert, serve *paletas* (popsicles) and watch everyone have a great time.

Make it very easy on yourself, and invite neighbors to an informal barbecue party and grill the versions of hamburgers or hot dogs that are served on Latin American streets. Serve them French fries with the toppings found south of the border. Cookies are easy to eat outdoors, and you'll find a few versions here that will fit the bill.

When the weather gets nippy and a fireplace becomes more inviting than an outdoor *chimenea*, plan an indoor party. One of the most casual ways to entertain is to throw what I call a Hug a Mug Party and build an entire menu around soups. For this kind of soiree, I make two or three large pots of soup and set them on a low simmer on the stove. Then I have a blast putting together a fun assortment of toppings so my guests can eat to their heart's content. For this kind of party the setup couldn't be any easier: a nice selection of mugs and bowls, plenty of spoons, and extra napkins. Offer a basket of freshly made tortillas or arepas, an interesting selection of cheese, and some of the sweet empanadas options in this book.

For years, I've been introducing the flavors found on the streets of Latin America to my family, to my friends, and to my students. I hope that you'll find plenty of inspiration in the pages of this book and that you'll discover the joy of eating stimulating, new, vibrant, refreshing, and fun foods. This is the happiest food in the world. Every day is a party on the streets. Open up your kitchen and invite the festive spirit and fabulous flavor of Latin streets into your home.

A typical beverage and snack kiosk on a Brazilian beach.

(inset) A fruit stand in a market in Antigua, Guatemala, featuring cashew fruit (center, left).

THE RAW BAR

Extending over a vast area of the Western Hemisphere, with terrain as varied as its people, Latin America is blessed with a bounty of fresh fruits and vegetables. The Pacific Ocean on one side and the Atlantic on the other yield a rich variety of seafood. Mountains and ridges and valleys and high plains (*altiplanos* or *mesetas*) are prime territory for raising cattle, pork, and fowl. Latin America is rich in fertile green lands and arid deserts, beautiful beaches with multicolored sand, and tropical rainforests filled with all kinds of flora and fauna. It offers a cornucopia of ingredients to cook with.

Fresh foods abound, and nowhere is this abundance more visible than on the streets, particularly when you eat at an establishment that sells raw food. A slice of watermelon sprinkled with lime, fresh coconut water poured directly from its edible vessel, and a piece of fish thinly sliced and simply macerated in citrus are all ways in which simple but good-quality natural ingredients are transformed into edible morsels on the streets. There is no pretense in these dishes, just pure, simple goodness. Latin Americans don't eat fruit only because it's healthy; we eat it because it's good.

This chapter includes many raw foods that street vendors prepare quickly and serve cold so that they retain all of their fresh qualities. Here you'll find ceviches, salads, fruits delicacies, and seafood cocktails. This selection will give you an opportunity to sample many of the healthy offerings found on Latin American streets on any given day.

Latin America boasts a great variety of fruits, many of which are unavailable in the United States. In Guatemala, for example, I grew up eating all kinds of delicious fruits bought from street food vendors, like *jocotes*, also known as tree tomatoes, which are small, oval-shaped fruits about the size of small eggs; they vary in color from green to yellow, to orange, to vibrant reds. When they're ripe, their flesh turns soft and juicy; the large pit in the center has the texture of a loofah sponge. Jocotes are sold by their weight in bags, and people eat them as they walk.

Fruit cups in Cartagena, Colombia, offer a great portable snack.

The fruit salads food vendors sell often include the vibrantly fuchsia-colored *pitahaya* (dragon fruit) that is usually cut into little squares and served with a toothpick.

On the streets of Costa Rica, customers eat clusters of the red or yellow fruits of a palm tree called *pejibayes*. These oval-shaped fruits are served peeled with a side of mayonnaise to dunk them in. It sounds unusual, but people love them. On the streets of Mexico, fruit is often simply sprinkled with chile and salt. The fruits that are generally available in your local grocery store, including oranges, melons, bananas, mangoes, grapes, papayas, guavas, passion fruits, pineapples, and strawberries are found all over Latin America. Others, like *zapotes*, the delicious and nectarous football-shaped fruits with shiny black seeds and orange flesh, and the *chico zapote* (gum-tree fruit) are common sights all over Latin America. (These are harder to find here in North America, but you may find them in specialty grocery stores.) Seldom is there a day when you walk through a Latin American street and not see at least one fresh fruit offering. This is street food at its most local.

There are certain seafood dishes that are only available in fine-dining establishments in Latin America, but some seafood dishes lend themselves to eating on the run because they're quick, easy, and inexpensive to make. These are the dishes you'll find on the streets, and this chapter includes some of my favorite renditions.

Before the Europeans arrived in the New World carrying citrus along with them, ceviches—raw seafood concoctions native to Peru and Ecuador but found all throughout Latin America—were cured with fermented corn called *chicha*. After the *Conquista*, it became commonplace to cure them with citrus juice instead. In a process called denaturation, the acid in the citrus "cooks" the flesh of the fish, causing it to become opaque and firm. Ceviches can also be made with shellfish, such as lobster and shrimp, which must be blanched briefly before they're marinated to make them safe to eat. This chapter is filled with fun and versatile recipes for ceviches, from the traditional flounder ceviche you'll find on the streets of Peru, to the spicy renditions available in Mexico. And true ceviches are made without oil or fat. Talk about figure-friendly street food! To me, a bowl of ceviche beats eating one of those diet bars any day!

There are some salads that have cooked components, such as the two renditions of layered salads I offer you here (one from Peru, the other from Nicaragua), but since they both feature lots of raw ingredients, I included them here. Slaws are extremely popular in Latin America, and here you'll find them made with cabbage and radishes. These are usually paired with salty fried foods to balance them with a refreshing and clean taste. I think you'll enjoy them very much. They're different, but they'll make a worthy addition to your slaw repertoire.

Whenever the first warm air of spring begins to tame the lion of winter each year, these are the refreshing recipes that turn my culinary weathervane. You'll find fascinating new ways to prepare favorite ingredients in this chapter, and I hope that you'll reach for it any time you want to whip something together without a lot of work.

An oyster ceviche stand on a beach in Ecuador offers a fresh feast.

Orange, Onion, and Pepita Salad

Here is perhaps the easiest salad you'll ever make and one of the most popular in my cooking classes. It's also one of the most refreshingly delicious salads you'll ever have. Cut-up oranges with salt and chile are a welcome sight on the streets of Mesoamerica, where they make a great light snack in the middle of the day. You may be surprised to see lime juice in this dish, but the addition of lime actually brings out the sweetness in the oranges. This salad makes a frequent appearance on my table during the winter months, when oranges are abundant.

Serves 6

> ¼ cup raw pumpkin seeds (pepitas)
> 4 navel oranges, peeled and thinly sliced
> ¼ cup thinly sliced red onion
> 1 tablespoon fresh lime juice
> 1 teaspoon guajillo chile powder
> Salt, to taste

Place the pumpkin seeds in a dry skillet over medium heat and toast them, stirring constantly, until they begin to puff and turn a golden color, about 3–4 minutes, being careful not to burn them. Remove them from the heat and cool completely. Chop them finely (or grind to a powder in a spice grinder), and set aside.

Arrange the orange slices on a large platter; top with the sliced onions. Sprinkle the salad with lime juice, chile powder, salt, and pumpkin seeds. Serve immediately. ✳

Orange, Onion, and Pepita Salad

Jicama Salad

Jicama is indigenous to the Americas, and since it looks like a giant turnip, it's also known as *navo mejicano* (Mexican turnip). Its brown skin hides a whitish bulb that smells like a raw potato but tastes deliciously like unripe pear. My first contact with jicama came at the tender age of six, during a Christmas holiday when we traveled to Mexico to see relatives. I recall a large party, a huge piñata made out of clay that only grownups were allowed to hit—unlike the colorful paper contraptions that I was used to seeing at kid's parties in Guatemala—and my great disappointment when it was broken and instead of candies, fruits and vegetables fell to the ground. I left the party with a giant, brownish root that resembled a child's top in my tiny hands, a shard of red clay for my trinket collection, and a very heavy heart. The next morning, my parents asked if I would share my delicious gift with them. In no time, my mother whipped together a salad with lime juice and salt that had me smiling again and thinking that perhaps mine had not been such an unlucky find after all. This is a dressed-up version of the salad sold on the streets of Mexico City.

Serves 6

1 (2–2.5 pound) jicama
1 cup fresh lime juice
½ cup roughly chopped cilantro (leaves and tender stems)
½ teaspoon pasilla chile powder
¼ teaspoon chipotle chile powder, or to taste
2 teaspoons salt, or to taste
¼ teaspoon freshly ground black pepper, or to taste

Using a sharp knife, slice off the top and bottom of the jicama (to make a flat base). Using a serrated potato peeler or a sharp knife, peel the jicama from top to bottom (see note). Cut the jicama into 2 × ¼–inch matchsticks (see note) and place them in a large bowl.

In a small bowl, whisk together the lime juice, cilantro, chile powders, salt, and pepper and combine the mixture with the jicama. Cover the bowl and marinate the jicama, stirring occasionally, for 30 minutes (or up to 4 hours). Serve chilled.

NOTE: If you don't use the jicama immediately after peeling, submerge it in water mixed with a little bit of lime or lemon juice to prevent it from browning.

I like cutting the jicama into matchsticks, but slice them any way you like; this salad tastes great no matter how you cut the jicama!

. . . .

Tropical Fruit Salad (Macedonia)

Not all street food is heavy. Even before smoothies and raw food became a modern trend in North America, they were already popular in Latin American streets. Delectable fruit salads are ever-present from Mexico to Brazil, made possible by the bounty of fruit available year-round. In Latin America, fruits are relatively inexpensive and can be very refreshing on hot summer days. Those fruits that aren't turned into juice are chopped to make delicious salads, like this one made with tropical fruits. It couldn't be any easier to make. Always slice the bananas right before serving and brush them with citrus so that they don't get brown.

Serves 6–8

    2 cups peeled, seeded, and cubed papaya
    2 cups peeled, seeded, and cubed cantaloupe
    2 cups peeled, seeded, and cubed ripe mangoes
    2 cups peeled, seeded, and cubed watermelon
    2 cups peeled, cored, and cubed pineapple
    1 cup fresh orange juice
    2 tablespoons sugar (optional)
    2 bananas
    2 tablespoons fresh lime juice

In a large bowl, toss together the papaya, cantaloupe, mango, watermelon, pineapple, orange juice, and sugar (if using). Chill and marinate for 1 hour, tossing once in a while.

Right before serving, peel and cube the bananas; brush them with lime juice and toss into the salad. Serve immediately. ⁑

Green Mango Salad (Ensalada de Mango con Limón, Pepitoria y Chile)

This sour, spicy, crunchy salad is similar to the one my brothers and I used to eat on the streets of Guatemala City when we were little kids. The combination of fruit and salty chile is also a favorite in Mexico, where mangoes are sold already peeled and on skewers. They're cut in such way that you can easily pull off pieces as you walk. In Guatemala, where all sorts of mango varieties also abound, this salad is traditionally made with small green mangoes that have sour flesh. Sometimes Asian markets will carry green mangoes, but if you can't find them, purchase unripe mangoes of any variety. Just make sure they have green skins and very firm flesh. Raw, unhulled, and green pumpkin seeds, called *pepitas*, usually can be found in any store that carries organic products. At home, I serve this salad with grilled or fried foods.

Serves 4–6

> 4 large, very firm mangoes (the greener the better), peeled
> ½ cup fresh lime juice
> Salt and freshly ground black pepper, to taste
> ⅓ cup raw pumpkin seeds (pepitas) (see note)
> Chipotle chile powder, to taste

Cut the mangoes into very thin ribbons with a serrated vegetable peeler or a very sharp knife, working around the large pit in the middle. Place the mango in a bowl and toss with the lime juice; season with salt and pepper. Chill for at least 20 minutes (up to 8 hours) before serving.

In the meantime, place the pumpkin seeds in a dry skillet over medium heat and toast them, stirring constantly, until they begin to puff and turn a golden color, about 3–4 minutes, being careful not to burn them. Remove them from the heat and cool completely. Chop them finely (or grind to a powder in a spice grinder).

Serve the mango salad in small bowls; top with pepitas and chile powder.

NOTE: I keep raw pumpkin seeds in the freezer (up to 6 months) and toast them as needed. If the seeds are frozen, they may take a couple of extra minutes to toast. Once toasted and chopped, they can be frozen for up to 2 months, but let them come to room temperature before using.

Quince Salad (Membrillo con Limón y Sal)

Quince is a round fruit with a flavor reminiscent of both apples and citrus. It's well known for its high pectin content and considered the ideal fruit for making preserves or jelly (such as the one used in the Miniature Quince Empanadas on page 235). I've heard it said that quince shouldn't be eaten raw, but for more than a century, Guatemalans have been eating raw quince after marinating it in lime juice; and for just as long, they've been purchasing salads like this one, which is sold in little plastic bags in street corners. Make it with yellow, fully ripened quinces only. Quince is extremely astringent, which helps it soak up citrus juice like a sponge. This salad is definitely an acquired taste, but I love it.

Serves 4–6

  4 ripe yellow quinces, peeled, cored, and diced
  ½ cup fresh lemon juice
  ½ cup fresh lime juice
  Salt, to taste

In a large bowl, stir together the quince, lemon juice, and lime juice. Chill and marinate for 2–3 hours, stirring often; season with salt, and serve. ❉

Radish Slaw with Pork Rinds (Chojín)

Radish Slaw with Pork Rinds (Chojín)

This beautiful salad is tart, tangy, and vibrantly colorful. The delicate white flesh of the freshly chopped radishes turns a bright pink color when it comes into contact with the acid of limes. Radishes can be bitter, but when treated in this manner, they lose all traces of bitterness and take on a deliciously sour taste. This slaw is great all on its own, but it also pairs beautifully with boiled meats and makes a delectable condiment for tacos. In Guatemalan streets, it's sold with a crunchy topping of ground *chicharrones* (pork rinds); omit them for a vegetarian option.

Serves 4–6

> 30 small, red radishes, beards and stems removed, quartered
> ½ cup fresh lime juice, or more, to taste
> Salt and freshly ground black pepper, to taste
> 2 cups crushed pork rinds (chicharrones) (optional)

Place the radishes in the bowl of a food processor fitted with a metal blade. Process for 15–18 one-second intervals, stopping several times to scrape the sides of the processor—the radishes should be very finely minced. (You can also chop them by hand.)

In a medium bowl combine the radishes and lime juice; season with salt and pepper. Set aside for 10 minutes, stirring occasionally. Chill for at least 30 minutes or up to 2 hours. If you're using pork rinds, sprinkle them over the top of the salad just before serving. ❊

Brazilian Hearts of Palm Salad (Salada de Palmito)

I grew up eating hearts of palm—the inner core of a palm tree—stirred into salads just like this one. To me, the flavor of hearts of palm is reminiscent of artichokes, but it's a bit sweeter, with a smooth, less fibrous texture. This salad delivers a colorful and refreshing mélange of tropical elements, scantily dressed in lively green vinaigrette. In Brazilian streets, this is sometimes chopped into very small dice and served with *acarajés* (black-eyed pea fritters, page 176). Make it anytime you want to make a colorful, chopped salad. It's simple to make and is the perfect pairing for my Bulgur, Beef, and Pine Nut Fritters (page 173), and it's delicious as a side to grilled meats and seafood. For a striking presentation, I like to serve this salad in martini glasses.

Serves 4–6

½ cup packed flat-leaf or Italian parsley (leaves and tender stems)
½ cup packed cilantro (leaves and tender stems)
2 tablespoons thinly sliced basil (chiffonade)
1 large garlic clove, roughly chopped
⅓ cup fresh lime juice
¼ cup sherry vinegar
1 tablespoon Dijon mustard
¾ cup extra-virgin olive oil
Salt and freshly ground black pepper, to taste
3 cups seeded and chopped plum tomatoes
2 cups drained and sliced hearts of palm
1 cup roughly chopped white onion

In a blender, combine the parsley, cilantro, basil, garlic, lime juice, vinegar, and mustard. Blend until the herbs are finely chopped. With the motor running add the olive oil (through the feeding hole at the top of the blender) in a thin stream until incorporated and the dressing is smooth, about 30 seconds; season with salt and pepper.

In a large bowl, combine the tomatoes, hearts of palm, and onions. Toss with dressing and serve immediately. ✳

Latin Slaw (Curtido)

Renditions of this refreshing slaw abound throughout Central America and the Latin Caribbean. It's the base for my Yuca, Cabbage, and Pork Rind Salad (page 43) and the topping for pupusas (pages 68 and 71). The secret is to blanch the slaw for *exactly* one minute so that it retains both crunch and color. Make it a day ahead of time; its flavor gets better as it marinates. What I love most about this slaw is that it's got some acidity but not enough to offend, so it pairs well with so many other dishes. For your next picnic, substitute your mayonnaise-based coleslaw with this version or use it in place of sauerkraut to top hot dogs, including ones on pages 89 and 153.

Serves 6

> 6 cups finely shredded cabbage
> 2 cups shredded carrots
> ¼ cup minced jalapeño peppers (seeded and deveined
>   if less heat is desired)
> 1 cup peeled, seeded, and minced plum tomatoes
> ⅓ cup white vinegar, or to taste
> 2 teaspoons oregano (preferably Mexican oregano)
> 2 teaspoons salt, or to taste
> ¼ teaspoon freshly ground black pepper, or to taste

Place a strainer over the sink. In a large bowl, combine the cabbage, carrots, and jalapeños; pour in enough boiling water to cover them, and stir. Let it sit for 1 minute. Strain the slaw, draining it well, and return it to the bowl; cool for 10–15 minutes.

Stir in the tomatoes, vinegar, oregano, salt, and pepper. Chill for 1 hour, or cover with plastic wrap and refrigerate overnight. This keeps for up to 1 week in the refrigerator. ❊

Yuca, Cabbage, and Pork Rind Salad (Vigorón)

Yuca, Cabbage, and Pork Rind Salad (Vigorón)

I first learned of this fun and colorful layered salad through my sister-in-law, Tey, who grew up eating it on the streets of Nicaragua, where it's wrapped in cones made of banana leaves. It offers a gustatory collision of soft and crunchy textures, where savory, sour, and spicy flavors meet in every bite. Pork rinds add an addictive crunch. It's a great vehicle to introduce you to yuca root if you've never tasted it before because here, its potatolike flesh takes on a subtle, sweet flavor. Because Nicaraguan cooks use a dark vinegar called *vinagre negro*, and since it's nearly impossible to find it in the United States, Tey suggests using white vinegar instead. The results are irresistible. Use large, freshly made pork rinds, if they're available. Chiltepines (also known as *chile congo* or bird's eyes) are tiny, fiery peppers; you'll find them preserved in jars and sold in Latin stores, called *tiendas*. In a pinch, use minced serranos or pickled jalapeños found canned in stores. You can also use the recipe for Jalapeños, Onions, and Carrots in Escabeche (page 266). The slaw and the yuca can be made ahead of time and refrigerated for up to 6 hours. However, add the pork rinds only when you're ready to eat it, or they'll get soggy.

Serves 6

- 2 pounds yuca, peeled and cut into large chunks (see note)
- 8 cups finely shredded cabbage
- 1 cup white vinegar, divided (or more, to taste)
- 1 cup seeded and minced plum tomatoes
- 1 cup shredded carrots
- 2 teaspoons salt, or to taste
- ¼ cup chiltepines or chile congo, stems removed and minced
- 1 cup minced white onion
- 3 cups roughly chopped chicharrones (pork rinds)

Place the yuca in a large pot and cover it with cold water; bring the water to a boil over high heat. Reduce the heat slightly and boil the yuca until it is fork-tender, about 15–25 minutes (see note). Just before it's finished cooking, fill a bowl with iced water; drain the yuca and plunge it into the iced water to stop the cooking process. Let stand for 5–10 minutes; drain.

Slice each chunk of yuca in half, lengthwise, and remove the inner fiber (some will have it, some will not); discard. Chop the flesh into ½-inch cubes and set aside.

In a large bowl, toss the cabbage with ½ cup of the vinegar and ¼ cup cold water. Using your hands, press the cabbage with your hands, crushing it for about 1 minute (this breaks the membranes of the cabbage, softening it). Add the tomatoes, carrots, and salt; toss with the cabbage, and set aside.

In a small bowl, stir together the chiles, the onion, the remaining ½ cup of vinegar, and 1 tablespoon cold water. Season with salt and set aside.

To serve, place the yuca on a large platter; top it with the cabbage slaw, then sprinkle the pork rinds over the slaw; serve with the chile sauce on the side.

❋⟩ NOTE: Raw yuca should have firm, white flesh; discard any that is brown or soft. Yuca roots are dipped in wax to preserve them, so always peel them before cooking.

The cooking time for yuca root will depend on how thick it is, so, to determine doneness, pierce it with a fork, as you would for potatoes. As soon as it's fork-tender, it's ready.

Cold foods like salads with dressings need to be re-seasoned just before serving, so taste this one before serving it and add more salt and/or vinegar as needed.

Crab Ceviche (Ceviche de Cangrejo)

Here, in one of the quickest versions of ceviche you'll ever make, delicate crabmeat is lightly dressed with a mixture of citrus. This is the kind of ceviche served at beach stands in Mexico and Central America, and this one features some heat and a smoky undertone lent by fiery chipotles. I'll never forget my first encounter with these smoky chiles. My grandmother brought my family a jar of pickled and puréed chipotles she'd purchased during one of her visits to Mexico. The taste of heat, smoke, and acidity was new to me, and at that very moment I was hooked to their flavor. Chipotles are so easy to find canned that I no longer pickle my own. Like many other spicy dishes, this ceviche is traditionally served with creamy avocados to offset the heat. The true star of this dish, however, is the crabmeat, and since it's already cooked, you can serve this ceviche immediately after making it, without having to wait for the seafood to get cured. This ceviche makes a great topping for tostadas; serve it with *tostones* (fried plantains, page 186) or with tortilla chips.

Serves 4–6

> 1 pound crabmeat (preferably claw meat), picked for
>   shell fragments
> ½ cup seeded and minced plum tomatoes
> ⅓ cup minced white onion
> ⅓ cup minced cilantro (leaves and tender stems)
> ¼ cup fresh lemon juice, or to taste
> ¼ cup fresh lime juice, or to taste
> 1 tablespoon minced mint
> 1 tablespoon plus 1 teaspoon minced chipotle chile, or to taste
> ½ teaspoon adobo sauce (from the canned chipotles)
> 2 Hass avocadoes
> Salt and freshly ground black pepper, to taste

In a medium nonreactive bowl, gently stir together the crabmeat, tomatoes, onions, cilantro, lemon juice, lime juice, mint, chipotles, and adobo sauce, being careful not to break up the crabmeat too much; season with salt and pepper. Cover and chill until ready to serve (up to 6 hours). Peel, pit, and slice avocados; serve on the side. ❊

Scallops with Creamy Yellow Ají Sauce (Tiradito)

Tiradito is very similar to ceviche. It is reminiscent of Asian sashimi or Italian *crudo* in that the seafood is thinly sliced and eaten raw, but the Peruvian version is always served with spicy sauces. Here, raw sea scallops are sliced paper-thin and drenched in a velvety, spicy, and vibrantly yellow sauce. Most of the time we think of street food as casual food, but in my opinion, this is one of the most elegant dishes that the streets of Latin America have to offer. Of course, you'll find tiraditos in some of the finest restaurants in Peru, but they're also found on a daily basis at road stands and outdoor market stalls. Purchase only the freshest possible scallops, preferably dry-packed and not injected with water. They should be firm to the touch and not mushy. Freezing the scallops for ten minutes makes them easier to slice. Remember to remove the abductor muscle on the sides of scallops (they pull off easily). In Peru, the curing time is cut short, but I suggest that you marinate the scallops for at least one hour to ensure their proper curing. Use ajíes preserved in jars—they're the easiest to peel—or purchase them already puréed into paste. Offer boiled potatoes with this dish to sop up the sauce and serve it with spoons so your guests can eat every last drop—it really is that delicious! You'll need a blender to make the pretty and delicate sauce.

Serves 4–6

- 1 pound sea scallops, sliced crosswise, paper-thin
- 4 preserved ají amarillos, peeled, seeded, deveined, and roughly chopped (see note)
- ½ cup fresh lime juice
- 1 large garlic clove, roughly chopped
- ¾ teaspoon salt, or to taste
- Pinch freshly ground black pepper, or to taste
- ½ cup extra-virgin olive oil
- Saltine crackers
- 4 boiled sweet or regular potatoes, peeled and thickly sliced (optional)

On a large platter with a high rim, arrange the sliced scallops in a single layer, fanning them attractively.

In a blender, combine the ají, lime juice, garlic, salt, and pepper. Blend until the sauce is completely smooth, about 45 seconds to 1 minute. With the motor running, slowly add the olive oil in a thin stream until the mixture is emulsified, about 30 seconds. Adjust salt and pepper, to taste.

Pour the sauce evenly over the scallops (they should be completely covered in the sauce); cover and chill for 1 hour (up to 3 hours). Serve well chilled with the crackers and/or potatoes (if using). For an elegant presentation, divide the scallops onto individual plates and top with lots of sauce.

❊} NOTE: If you can only find ají amarillo ground into a paste, use ¼ cup. Modern renditions are served with garnishes, such as chives, but the classic version is served just with the sauce.

Flounder Ceviche with Corn Nuts (Ceviche de Lenguado)

You'll find ceviches throughout Latin America, where each country gives them its own spin. The most classic presentation is found on the street stalls of Lima, Peru, where flounder is abundant. The fish is bathed in a spicy and sour essence of citrus and chiles and topped with crispy *canchita* (corn nuts). Although in Peru, the fish in ceviches like this one is only briefly marinated, sometimes as little as a few seconds, I prefer to marinate it a bit longer and until its flesh has turned opaque. Ají amarillo is the yellow pepper native to Peru, and here it provides gutsy heat and vibrant color. The corn you'll need for this recipe is found only in Latin stores. It's larger and flatter than popping corn, and since it will jump out of the pan just like popcorn does, it's imperative to cover the pan while it toasts. Unlike popcorn, canchita won't fully pop; instead it will toast and become crunchy. I love it, because it's like eating the center part of the popped corn kernels, and it's quite addictive. I like to think of canchita as the original corn nut. When canchita is not available, I serve this ceviche with saltine crackers or plantain chips. Here's a great low-fat dish to enjoy all summer.

Serves 4

1 pound flounder fillets, sliced into 2 × ⅙-inch strips

1 cup fresh lime juice

1 ají amarillo, deveined, seeded, and sliced into thin strips

¾ cup thinly sliced red onion (sliced into strips)

1½ teaspoon salt, or to taste

¼ teaspoon freshly ground black pepper, or to taste

2 tablespoons vegetable oil

1 cup *cancha* corn

Salt, to taste

In a large nonreactive bowl, toss together the fish, lime juice, ají, onions, salt, and pepper. Cover with plastic wrap, refrigerate, and marinate for at least 30 minutes (up to 2 hours). See note.

In the meantime, make the canchita: Heat the oil in a medium skillet over medium heat; add the corn and stir to coat with the oil. Partially cover the skillet with a lid. As soon as you can hear the corn popping, shake the pan. Continue shaking over the heat for 1–1½ minutes or until the kernels are toasted, being careful not to burn the corn. Transfer the corn onto a plate and season with salt.

Serve the ceviche well chilled with the corn as a topping or on the side.

✳ NOTE: The residual whitish juice left after marinating ceviches is called *leche de Tigre* (tiger's milk), and it's prized for its nutritional value. It is typically not strained from the ceviche before eating, but sometimes there is enough of it to spare. In Peru, you can buy small glasses of this to gulp down. Sometimes it's used as a base to start another ceviche. I often pour it over boiled potatoes and let them soak it up before eating them. Just make sure to consume it shortly after eating the ceviche for it won't keep long (about 2 hours, if chilled). Since Peruvians often serve ceviches with boiled potatoes, I make sure to have them at the ready whenever I make this recipe.

Once toasted, canchita will stay fresh in a tightly sealed container for up to 1 week.

Flounder Ceviche with Corn Nuts
(Ceviche de Lenguado)

Tuna Ceviche

Refreshing, low-fat ceviches such as this one are very easy to make, and this one can be assembled in no time. This ceviche is particularly festive because it's so pretty and colorful. If you eat it as a first course, serve it with corn nuts (page 48), plantain chips (page 182), or saltine crackers. For a main course salad, eat it the way Peruvians do: with boiled sweet or yellow potatoes, to soak up the sour marinade. I love to serve this ceviche in well-chilled martini glasses, to showcase all of the colors. Use only the highest quality, sashimi-grade tuna for this recipe. For an impressive appetizer, serve spoonfuls of this ceviche on the ends of endive leaves. It's simple, pretty, and fun.

Serves 8 as an appetizer or 4 as a main course

> 1½ pounds fresh, sashimi-grade tuna, cut into ¼-inch dice
> 1½ cups fresh lime juice
> ½ cup minced roasted red bell pepper
> ½ cup minced cilantro (leaves and tender stems)
> ½ cup seeded and minced plum tomatoes
> ⅓ cup minced red onion
> ¼ cup minced jalapeño peppers (seeded and deveined
>   if less heat is desired)
> ¼ cup minced chives
> Salt and freshly ground black pepper, to taste

In a large nonreactive bowl (preferably glass), combine the tuna, lime juice, bell peppers, cilantro, tomatoes, onions, jalapeños, and chives; stir well to combine. Cover with plastic wrap and chill for 1 hour (up to 4 hours). Season with salt and pepper and serve well chilled. ❖

Tuna Ceviche

Tuna Ceviche with Soy Sauce and Seaweed (Ceviche Nikkei)

Sushi meets ceviche! Sour, salty, and spicy flavors epitomize this dish so popular in Lima, Peru. Although this ceviche has very few ingredients, they come together perfectly to create a delicate balance of flavors. The Japanese culinary influence in the food of Peru is enormous, and this dish exemplifies this exciting blending of cultures. Flounder and scallops also work perfectly with this Asian interpretation. Serve it with Japanese rice crackers.

Serves 8 as an appetizer or 4 as a main course

> 1½ pounds fresh, sashimi-grade tuna, cut into ¼-inch dice
> 1½ cups fresh lime juice
> ¼ cup soy sauce
> Salt and freshly ground black pepper, to taste
> ½ cup thinly sliced red onion, soaked in cold water for 1 hour
>   and drained
> 1 ají amarillo, seeded, deveined, and sliced into thin strips
> 1 garlic clove, minced
> 1 teaspoon peeled and grated ginger root
> ¼ cup sliced green onions (light and dark green parts)
> 2 seaweed sheets (nori), cut into thin 2- to 3-inch-long strips

In a nonreactive bowl (preferably glass), combine the tuna, lime juice, and soy sauce; stir well to combine. Cover with plastic wrap and chill for 1 hour (up to 4 hours).

When ready to serve, season with salt and pepper. Stir in the onions, ají, garlic, ginger, and green onions. Serve immediately in individual bowls topped with the nori strips. ❈

Fried Squid Ceviche (Ceviche Frito)

This is a newcomer to the ceviche repertoire in Peru: fried seafood, topped with a traditional marinade made with lime, onion, and ají amarillo. It's a very loose interpretation of ceviche, but it's all the rage in Latin America, and it blends seafood and marinade beautifully. Most ceviches using shrimp, lobster, or squid require them to be blanched briefly; here, they're fried instead. My rendition is similar to those you'll find at market stands in Lima. Rice flour is available in most supermarkets and in health food stores. It doesn't turn golden when fried, and it makes a very light crust that's only slightly crunchy. If you like, use a combination of shrimp, scallops, and squid. Make the marinade up to a day in advance, but fry the seafood only just before you're ready to eat.

Serves 4–6

    ½ cup fresh lime juice
    1 ají amarillo, seeded, deveined, and sliced into thin strips
    ¾ cup red onion, sliced into thin strips
    2 pounds cleaned squid (or 2 pounds mixed shrimp, scallops,
        and squid)
    1 cup rice flour
    1 teaspoon salt
    ½ teaspoon freshly ground black pepper
    Peanut or canola oil for frying

In a large bowl, combine lime juice, ají, and onions; set aside and allow it to marinate for 30 minutes.

Place the squid in a strainer and rinse it under cold running water. Drain them well and lightly pat between paper towels (but don't dry them too much; you'll want to leave some moisture so that the flour can adhere). Cut the squid into ⅓-inch-thick rings, leaving the tentacles whole.

In a medium bowl, whisk together the rice flour, salt, and pepper; set aside. Fit a large baking pan with a metal cooling rack; set aside.

In a medium skillet, heat 2–3 inches of oil to 375°F (or use a deep fryer according to the manufacturer's directions). Working in batches, place a handful of squid (or seafood) into the flour, coating them on all sides; transfer them to a fine sieve and shake the excess flour back into the bowl. Fry the squid for 1–1½ minutes, turning them over with a fork to keep them separate. Using a slotted spoon, transfer them to the prepared rack to drain; repeat with the rest of the squid until done.

Transfer the fried squid to a large platter; season the marinade with salt and pepper and pour it liberally over the squid. Serve at once. ❊

Shrimp Ceviche

Plump, meaty shrimp swim in a generous amount of sweet, sour, and spicy citrus marinade. Believe it or not, the addition of ketchup is traditional to Ecuadorian ceviches; it adds a slight sweetness to the otherwise sour marinade while imparting beautiful color. In Ecuador, some ceviches are drizzled with yellow mustard, but I prefer not to include it in mine. What really makes Ecuadorian ceviches different and so much fun to eat are the toppings: from crispy plantain chips, to lighter-than-air popcorn, to chopped salads, and, yes, to peanut butter! This ceviche was inspired by the one made by my friend Maricel Presilla, restaurateur and cookbook author, during our panel presentation at the International Culinary Center in New York City. Mine features an avocado salad with a creamy texture that contrasts nicely with the crispy elements featured in this ceviche.

Serves 4–6

> 1½ pounds shrimp (26–30 count), peeled and deveined
> 1½ cups fresh lime juice, divided
> ½ cup ketchup
> 2 teaspoons Worcestershire sauce
> ¾ teaspoons salt, or to taste
> 1 cup very thinly sliced red onion
> ¼ cup minced serrano chiles or jalapeños (seeded and deveined
>   if less heat is desired)
> 1–2 Hass avocados
> ¼ cup minced cilantro (leaves and tender stems)
> ¼ cup minced flat-leaf or Italian parsley (leaves and tender stems)
> Fried Plantain Chips (page 182)

Fill a bowl with iced water; set aside. Bring a pot of water to a boil; add the shrimp and cook for 2–3 minutes or until just barely pink. Immediately drain them and plunge them into the iced water; let stand for 5–10 minutes. Drain and set aside while you make the marinade.

In a large bowl, combine all but 1 tablespoon of the lime juice (reserving the tablespoon for later), ketchup, Worcestershire, and salt, whisking until the ketchup is dissolved. Stir in the shrimp, onions, and chiles; cover and chill for 20–30 minutes.

Right before serving, peel, seed, and chop the avocados; toss them with the reserved lime juice, cilantro, and parsley. Top the ceviche with the avocado salad and serve immediately, with plenty of plantain chips. For a striking presentation, I serve this colorful ceviche in individual white bowls and then top each with the avocado salad. ✳

Kick-in-the-Pants-Spicy Shrimp in Chile-Lime Dressing (Aguachile de Camarones)

Aguachile (chile water) is a very spicy combination of green chiles—usually serranos—and lime. Aguachile is the cevichelike dish of Sinaloa, Mexico, but it differs from ceviches in that the raw shrimp is cured only for a few seconds rather than blanched. On Mexican beaches, shrimpers featuring their day's catch will simply clean the shrimp and combine them with the dressing. It's much safer to blanch the shrimp before giving them their spicy bath, so I combine both methods here. Aguachiles are meant to be very spicy, so it's traditional to serve them with a generous amount of buttery avocado, which tempers the heat. If you wish to further tame the spiciness, reduce the amount of chiles. It's best to make this dressing in a blender so that the chiles can be fully crushed. Serve this with tortilla chips and either an icy, cold beer or a margarita.

Serves 4

> 1 pound shrimp (16–21 count), peeled, deveined, and butterflied
> 1 cup fresh lime juice
> 3–4 serrano chiles, or to taste (stemmed, but left whole)
> ½ cup packed cilantro (leaves and tender stems)
> 1 garlic clove, minced
> Salt and freshly ground black pepper, to taste
> ½ cup very thinly sliced red onion
> 2 Hass avocados, pitted, peeled, thinly sliced and brushed with
>   fresh lime juice (to prevent browning)
> Fried tortilla chips

In a large pot, bring 6–7 cups of water to a rolling boil. Fill a large bowl with iced water and set aside. Add the shrimp to the boiling water and cook for 20–30 seconds or until just barely pink. Drain the shrimp and immediately plunge them into the iced water; let them stand for 5–10 minutes. Drain and set aside.

In the meantime, make the dressing. In a blender, combine the lime juice, serranos, cilantro, and garlic; blend until smooth, and season with salt and pepper.

Arrange the shrimp on a large platter in a single layer; pour the dressing over them. Sprinkle with the sliced onions. Serve immediately, with the sliced avocados and tortilla chips on the side. ❄

Shrimp Cocktail (Coctel de Camarones)

Seafood cocktails such as this one, in which plump shrimp are bathed in creamy, sweet, and sour dressing, are sold in the many *casetas* or *ranchos* (little huts) that line the beaches along the Pacific coast of Guatemala. They're typically served in small, white paper cups with a toothpick for spearing the shrimp. I recall eating this cocktail in my youth, during family vacations at the beach and being amazed at how its pink color contrasted with the volcanic, black sandy beaches. Serve it with saltine crackers or tortilla chips. You could leave the shrimp whole, but they're easier to mound on crackers if they're chopped coarsely. This is a quick and easy recipe that delivers great flavor. For an even quicker version, buy frozen, precooked and peeled shrimp; just thaw, stir, and enjoy.

Serves 4–6

> 2 pounds shrimp (16–20 count), cooked, peeled, and deveined
> ¾ cup Golf Sauce, or to taste (page 276)
> ½ cup thinly sliced celery
> ¼ cup chopped green onions
> Salt and freshly ground black pepper, to taste
> Saltine crackers

Chop the shrimp coarsely and place them in a large bowl; stir in the sauce, celery, and onions. Season it with salt and pepper and serve, well chilled, with plenty of saltine crackers.

❄ NOTE: This keeps in the refrigerator for up to 8 hours; it's not suitable for freezing.

Shrimp Cocktail (Coctel de Camarones)

Layered Potato, Crab, and Avocado Salad (Causa Limeña de Cangrejo)

Causas are beautiful salads made by layering chile and lime–infused mashed potatoes with mayonnaise-laden salads. This one is made with crab, but chicken, tuna, or shrimp may easily be substituted. Causas are the most famous potato salads of Peru, and they're said to have pre-Columbian origins. Like many other recipes, its name is a matter of lore. Some historians say the term "causa" derives from the Quechua word for potato, *kausac*. However, the popular version of the story is that causas got their name when women began to sell them on the streets during Peru's war with Chile to help raise funds *por la causa* (for the cause). In the outdoor markets in Peru, causas are molded into individual portions or sliced off large timbales, like this one. Use a 9-inch springform pan or shape them into individual portions by layering them into smaller rings (tuna cans without lids work well in lieu of baking rings).

Serves 8–10

3½ pounds Yukon Gold potatoes

½ cup fresh lime juice, or to taste, divided

¼ cup extra-virgin olive oil

2 tablespoons ají amarillo paste, or to taste

2 teaspoons salt, or to taste

¼ teaspoon freshly ground black pepper, or to taste

½ cup minced white onion

1 pound lump crabmeat, picked for shell fragments, drained well
    (I prefer claw meat)

½ cup mayonnaise

2 tablespoons minced red onion

2 tablespoons minced flat-leaf or Italian parsley
    (leaves and tender stems)

2 Hass avocados, sliced and brushed with lime juice
    (to prevent browning)

1 cup sliced black olives

1 large roasted red bell pepper, cut into strips (optional)

¼ cup chopped flat-leaf or Italian parsley, for garnish

Place the potatoes in a large pot filled with cold water; boil the potatoes until tender (about 20–30 minutes); drain, peel, and mash them until smooth (use a potato ricer, if you have one).

In a large bowl, combine the mashed potatoes, ⅓ cup of the lime juice, oil, and ají paste, salt, and pepper; stir well and set aside.

In a large bowl, gently stir together the crab, mayonnaise, red onions, and parsley, being careful not to break up the crab too much; add the remaining lime juice, and season with salt and pepper; set aside.

Remove the ring from a springform pan and brush it with oil (or use oil spray); set it directly on a large serving platter. Pour half of the potato mixture into the ring and spread it evenly to form one layer; top with the crab salad. Place the avocado slices in one layer over the crab; top with the remaining potato mixture, spreading it evenly with a spatula. Cover with plastic wrap and chill for at least one hour (or up to 4 hours).

When ready to serve, gently lift the ring. Decorate the top with the olives, bell peppers (if using), and parsley. To serve, slice into thick wedges; serve cold. ✳

TORTILLA FLATS

There is nothing like the aroma of freshly ground masa, which has a clean smell of corn and *cal* (calcium hydroxide). The fragrance takes me back to my girlhood watching my grandmother's cooks grind the moist, swollen corn that had been previously soaked in lime water. On several occasions I tried my hand at it, kneeling on the tiled floor before the *metate*, a giant, rectangle-shaped, slightly concave, and roughly textured volcanic stone set over three legs made out of the same material. My tiny hands would hold the oblong shaped rolling pin, called a *tlejolote* or *metlapil*, which had to be moved swiftly back and forth over the corn to grind the kernels. The trick, if I remember correctly, was to keep the corn moist, so we kept a bowl of water next to us. The ground masa was then transferred to a large plastic *cubeta* or bowl and kept covered. Let's just say I was much better at patting tortillas flat between my tiny hands.

Frankly, the idea of making fresh masa from scratch—by soaking the corn in lime to remove the outer hull and then grinding it—to make fresh masa, is daunting by anyone's standards. And, unless you're lucky enough to live near a store that makes its own, you're unlikely to find fresh masa to work with. (There are lots of Mexican stores where I live, but I can't find fresh masa anywhere.) Truth be told, most cooks in Mexico and Central America use masa harina (dried masa) because it's simple to use and only needs to be reconstituted with warm water and kneaded slightly before it's ready. That is what I use for the recipes in this book.

Since masa harina varies so much from brand to brand, the amount of water each brand will require to reach its optimal texture will be different. I prefer Maseca or TortiMasa. Keep in mind that just as it is with any other kind of flour, the varying level of moisture in the air from day to day will dictate how much water the dried masa harina will need; more water may be needed in very dry days, and less water will be required on those days that are wet.

Although you can use store-bought tortillas for all of the recipes in this book, the most authentic taco trucks make their own. To encourage you to do the same, I developed a recipe that produces tortillas that are meatier than store-bought brands. Mine sit somewhere between the thick tortillas found in Guatemala and the thin versions found in Mexico. Making them thicker serves a dual purpose: first, they'll hold up to any fillings you may want to pile onto tacos, and, second, they'll always have a stellar role, because I believe a tortilla is meant to be tasted as much as its filling is. Thicker tortillas also make great tostada bases. Not only are they easier to handle while you're frying them, but they also make it easy to spread them with thick beans and salsas. The right thickness ensures also that tostadas will withstand the weight of some of the toppings you'll find in this chapter such as the beet salad and the spicy chicken that crown two of my favorite renditions here. Try putting heavy toppings on a flimsy corn tortilla!

What I do not give you here is a master recipe for masa, and there is a reason for this. Each recipe that uses masa in this book—whether it's in this chapter or elsewhere—requires that it be a different consistency. Some of the masa needs to be very moist so that it can be pressed thinly

A young Mayan woman wearing a traditional *güipil* makes tortillas in Chichicastenango, Guatemala.

with a tortilla press, while other recipes need it to be thicker so it can hold a particular shape. However, each of the recipes in this book requiring masa was formulated to give you the best results every single time you make it.

Not all flatbreads (unleavened bread) made in Latin America are tortillas. Mexicans and most Central Americans consume tortillas, but once you cross over into South America, the tortillas made with nixtamalized corn disappear. In their place you'll find thick corn cakes called arepas. In Ecuador, you'll find flatbreads made with a mixture of fresh corn and wheat flour that are a cross between arepas and tortillas. In the rest of South America, the term tortilla denotes a frittata, much in the same way that it does in Spain. As you can see, the nomenclature stays the same but the meaning changes completely. Another example of this is Guatemalan enchiladas (page 81), which don't at all resemble the filled and rolled tortillas from Mexico that have the same name. This happens because although most Latin Americans, with the exception of Brazilians, speak Spanish, we don't all speak it exactly the same way.

An elderly couple selling bread waits for customers in Cuzco, Peru.

I've included other popular flatbreads in this chapter. I introduce you to the amazingly delicious *arepas* of Colombia and Venezuela, give you a classic pizza recipe popular on the streets of Argentina, and showcase the fun *cachapas* (sweet corn pancakes) you'll find from Costa Rica down to Venezuela. Of course, you'll find some of the masa classics here as well, such as *sopes* with various options for fillings, a recipe for the elongated, sandal-shaped *huaraches* so beloved not only in Mexico but in this country, too. Here, every flatbread is given a stellar role. All of the other ingredients will work in unison with each base so their flavors will stand out.

I invite you to play around with the recipes in this book. Use the salsas, fillings, and condiments in an interchangeable fashion according to your taste so that you, too, can create new recipes out of old favorites. Street food is meant to be customized by each individual palate. To me, that's precisely what makes it so much fun. The world may not be flat, but the world of flatbreads certainly is a tasty reality.

Handmade Corn Tortillas

The best corn tortillas are handmade. My formula calls for more water than most recipes you'll find, as the masa must be moist enough so that the resulting tortillas will have smooth edges that won't break. A tortilla press will come in handy here, but using a rolling pin or flattening them down with a plate also work. When making these tortillas, keep your hands moist so that the masa doesn't stick to them. Use a plastic bag, cut open on three sides, to encase the masa as you shape it; this will prevent it from sticking to the press. Resist the temptation to make thinner tortillas than what I suggest here (⅛ inch is ideal). These are thicker, sturdier than store-bought tortillas and they hold up to any filling. There'll be no more stacking two of them together every time you make a taco. These will roll beautifully whether you're shaping taquitos or frying tostadas. These are traditionally cooked on a *comal*, but a griddle works just as well. Flipping them onto the griddle takes practice, but you'll get the hang of it. Like pancakes, tortillas release from the cooking surface only when their exteriors are fully cooked. Fight the urge to flip them until they're ready, or you'll destroy their shape. Tortillas are always flipped three times, and if you're lucky, they'll puff up beautifully on the griddle—the sign of the perfect tortilla—but they'll taste just as delicious if they don't. Sometimes pressing them down slightly with a spatula at the last minute helps them to inflate. At first, these tortillas will seem tough, but if you stack and wrap them in moist towels immediately after cooking them and let them rest, their own steam will make them pliable. My tortillas take a few minutes longer to cook than the average recipe. Make sure they are still warm when you use them for any of the recipes in this book; they can be reheated wrapped in a damp towel in the microwave or wrapped in aluminum foil and baked in a 350°F oven for 10–12 minutes.

Makes 12 tortillas

> 2¼ cups masa harina
> 1¾–2 cups warm (100°F) water (or more if needed; see note)

In a medium bowl, combine the masa harina with 1¾ cups of the water. With your hands, mix to form a lump-free dough with the consistency of soft mashed potatoes. Add more water as necessary. When the dough has reached the desired consistency, cover the bowl with plastic wrap and let it rest for 10 minutes (the masa will continue to absorb the liquid as it sits).

In the meantime, line a tortilla press with a freezer bag cut open along the sides (so the bag opens like a book). With moistened hands, divide the dough into 12 equal portions (about ¼ cup each). Roll each into a ball, keeping them covered with a damp towel as you work.

Heat a nonstick griddle or skillet over medium-high heat (or heat an electric griddle to 375°–400°F). Keep a bowl of water nearby to moisten your hands as you shape the masa. Working quickly so the dough doesn't dry out, place a ball of masa in the center of a tortilla press, cover it with the top of the plastic, and flatten it into a 5- to 6-inch disk, ⅛ inch thick. If the edges break, moisten your hands, roll the dough into a ball again to moisten it, and press it again. Pull back the plastic from one side of the tortilla (to loosen the plastic), cover it again, then flip the tortilla (still using the plastic) and pull the plastic off that side. Lay the side of the tortilla without plastic gently on the extended (and moist) fingers of your dominant hand. Pull off the plastic completely and flip the tortilla directly onto the center of the griddle. If it folds, flatten it with wet fingers (it won't stick to your fingers if they're wet). Cook the first side until it has golden flecks, about 2–2½ minutes. Flip the tortilla over with a spatula, and cook until it has golden flecks, about 2–2½ minutes. Flip the tortilla again and cook it for 30 seconds to 1 minute. Wrap the tortillas in a moist kitchen towel, making sure to stack one on top of the other as you finish the rest. See note.

NOTE: Since masa brands vary, the amount of water required to make the dough will vary. Always start with the minimum amount of water called for and test the dough by pressing a bit of it into a tortilla; if the edges break, add more water, a few tablespoons at a time. If the dough is too wet to form a patty, add more masa harina, a few tablespoons at a time. Make sure you keep a bowl of water nearby to moisten your hands when you shape the masa.

The tortillas can be wrapped in plastic and frozen for up to 2 months. To reheat, wrap them in a damp towel and microwave them on HIGH for 1–2 minutes or wrap them in aluminum foil and heat in a 350°F oven for 20–25 minutes. They also can be reheated one at a time on a hot griddle for a few seconds until warm; stack and wrap them in a damp towel and allow them to steam again.

Potato and Chorizo Masa Boats
(Sopes de Papa y Chorizo)

These crispy, flaky, and dainty masa cakes have pinched edges thick enough to hold a classic Mexican filling of finely diced potatoes and spicy sausage, called *chorizo*. Sopes can be filled with virtually anything, and popular toppings include red or black refried beans, shredded beef or chicken, and sautéed vegetables like zucchini or mushrooms. They're topped with succulent and fun garnishes, such as crumbled Cotija (a feta-like cheese) or cabbage and salsas like Avocado-Tomatillo Taco Truck Sauce (page 270) or Sweet Dried Chile Sauce (page 278). Some sopes are cooked on a griddle, and their edges are pinched after they're cooked, making them soft rather than crunchy. These are pan-fried until golden and crispy. Serve them as a first course, or make them smaller for appetizers. For variety, fill them with Beef Picadillo (page 288), Spicy Chicken (page 76), or Crab Ceviche (page 45).

Makes 12 sopes

> 8 ounces Mexican chorizo, casings removed
> 1 pound white potatoes, peeled and minced
> 1/3 cup minced white onion
> 2 cups masa harina
> 1/2 teaspoon salt
> 1 1/3–1 1/2 cups hot (approximately 125°F) water
> Vegetable oil for frying
> 3 cups shredded iceberg lettuce
> 1 1/2 cups seeded and minced tomatoes
> 3/4 cup crumbled Cotija cheese

Line a baking pan with a metal cooling rack; set aside. In a large skillet over medium-high heat, cook the chorizo, breaking it up with the back of a spoon as it cooks, until it begins to render its fat, about 2–3 minutes. Add the onions and cook for 1 minute; add the potatoes and stir well. Cover the skillet; reduce the heat to medium-low and cook, stirring on occasion, for 8–10 minutes or until the potatoes are fork-tender. Set the filling aside and keep it warm (the filling can be prepared the day before and chilled; reheat before using).

Potato and Chorizo Masa Boats (Sopes de Papa y Chorizo)
with Avocado-Tomatillo Truck Sauce (page 270)

In a large bowl, stir together the masa harina and salt. Gradually add 1⅓ cups of the water and mix with your hands until the masa comes together into a ball with the consistency of mashed potatoes (if it's too dry add more water a few tablespoons at a time); cover with a damp towel and let it rest for 10 minutes.

Line a tortilla press with plastic wrap (a plastic bag split down the sides also works great). Keep a bowl of cold water on hand. Divide the masa into 12 equal portions (about ¼ cup each). With moist hands, roll each piece into a ball, keeping the balls covered as you work. Press each ball into a 3½-inch patty, ¼ inch thick (if the masa breaks around the edges, moisten your hands with the water, reroll it into a ball, and shape again). Use your fingers to pinch the edges to form a small rim (like you would for a tart). Don't make the rims too thin or too tall or they'll break when they're frying. Heat ½ inch of oil in a large skillet over medium-high heat. Fry the sopes until golden on the bottom, about 4–5 minutes, occasionally spooning the hot oil into the sope to cook the centers; flip them over (it's okay if their rims touch the bottom of the pan) and fry until golden, about 2–3 minutes. Be careful not to burn them; lower the temperature of the oil if they start browning too quickly. Transfer them to the prepared rack.

While the sopes are still hot, fill each with about ¼ cup of the chorizo filling. Top them with shredded lettuce, tomatoes, and cheese.

✳} NOTE: Shaped sopes can be kept covered in the refrigerator for up to 3 hours before frying. The fried sopes can be kept warm on baking sheets in a 250°F oven for up to 1 hour before serving.

To shape a sope, use your fingers to form a rim around the edge of the dough.

Fry the sopes on each side until golden.

Bean-Stuffed Masa Cakes
(Pupusas de Frijol Negro)

Tender masa gives way to creamy beans and crispy cabbage slaw, called *curtido*. Pupusas can be filled with cheese, refried beans, *chicharrón* (seasoned ground pork) or a combination of all three, in which case they're called *revueltas*. Your first attempts may result in some of the filling seeping out of the masa as they cook, and that's okay. The amount of beans you'll need may vary slightly depending on how much you're able to stuff inside them. Kids can help make these; just know that tiny hands will make smaller pupusas. I was a little girl the first time I ate pupusas on the streets of San Salvador and can vividly recall watching in awe as the *pupuseras* expertly shaped, filled, and patted round cakes before cooking them on giant griddles. Years later, I taught my young niece, Marcela, to make these. Now, every time I make them, I think of her.

Makes 12 pupusas

> Latin Slaw (page 41)
> All-Purpose Tomato Sauce (page 268) or sauce for
>   Cheese Pupusas (page 71)
> 3 cups masa harina
> 3¼–3½ cups warm (110°–120°F) water
> 1–1½ cups Refried Black Beans (page 284) (or used canned)
> ½ cup vegetable oil

In a large bowl, combine the masa harina with 3¼ cups of the water and knead with your hands until a soft dough with the consistency of thick mashed potatoes is formed (add more water, one tablespoon at a time, if needed); cover with plastic wrap (or a kitchen towel) and let it rest for 10 minutes.

Line a baking pan with a damp kitchen towel. Heat a nonstick griddle or skillet over medium-high heat (or heat an electric griddle to 375°–400°F). Moisten your hands with a little bit of the oil and divide the masa into 12 equal portions (⅓ cup each); pat each into a ½-inch-thick disk. Keep them covered with a moist towel so they don't dry out.

Working with one disk at a time, place 1 heaping tablespoon of the beans in the center; bring the outer edges of the dough up and together over the filling to enclose it. With oiled hands, roll the pupusa into a ball

Bean-Stuffed Masa Cakes (Pupusas de Frijol Negro) with Latin Slaw (Curtido) (page 41) and All-Purpose Tomato Sauce (Salsa Casera) (page 268)

and then pat it again into a ½-inch-thick disk (or press it down with a tortilla press lined with plastic), making sure the filling does not escape. Repeat with the remaining dough and filling.

Place the pupusas on the griddle and cook until they are golden, with brown flecks, about 4–5 minutes per side. (If the griddle is too hot, the exterior of the pupusas will burn before they're cooked through. If you see black rather than brown flecks forming as they cook, reduce the heat of your griddle.) Transfer the finished pupusas to the prepared pan, enclosing them in the damp towel (this allows them to steam and become tender).

Serve the pupusas topped with the slaw and a generous spoonful of the tomato sauce.

⁕⸩ NOTE: Pupusas are best made just prior to eating, but they can be kept warm for up to 1 hour wrapped in a damp kitchen towel and placed in a baking pan in a 250°F oven. Be sure to keep the towel damp by sprinkling it with water occasionally.

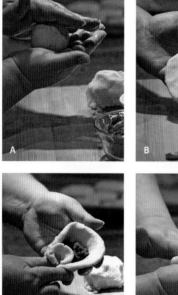

A. To shape and fill the pupusas, roll a portion of masa into a ball and flatten it into a disk.

B. Place a heaping tablespoon of the filling in the center.

C. Gather the edges of the masa up and over the filling to enclose it; roll the dough into a ball.

D. Pat the ball back into a disk.

Tortilla Flats

Cheese Pupusas

Pupusas are Salvadorian masa cakes stuffed with myriad fillings, among them beans and pork mince. They're prepared street-side by *pupuseras* who cook them on griddles. These pupusas are filled with gooey, creamy, melting cheese, topped with refreshing and crunchy Latin Slaw and finished with a quick and easy tomato sauce. Make sure your griddle is not too hot or the exteriors of these pupusas will burn before their centers cook through. When the pupusas are cooked, keep them in a clean kitchen towel so that the steam can soften them as they sit, which will make them tender. If you love grilled cheese sandwiches and quesadillas, give these a try.

Makes 12 pupusas and 1 ½ cups sauce

Latin Slaw (page 41)

FOR THE TOMATO SAUCE
1 (14-ounce) can of fire-roasted tomatoes
2 garlic cloves, roughly chopped
1 teaspoon salt
¼ teaspoon freshly ground black pepper
2 tablespoons vegetable oil

FOR THE PUPUSAS
3 cups masa harina
3¼–3½ cups warm (110°–120°F) water
2 cups shredded Muenster cheese or queso blanco
½ cup vegetable oil

In a blender, combine the tomatoes, garlic, salt, pepper, and oil; blend until smooth. Place the sauce in a medium saucepan over medium-high heat and bring it to a boil; cover, reduce the heat to low, and simmer for 15 minutes. Keep it warm, covered, until ready to use.

In a large bowl, combine the masa harina with 3¼ cups of the water and knead with your hands until a soft dough with the consistency of thick mashed potatoes is formed (add more water a tablespoon at a time, if needed); cover with plastic wrap (or a kitchen towel) and let it rest for 10 minutes.

Line a baking pan with a damp kitchen towel. Heat a nonstick griddle or skillet over medium-high heat (or heat an electric griddle to 375°–

400°F). Moisten your hands with a little bit of the oil and divide the masa into 12 equal portions (⅓ cup each); and pat each into a ½-inch-thick tortilla. Keep them covered with a moist towel, so they don't dry out while you shape them.

Working with one tortilla at a time, place 1 heaping tablespoon of the cheese in the center; bring the outer edges of the dough up and together over the cheese to enclose it. With oiled hands, roll the pupusa back into a ball; then, pat it again into a ½-inch-thick disk (or press it down with a tortilla press lined with plastic), making sure the filling does not escape. Repeat with the remaining tortillas.

Place the pupusas on the griddle and cook until they are golden, with brown flecks, about 4–5 minutes per side. (If the griddle is too hot, the exterior of the pupusas will burn before they're cooked through. If you see black rather than brown flecks forming as they cook, reduce the heat of your griddle.) Transfer the finished pupusas to the prepared pan, enclosing them in the damp towel.

Serve the pupusas topped with a generous amount of slaw and a hefty spoonful of the tomato sauce. Leftover sauce can be spooned over eggs or chilled and served as salsa with chips.

✻⟩ NOTE: Pupusas are best made just prior to eating, but they can be kept warm for up to 1 hour wrapped in a damp kitchen towel and placed in a baking pan in a 250°F oven. Be sure to keep the towel damp by sprinkling it with water occasionally.

Sandal-Shaped Stuffed Tortillas with Assorted Toppings (Huaraches)

Huarache means "sandal," and the shape of these colorful and fun morsels explains their name. Huaraches (also known as *tlacoyos*) are sold throughout Mexico City and are sometimes so large that vendors require a special press to make them. However, these can be made with a regular tortilla press—which can be inexpensively purchased in a Latin market—or with a flat, heavy plate. Huaraches are not hard to make, but they do take some time to craft. First, the masa is flattened and spread with a filling—usually beans, but cheese, mashed potatoes, and chorizo are also popular—then, it's folded in half, like an empanada, and flattened again. Huaraches are cooked twice: first on the griddle and then in oil. After they're cooked on the griddle, they can be kept warm for an hour or chilled for up to two hours. They should be fried just before you plan to eat them. My recipe makes medium-size huaraches, but you can make them any size your press allows. Tiny huaraches make beautiful appetizers. Street vendors will transport the filled and grilled huaraches to their stations and fry them to order, often allowing customers to top them with the condiments of their choice.

Makes 10 huaraches

> 4 cups masa harina
> 1 teaspoon salt
> 3½–4 cups warm (110°–120°F) water
> ¼ cup melted lard
> 1½–2 cups Traditional Mexican Refried Beans (page 286)
>   (or use canned)
> Vegetable oil for frying
> 2 cups crumbled queso fresco, or to taste
> 1 cup very thinly sliced red onion, or to taste
> 1 cup roughly chopped cilantro (leaves and tender stems), or to taste
> Avocado-Tomatillo Taco Truck Sauce (page 270)

In a large bowl, stir together the masa harina and salt. Gradually add the water and mix with your hands until the masa comes together into a ball with the consistency of playdough. Add the lard and knead it into the dough; cover with a damp towel and let it rest for 10 minutes.

In the meantime, line a tortilla press with plastic wrap (a freezer bag cut open along the two sides adjacent to the opening—so the bag opens like a book—also works great). Keep a bowl of cold water on hand. Divide the dough into 10 equal portions (about ½ cup each), and with moist hands, roll each into a football (5 inches long), keeping them covered with a damp towel as you work.

Heat a nonstick griddle or skillet over medium-high heat (or heat an electric griddle to 375°–400°F). Working with one football at a time, press the dough into ¼-inch-thick ovals (they'll measure roughly 8×6 inches). If the masa cracks on the edges when first pressed, roll it back into a ball, moisten it a bit, and reshape it into a football. Peel off the plastic from the top side and then cover it again; flip the masa over and peel off the plastic from this side and cover it with the plastic again (this is done to prevent the masa from sticking to the plastic). Once shaped, transfer it to a flat surface and uncover the plastic from the top only.

Leave the huarache on the plastic and turn it so that one of the long sides is facing you. Spread 2 tablespoons of the refried beans on the lower half, making sure to leave a ½-inch rim. Without removing the plastic, fold the top of the huarache over the beans to form a half moon. Using the plastic to help you, press the seams together well to seal (the half moon will be encased in the plastic). Place the huarache back into the tortilla press and press slightly, until it's ¼ inch thick (a bit thicker than a tortilla) and you can begin to see the beans through the masa; it will measure about 9 × 4½ inches.

Remove the plastic from the top of the huarache; flip the side of the huarache without plastic gently onto the extended (and moist) palm and fingers of your dominant hand. Pull off the plastic completely and flip the huarache onto the center of the griddle; cook on the first side until golden flecks are visible on the bottom, about 2 minutes (at this point, it should slide easily on the griddle); using a spatula (ideally, a very long one, such as the kind used to lift fish), flip it onto the other side and cook until golden flecks are visible on the bottom, about 2 minutes. Flip again to the first side and continue cooking for 1 minute. Place the huarache on a baking pan and cover with a moist kitchen towel. Repeat with the rest of the dough (layering the huaraches on top of one another as you go).

Place the huaraches, still covered with the moist towel, in a preheated 250°F oven to keep them warm for up to 1 hour (sprinkle the towel with water occasionally so they'll stay moist or wrap them in plastic and re-frigerate them for up to 8 hours).

When ready to eat, fit two baking pans with metal cooling racks; set aside. In a large skillet, heat ½ inch of oil over medium-high heat; work-ing in batches, sauté the huaraches on both sides until crispy and lightly golden, about 1–1½ minutes total. Remove them from the pan with a slotted spoon and place them on the prepared racks.

To serve, spread each huarache with the Avocado-Tomatillo Taco Truck Sauce and sprinkle with cheese, onions, and cilantro. ❖

Corn Pancakes with Cheese (Cachapas)

These savory corn crepes made with fresh corn are filled with deliciously melting cheese and luscious cream. *Cachapas*, stuffed with a huge variety of fillings, are sold at street stands across Venezuela for breakfast and lunch or as a midday snack. Other than cheese, popular fillings include shredded beef, pork rinds, or jam. In Costa Rica, you'll find sweeter versions called *chorreadas*. Serve these as a side dish for grilled meats or make them for brunch, stuffed with scrambled eggs and ham or bacon. On the streets, cachapas are often served on paper plates to hold the hefty amount of cheese. At home, I like to serve these with a side of eggs and sausage for breakfast or filled with Shredded Beef and Vegetable Stew (page 123) for lunch.

Makes 8–9 cakes

> 5 cups fresh corn kernels (9–10 ears)
> ½ cup, plus two tablespoons all-purpose flour
> 2 large eggs
> 1 teaspoon salt
> ¼ cup unsalted butter, softened to room temperature
> 9 ounces fresh mozzarella cheese, cut into 9 slices
> 1 cup Mexican crema or crème fraîche

In a blender, combine the corn, flour, eggs, and salt; blend for 1 minute or until almost smooth. Cover and set aside for 10 minutes.

Heat a nonstick griddle or skillet over medium heat and brush with butter. Pour a scant ½ cup of batter onto the pan and spread it to form a 5-inch pancake; cook until the edges look set and the centers are cooked, about 2–2½ minutes on the first side. Use a spatula to flip them onto the other side and cook until cakes are golden and cooked through, about 1 more minute. (The pan will get hotter as you cook, so if the pancakes are browning too quickly, reduce the heat and cook for less time.)

Remove the pancakes to a plate, brush them with butter, top with cheese, and drizzle with crema. Serve immediately. ❊

Tostadas with Spicy Chicken (Tostadas de Tinga)

Balancing a tower of toppings on a toasty base is an exciting thing to do, especially when biting into such a soaring creation gets you a step closer to culinary nirvana. Tostada means "toasted," and one of the most popular taco truck offerings in Mexico is this crunchy tortilla topped with beans and a spicy chicken called *tinga*. What makes tostadas all the rage is the variety of toppings that can be used to crown them: cream, salsas, cheese, avocado—you name it! In the Yucatán Peninsula, tinga is traditionally topped with pickled onions, which offer a refreshing contrast, so I use them here, too. The fried tortilla bases are very easy to make, but the prepackaged ones found in grocery stores work, too. Tostadas are a lot of fun to assemble, and given all of the toppings they can be loaded with, they're perfect for a casual party, where guests can fix their own.

Makes 8 tostadas

2 tablespoons vegetable oil (plus more for frying the tortillas)
1 cup minced white onion
2 large garlic cloves, minced
2 cups seeded and chopped plum tomatoes
1 cup chopped tomatillos (remove husks and rinse before chopping)
1–2 chipotle chiles in adobo, or to taste, minced
2 teaspoons adobo sauce (from the canned chipotles)
1 teaspoon dried Mexican oregano
½ teaspoon dried thyme
2½ cups packed shredded cooked chicken
1 cup chicken broth
1 teaspoon salt
8 Handmade Corn Tortillas (page 63)
1–1¼ cups Traditional Mexican Refried Beans (page 286) (or use canned)
2 Hass avocados (pitted, peeled, sliced, and brushed with fresh lime juice to prevent browning)
3–4 cups shredded iceberg lettuce
1–1½ cups Mexican crema
1–1½ cups Cotija cheese
Yucatán Pickled Onions (page 281)

Heat the 2 tablespoons of oil in a large skillet over medium-high heat; add the onions and sauté until softened, about 3 minutes. Add the garlic, tomatoes, tomatillos, chiles, adobo sauce, oregano, and thyme; reduce the heat to medium-low and simmer, uncovered, for 10–15 minutes. Add the chicken, broth, and salt; continue cooking until it has thickened, about 20–22 minutes; keep warm. See note.

Fit a baking pan with a metal cooling rack; set aside. In a large skillet with high sides, heat 1–2 inches of oil to 360°F (or use a deep fryer according to the manufacturer's directions); using tongs, slide the tortillas into the oil, one at a time. Fry them for 3–4 minutes or until golden, turning them over halfway through (keep them flat by pressing them down with the tongs). Using the tongs, transfer them to the prepared rack to drain.

Spread each tostada with 2–3 tablespoons of refried beans; top with chicken, avocado, lettuce, crema, cheese, and pickled onions.

*⸳} NOTE: For a party, and as a time-saving measure, I suggest that you make the chicken a day in advance and then reheat it when ready to eat. Homemade tostada bases (without toppings) kept in an airtight container will keep for up to 3 days.

Tricolor Tostadas (Tostadas de Feria)

Tricolor Tostadas (Tostadas de Feria)

If you ask Guatemalans what they're most likely to snack on on the streets, chances are you'll hear about these very thin tortilla crisps that are topped with beans, avocado, and tomato sauce. Each tortilla features only one main topping at a time and a little sprinkling of cheese. They're simple snacks, known as *tentenpiés* (roughly, "keep-me-uppers"), to tide you over until mealtime. A platter of different color tostadas is a festive sight. When I entertain a small group of friends, I sometimes use cookie cutters to cut store-bought corn tortillas into smaller rounds or I make very thin miniature corn tortillas by hand and fry those instead. Then I serve the delightful tostadas as finger food. They're very simple, but if you ever needed proof that sometimes simple can indeed be better, look no further.

Makes 12 tostadas

> 12 (6- to 8-inch) store-bought yellow or white corn tortillas
> Vegetable oil for frying
> 1 Hass avocado
> 1 tablespoon grated onion
> Fresh lime juice, to taste
> Salt, to taste
> 1 cup Refried Black Beans (page 284) (or use canned)
> ½ cup All-Purpose Tomato Sauce (page 268)
> ⅓ cup Cotija cheese (or more, to taste)
> ¼ cup minced flat-leaf or Italian parsley (leaves and tender stems)

Fit a large baking pan with a metal cooling rack; set aside. In a large skillet with high sides, heat 1–2 inches of oil to 360°F (or use a deep fryer according to the manufacturer's directions). Working with one or two tortillas at a time and using tongs, place the tortillas in the oil. Fry them for 45 seconds to 1 minute or until golden, turning them over halfway through (keep them flat by pressing them down with the tongs). Using the tongs, transfer them to the prepared rack to drain.

Halve, seed, and peel the avocado. In a small bowl, mash the avocado, onions, and lime juice until very smooth; season with salt. Spread four of the tostadas with beans; sprinkle with cheese. Spread four of the other tostadas with a thin layer of sauce; top with cheese and parsley. Spread the remaining four tostadas with the mashed avocado; top with cheese and parsley. Serve immediately. ❖

Beet Salad Tostada
(Guatemalan Enchilada)

Beet Salad Tostadas (Guatemalan Enchiladas)

When is an enchilada a salad? In Guatemala, enchilada means only one thing: a crunchy tostada topped with luscious beet slaw. Here is one of the loveliest composed salads you'll ever see on the streets; it features a virtual rainbow of colors that combines vibrant fuchsia, red, yellow, white, and green ingredients. The sweet and sour slaw crowns the crunchy base in the ultimate juxtaposition of textures. All of the different parts can be made ahead of time and assembled just before serving. These will impress your guests. For a vegetarian option, omit the pork.

Makes 12 enchiladas

> 1½-pound pork shoulder blade or butt
> All-Purpose Tomato Sauce (page 268)
> ¼ cup extra-virgin olive oil
> 5 cups finely shredded cabbage
> 2 cups finely shredded yellow onion
> 6 large beets, peeled, boiled, and minced (about 4 cups)
>   (or use canned beets)
> 1 cup frozen peas, thawed
> ½ cup white vinegar
> 1 tablespoon sugar
> 1 tablespoon stone-ground mustard
> 1 bay leaf
> 1 fresh thyme sprig (or 1 teaspoon dried)
> Salt and freshly ground black pepper, to taste
> 12 Handmade Corn Tortillas (page 63)
> Vegetable oil for frying
> 12 large iceberg lettuce leaves
> 2 sliced hard-boiled eggs
> 1 cup grated queso seco (or Pecorino Romano, in a pinch)

In a small saucepan over medium-high heat, place the pork; cover it with water. Bring to a boil; reduce the heat and simmer for 30–35 minutes or until the juices run clear when the pork is pierced with a fork. Remove the pork from the broth (reserve the broth for other uses, such as soup). When the pork is cool, shred or chop it finely. Combine the pork and tomato sauce in a small saucepan and simmer over low heat for 15 minutes; remove from the heat and chill until ready to use.

In a large Dutch oven, heat the olive oil over medium heat. Add the cabbage and onions; cook until the onions are translucent, about 2 minutes. Add the beets, peas, vinegar, sugar, mustard, bay leaf, and thyme; stir and simmer for 3–4 minutes. Season with salt and pepper and cool completely. Transfer to a bowl, cover, and chill for an hour (or up to 3 days).

Fit a baking pan with a metal cooling rack; set aside. In a large skillet with high sides, heat 1–2 inches of oil to 360°F (or use a deep fryer according to the manufacturer's directions); using tongs, slide the tortillas into the oil, one at a time. Fry them for 3–4 minutes or until golden, turning them over halfway through (keep them flat by pressing them down with the tongs). Using the tongs, transfer them to the prepared rack to drain.

To assemble the enchiladas, reheat the pork. Place a lettuce leaf on each tortilla. Divide the pork among the tortillas, top with a mound of beet salad (about ¾ cup) and a slice of egg. Sprinkle with cheese and serve immediately. ❋

Grilled White Corn Arepas (Arepitas Blancas)

There are many variations of these dense and hearty corn cakes sold on the streets of Colombia and Venezuela. Some are flat like tortillas and simply grilled; some are stuffed with eggs and fried. You can make arepas any size you want, but these are meant to be plump and about the size of dinner rolls. Arepas like these are often skewered at the ends of kabobs called *chuzos* (see pages 203 and 208), so that customers can eat a piece of meat and follow it with a bite of this bread. Here, I offer you different ways of cooking these arepas: directly on a grill, on a grill pan, on the stove on a nonstick pan, on an electric griddle, and on a panini press. Although a panini press is by no means a traditional appliance in Colombia, it makes perfect arepitas, as I found out one day when my outdoor grill broke. Panini presses reproduce perfect grill marks, plus you can flatten arepas as much as you like, as long as you adjust the cooking time. These arepitas, slathered with butter and jam or stuffed with sliced ham and cheese, make a great snack.

Makes 6 arepitas

 1½ cups white arepa flour (masarepa or harina pan)
 1 teaspoon salt
 1 cup warm (110°–120°F) milk
 ¾–1 cup warm (110°–120°F) water (or more if needed;
    see note on page 136)
 1–2 tablespoons vegetable oil, for brushing on the arepas

In a medium bowl combine the arepa flour and salt; slowly add the milk and ¾ cup water, stirring constantly, until the dough starts to come together and is lump-free (the texture should be like thick mashed potatoes; add more water as needed). Knead the dough with your hands for 1 minute or until the dough thickens (it will continue to thicken as it sits, and you should be able to form a patty when it's done resting). Cover the bowl with plastic wrap; let it sit at room temperature for 10–15 minutes.

Preheat an outdoor grill (for indirect heat) until hot. Line a plate or baking pan with parchment paper. Moisten your hands and divide the dough into 6 equal portions (about ½ cup each); shape each into a 3-inch patty, ¾ inch thick. (You can shape the arepas up to 2 hours ahead of time; cover, chill, and cook them right before serving.) Brush the arepas lightly with oil and grill for 5–7 minutes on each side or until grill marks are clearly imprinted on each side and the arepas are cooked through.

If using a nonstick grill pan, griddle, or skillet, heat it over medium-high heat and cook the arepas until black and brown flecks appear, about 5–7 minutes on the first side, and 3–4 minutes on the second. Serve hot. To keep them warm, place them on a baking sheet lined with parchment paper in a 250°F oven for up to 1 hour before serving.

※ NOTE: To cook arepas with a panini press, preheat the press. For thick arepas, use only the bottom of the press. Grill for about 6–8 minutes on each side or until grill marks are clearly imprinted on each side and the arepas are crispy. For thinner arepas, place the arepas on the panini press and lower the top of the press over them; let the press alone flatten them slightly without applying any pressure. Cook them for 6–8 minutes. Keep in mind that cooking times will vary depending on the panini press.

Tomato and Basil Pizza

The Italian influence on Argentinean cuisine is clearly found in its street food. Here, crispy crust meets creamy cheese in this classic pizza found on the streets of Buenos Aires, where pizza is one of the most popular offerings. You'll need to start the dough three hours before you intend to bake it. I prefer baking pizzas on rectangular baking sheets rather than round pizza pans so I can cut them neatly into squares, but use what you like best. I also like to shape pizza with my hands in a rustic fashion rather than rolling out the dough, but this dough rolls out beautifully. This recipe calls for only basil, salt, and pepper for seasoning, but feel free to add your own, such as oregano or dried red pepper flakes. One bite of this pizza and you'll see why my family prefers this to any take out!

Makes 1 large pizza

FOR THE DOUGH
1 package active dry yeast (1½ teaspoons)
1½ cups warm (75°-90°F) water
¼ teaspoon sugar
2 tablespoons extra-virgin olive oil
4½ cups all-purpose flour, divided
2 teaspoons salt

FOR THE TOPPING
2 pounds canned plum tomatoes, drained and chopped
   (may use petite diced canned tomatoes, but NOT crushed)
2–3 tablespoons extra-virgin olive oil, or to taste
1 pound fresh mozzarella cheese
4 ounces freshly grated Parmigiano-Reggiano
16–20 fresh basil leaves
Salt and freshly ground black pepper, to taste

In the bowl of a stand mixer, combine the yeast and the water; add the sugar and stir with a fork. Set aside for 5–10 minutes or until creamy; stir in the olive oil and gradually add 2¼ cups of flour, stirring with a spatula until it's incorporated. Scrape down the sides of the bowl, cover, and let it sit in a warm place for 1½ hours or until the sponge has doubled.

Deflate the sponge with a rubber spatula; add 2 more cups of the flour and the 2 teaspoons of salt. Mix at low speed on a stand mixer for 2–3 minutes (or knead by hand on a floured surface for 5–6 minutes). Scrape down the sides of the bowl, and mix 4–5 more minutes at medium speed (or knead 8–10 minutes by hand). If the dough is too sticky, add more flour, 1 tablespoon at a time, until the dough releases from your fingers and bounces back a bit when pressed (it will still be a bit sticky, but it should not stick to your fingers).

Oil a deep bowl lightly with olive oil; form the dough into a ball and roll it around in the bowl so that all sides are coated in oil. Cover the bowl with plastic wrap and let it stand in a warm place for 1½ hours or until it has doubled. (If desired, at this point, the dough may be frozen for up to 2 months; thaw in the refrigerator overnight, warm to room temperature, and proceed with the recipe.)

Preheat the oven to 450°F. With your hands (or a rolling pin) roll the dough into the desired shape, until it is about ⅓ inch thick. Transfer the dough to the baking pan; if desired, shape a rim by pinching the edges. Spread the tomatoes evenly over the top; drizzle with olive oil and sprinkle with salt to taste. Bake for 15 minutes; remove it from the oven and top with the mozzarella and Parmesan cheese. Return it to the oven; bake for 10–12 minutes or until the cheese is melted. Remove it from the oven and top with basil leaves. Drizzle with more olive oil, season with salt and pepper, and serve. ❊

TACO TRUCK

Stereotypes about both the food and the people of Latin America abound. I must confess to finding the stereotypical images of sombrero-wearing men taking daily long siestas under palm trees a bit humorous. I blame the Hollywood movie directors and socialites of the 1940s and 1950s who spent posh vacations in coastal resort areas of Mexico for perpetuating that cliché. That was around the same time the iconic image of the hip-swinging Carmen Miranda sporting fruit headpieces was immortalized. (And, by the way, that one is also funny.)

Sure, men who worked in the fields under the scorching heat of the sun took siesta breaks here or there, some even using their sombreros to shield their faces; and women toting fruit baskets on their heads are a still common sight, but they're working at making a living, not at seducing observers. I don't know why, but for some reason, these images have stuck.

I will confess to taking a siesta here and there. When I was little, I was forced to take a nap whenever we had a big event that would keep us up late at night. Christmas Day, New Year's Eve, and the weddings of relatives meant that my brothers and I were put to bed for a period of time midday. However, I never saw my dad tote a sombrero; nor did I ever see him take a siesta in a hammock under a palm tree. Personally, I think he would have loved to, as he worked long hours as a surgeon and was on call on what seemed to be a never-ending schedule. I'm also pretty sure my mother, a university professor and business owner, never dressed as Carmen Miranda, although I bet my father would have loved that, too.

Another common stereotype about Latin Americans is that we all eat tacos. That's not true. (Although, maybe we should, particularly when they are as delicious as the ones I've included in this chapter!) Francisco Santamaría, author of *El Diccionario de Mejicanismos*, traces the word "taco" back to the Aztecs, when the name of a tortilla eaten in those days, called *taqualli*, morphed into the word *tlaco* and then eventually into the word "taco." Other theories suggest that the word derives from the word

(opposite, from top)
A beautifully dressed woman selling fruit at a Cartagena, Colombia, market.

A woman makes tortillas at a street market in Mexico City.

tac, a wooden cylindrical tool or peg used by craftsmen or a contraption used to make bullets.

Tacos have revolutionized the way Americans eat fast food. Although, taco trucks have been around for decades in cities like Los Angeles and Austin, in the last few years, they've taken the rest of the country by storm, leading us on newfound culinary adventures.

In the Latin American countries where tacos are eaten, there are many different forms: soft, crunchy, rolled, long, grilled, or fried. However, what you will not find in the land of real tacos—which stretches from Mexico to Costa Rica— are the prefabricated taco shells so beloved here in the United States. Those were invented by the founder of a popular taco food chain—a man with the surname Bell.

All tacos are tortillas—sometimes made with corn, and others with wheat flour—used to hold some kind of filling. The quality of the tortilla, in my opinion, is what most distinguishes a taco. Use flimsy, bland tortillas and your tacos will be okay; but use artisan, handcrafted tortillas and you're talking gourmet tacos. Self-respecting taco vendors either make their own tortillas or source them out to somebody else who does it for them.

In the end, however, the filling is what separates a superb taco from an average one. Truly, when it comes to stuffing tacos, your only limit is your imagination. From expertly grilled meats to perfectly cooked vegetables, so many possibilities await you. I'm a purist when it comes to tacos. I grew up attending *taquizas* (taco-making parties)—and my grandmother threw the best ones I ever attended—where we made homemade yellow and blue corn tortillas and stuffed them with miniature chorizos called *copetines*, several kinds of meat, and finished them off with multicolored toppings.

Finding inspiration to build this chapter was easy. It features some of the most popular taco fillings sold on the streets of countries like Mexico, Guatemala, and Costa Rica. Here, you'll find favorites such as Shepherd's-Style Pork and Pineapple Tacos (*Tacos al Pastor*) and Grilled Beef (*carne asada*) Tacos; some renditions that are not as well known here in the United States, such as the whimsical Costa Rican Tacos Ticos; and a healthy recipe for tacos filled with a refreshing beef salad, Beef and Radish Soft Tacos. I also include two famous wraps made in Central America. The first is the Guatemalan answer to the question of what would happen if you married a hot dog with a taco, and the second is the Honduran way to eat breakfast all rolled up into a flour tortilla. All are colorful and tasty options that will make your palate laugh.

Finally, because taco trucks offer all sorts of other things on their menus, I've included what is perhaps the most popular Mexican recipe for leftover tortillas—my truly mind-blowing recipe for *chilaquiles*, which will satisfy any appetite, no matter what time of day.

The best part about making tacos is being able to top them with all sorts of sensational salsas. So go ahead, make yourself two or three tacos at a time and indulge a little. If you're not happy before you start cooking them, you certainly will be after you eat them.

Guatemalan Hot Dog Wraps (Mixtas)

These Guatemalan hot dog wraps combine traditional Mayan, American, and German influences. They're called *mixtas* (mixed) because they mix ingredients from different ethnic cuisines together in a perfect union of tastes and textures. You'll find these sold in street carts all over Guatemala City. This recipe epitomizes what modern Latin street food is all about: a juxtaposition of flavors, techniques, and ingredients of the different cultures that have shaped it.

Makes 10 hot dog wraps

> 10 (8-inch) Homemade Flour Tortillas (page 90)
>   or store-bought, warm (see note on page 94)
> 10 all-beef hot dogs, steamed or boiled (fully cooked)
> Avocado Sauce (page 268)
> 1½ cups prepared sauerkraut
> 3 corn husks (soaked and torn into 10 strips for ties)
>   or 10 (6-inch-long) pieces kitchen twine
> Parchment paper
> Jalapenōs, Onions, and Carrots in Escabeche (page 266)

Working with one tortilla at a time, spread each with 2–3 tablespoons of the Avocado Sauce; top with 2–3 tablespoons of the sauerkraut. Place a cooked hot dog on one end of the tortilla and roll it up tightly, as you would a cigar. Roll tightly in parchment paper and use a corn husk tie or piece of twine to secure it; repeat until all are assembled. Chill them in the refrigerator for 1 hour (up to overnight).

Remove the ties, slice each wrap in half, and serve with the escabeche on the side. ❊

Honduran Breakfast Wraps with Homemade Flour Tortillas (Baleadas)

Making flour tortillas is a lot of fun. On the streets of Honduras, you'll see women making the dough, then shaping the tortillas by slapping them against their hands, and cooking them on makeshift griddles. In Honduras, the tortillas are filled with a combination of scrambled eggs, refried beans, sliced avocado, crumbled cheese, and hot sauce, and they're called *baleadas*. At first, you may have a bit of trouble making the tortillas perfectly round, but you'll get the hang of it after you've made a couple of them. Part of the fun of this recipe is that no matter how rustic your tortillas appear to be, they always taste delicious. Of course, you can use store-bought flour tortillas instead. Use any leftover tortillas to make soft tacos or quesadillas. Baleadas are best served for breakfast or for brunch, but I serve them as a vegetarian option for any meal. Breakfast for dinner, anyone?

Makes 12 baleadas

- 3–3¼ cups all-purpose flour (plus more for kneading and shaping)
- 1 tablespoon baking soda
- 1 teaspoon salt
- ¾ cup lard
- 1½ cups warm (about 110°F) water
- 2–3 cups Refried Black Beans (page 284) (or use canned)
- 12 large eggs
- 1 tablespoon butter or vegetable oil
- 2 Hass avocados, sliced lengthwise and brushed with fresh lime juice to prevent browning
- 1 cup crumbled queso fresco

In a large bowl, whisk together the flour, baking soda, and salt. With two knives or a pastry cutter, cut in the lard until the mixture resembles coarse, lumpy sand. Slowly add the water, stirring with a wooden spoon to combine. Turn the dough out onto a clean, lightly floured surface; knead 1–2 minutes or until smooth and elastic, adding more flour as needed to prevent it from sticking to the surface. Place it in a clean bowl, cover it with a damp towel, and let it rest for 1 hour (this dough will not rise).

Divide the rested dough into 12 equal portions (about ¼ cup each). Roll each into a ball, keeping them covered with a damp towel as you work, and let them rest for 10 minutes.

With floured hands, pat each ball into a ½-inch-thick patty. Flour your rolling pin and surface well. Roll out each ball into a 9- to 10-inch circle (turn the dough a quarter turn each time you roll to keep it round). Gently toss each circle of dough back and forth between your hands to remove any excess flour. Cover them with a kitchen towel as you finish the rest.

Heat a nonstick griddle or skillet over medium-high heat (or heat an electric griddle to 375°–400°F). Place the tortillas on the griddle and cook until golden flecks are visible on the bottom side, about 45–60 seconds; flip them and cook the second side until golden flecks are visible, about 45–60 seconds. Flip them back onto the first side and cook for 20 seconds (see note). Wrap them, stacked, in a damp towel and set aside while you scramble the eggs.

Crack the eggs into a large bowl and whisk them well. In a large skillet over medium heat, melt the butter; add the eggs, season with salt, and scramble to the desired consistency. Fill the tortillas with the beans, eggs, avocado, and cheese. Serve immediately.

✳{ NOTE: The hotter your pan gets, the quicker your tortillas will cook. If the pan is getting too hot, reduce the heat, wait a bit, and continue cooking them. Flour tortillas can be wrapped and refrigerated for up to 2 days or frozen for up to 2 months.

Costa Rican Tacos Ticos

Costa Rican Tacos Ticos

I like to call these happy tacos because it's impossible not to laugh out loud when trying to eat them. Corn tortillas stuffed with shredded beef are fried until crispy and then topped with whimsical ingredients. I use leftover beef from my *cocido* and Handmade Corn Tortillas. Of course, you can use store-bought corn tortillas if you wish. The toppings are what make these so much fun to eat: first, a generous amount of shredded cabbage, and then the real enjoyment begins when they're drizzled with ketchup, mustard, and mayonnaise. I know it sounds funny to use the same condiments you'd usually reserve for hot dogs, but they really work! In Costa Rica, tacos ticos are served either singly or in pairs (called *dobles*) and are wrapped in plastic squares. If you're planning a taco party, fry the tacos ahead of time and keep them warm in a 250°F oven, for up to 1 hour. Place the condiments in squirt bottles and let everyone assemble and top them as they like.

Makes 12 tacos

> 5 cups shredded cabbage
> 1½ teaspoons salt
> 2½ cups leftover meat from the cocido (page 113)
>   or other cooked and shredded beef (see note)
> 12 Handmade Corn Tortillas (page 63) or store-bought, warm
>   (see note)
> 12 (8-inch-long) pieces kitchen twine
> Vegetable oil for frying
> Ketchup
> Mustard
> Mayonnaise

Place the cabbage in a large bowl; add enough boiling water to cover and let it sit for exactly one minute. Drain the cabbage well and return it to the bowl. Add the salt and stir; let it sit at room temperature for 30 minutes or until cool. Cover and chill for up to 24 hours.

Working with one tortilla at a time, place 2–3 tablespoons of the shredded beef on one end of it and roll it up tightly, like a cigar (it has to be tight or the beef will escape when the tacos are fried). Tie it snuggly with a piece of twine and set aside; repeat with the remaining tortillas and filling.

Fit a large baking pan with a metal cooling rack; set aside. In a large skillet with high sides, heat 1–2 inches of oil to 360°F (or use a deep fryer according to the manufacturer's directions). Working in batches, use tongs to place the tacos in the oil. Fry them until golden, about 3–3½ minutes, turning them over halfway through. Transfer them to the prepared rack to drain.

To plate, place two tacos on a plate, top with a generous amount of the cabbage, and drizzle with the condiments. Serve immediately.

*⁝} NOTE: If you don't want to make the cocido, simply boil a 1-pound piece of beef roast or flank steak in salted water until it's cooked through. Cool and shred. Shredded rotisserie chicken works well, too.

To prevent corn or flour tortillas from breaking when folded or rolled, heat them briefly. To do this, wrap several tortillas in a clean, damp kitchen towel; microwave at 1-minute intervals until they are warm. Alternatively, wrap them in foil and place them in a preheated 350°F oven for 10–15 minutes. You can also heat them, one at a time, directly over a flame of a gas stove (or an outdoor grill) for 20 seconds on each side. Keep the warm tortillas wrapped in a kitchen towel as you work. It's a good idea to have a few extra tortillas in case some break as the tacos are shaped.

Beef and Radish Soft Tacos (Tacos de Salpicón)

These healthy and refreshing tacos have a limey flavor and a delicious crunch that satisfies a hungry appetite. You can prepare the *salpicón* (beef salad) a couple of days ahead of time, either making it from scratch, as shown here, or using leftover beef from the cocido on page 113. A topping of sliced radishes or Radish Slaw (page 39) adds a peppery bite. These light tacos are sold on the streets of Guatemala and usually come three to a portion, and the broth left over from boiling the meat is usually seasoned and served in mugs, with a bit of lime juice and hot sauce. A splash of hot sauce, an extra squirt of lime juice, and a sprinkle of sea salt is all you'll need to complete this meal.

Makes 12 tacos

1 (2-pound) pot roast
½ cup minced white onion
½ cup minced cilantro (leaves and tender stems)
¼ cup minced mint
½ cup fresh lime juice, or to taste
Salt and freshly ground black pepper, to taste
18 Handmade Corn Tortillas (page 63) or 36 store-bought
    (see note), warm (see note on page 94)
1½ cups thinly sliced radishes or Radish Slaw
    (without the pork rinds)

Place the beef in a medium saucepan and cover with water completely; set it over medium-high heat. Bring the liquid to a boil; reduce the heat and simmer for 15–20 minutes, skimming off (and discarding) the foam that rises to the top. Bring the liquid back to a boil; cover, reduce the heat, and simmer for 1½–2 hours or until the beef shreds easily. Remove the beef from the heat and let it cool in the broth for 30 minutes.

Transfer the roast to a cutting board and reserve the broth for other uses, such as soups. Slice the beef thinly, trim off the fat, and place it in a food processor fitted with a metal blade; pulse it until it's very finely chopped (it will look like fine powder).

Transfer the beef to a large bowl and combine it with the onions, cilantro, and mint. Add the lime juice and season with salt and pepper; cover and chill, until ready to use.

To assemble the tacos, divide the beef mixture among the tortillas; top with the radishes and serve immediately.

❊⟩ NOTE: Store-bought corn tortillas can be flimsy, so use 2 for each serving so that the tacos hold up to the filling.

Beef Taquitos with Tomato Sauce

Beef Taquitos with Tomato Sauce

My husband and I dated long distance for many years. Every time he flew back to Guatemala for his holidays from college, I'd welcome him with a platter of these—his favorite—tacos. Almost three decades later, I can still make him smile whenever I make these for him. Taquitos such as these are sold on the streets, often in groups of three, wrapped in brown paper bags with a tomato dipping sauce on the side. I like to cook these ahead of time and freeze them so that anytime my husband craves them, I can reheat as many as he wants. Someone once told me that the way into a man's heart is through his stomach. I listened and learned it well.

Makes 20 taquitos

FOR THE TAQUITOS
Beef Picadillo (page 288)
24 Handmade Corn Tortillas (page 63) or store-bought
6 corn husks (soaked and torn into strips to make ties),
    or 12 (8-inch-long) pieces kitchen twine
Vegetable oil for frying

FOR THE TOMATO SAUCE
1 (28-ounce) can fire-roasted tomatoes
½ cup minced yellow onion
2 garlic cloves, minced
1 tablespoon vegetable oil
½ teaspoon dried thyme
1 bay leaf
Salt and freshly ground black pepper, to taste

FOR THE GARNISH
½ cup minced cilantro (leaves and tender stems)
¼ cup minced fresh mint
¼ cup minced flat-leaf or Italian parsley (leaves and tender stems)
1 cup grated queso seco (or Pecorino Romano cheese)
1 white onion, thinly sliced and separated into rings

Fit two large baking pans with metal cooling racks; set aside. Preheat the oven to 250°F. Heat the corn tortillas briefly in the microwave (see note on page 94) and keep them covered.

Working on a clean surface with one tortilla at a time, place 2 tablespoons of the picadillo on one end; roll it tightly, like a cigar and tie it snuggly with a strip of corn husk. Repeat with the remaining tortillas and filling, keeping them covered with a kitchen towel as you work.

In a large skillet with high sides, heat ½ inch of oil to 360°F (or use a deep fryer according to the manufacturer's instructions). Working in batches, carefully slide the taquitos into the oil and fry them until golden, about 4–5 minutes, turning them over halfway through. Using a slotted spoon, transfer them to the cooling racks; place them in the warm oven while you make the sauce. See note.

In a blender, combine the tomatoes, onion, and garlic; blend until smooth. In a saucepan over medium heat combine the tomato mixture, oil, thyme, and bay leaf; season with salt and pepper. Bring to a boil; cover, reduce the heat to low, and simmer for 10–15 minutes.

In a small bowl, combine the cilantro, mint, and parsley. Place the taquitos on a large serving platter; ladle sauce over them and garnish with queso seco, herbs, and onion rings. Serve immediately.

✳} NOTE: At this point, the taquitos can be frozen for up to 4 months. Freeze in a single layer until solid and then transfer them to an airtight container. To reheat, place them on a baking pan in a preheated 400°F oven until warmed through, about 8-10 minutes.

Carne Adobada Soft Tacos

Irresistibly tender pork enrobed in *adobo*, a sauce that marries cinnamon and chiles, is a favorite in Guatemala. On the streets, the pork is chopped into tiny pieces, wrapped in warm tortillas, and served with lime wedges. This adobo sauce, which is similar to my grandmother's, is spicy but not spicy-hot; the charred vegetables add layers of smokiness, and the roasted garlic adds a touch of sweetness. The pork is marinated twice: first in vinegar, to tenderize it; then in the sauce to infuse it with flavor. You'll need to start this recipe a couple of days ahead of time. It's great for entertaining because all the prepping can be done ahead of time and both the cooking and assembly can be done quickly. The recipe may be long, but this is not hard to make.

Makes 12 tacos

1½ pounds pork butt, thinly sliced (about ⅓ inch thick)

¼ cup white vinegar

5 plum tomatoes

5–6 medium tomatillos, husks removed, rinsed and left whole

½ large red bell pepper

2 large garlic cloves, unpeeled

½ cup roughly chopped white onion

¼ cup pumpkin seeds (pepitas)

2 tablespoons sesame seeds

1 guajillo chile, seeded and deveined (seeds reserved)

2 pasilla chiles, seeded and deveined (seeds reserved)

2 teaspoons annatto (achiote) paste

1 (2½-inch) stick Mexican cinnamon (canela) (see note)

1 teaspoon dried thyme

1 bay leaf, crushed

½ cup water

2 teaspoons salt, or to taste

¼ teaspoon freshly ground black pepper

½ cup plus 2 tablespoons vegetable oil, divided

12 Handmade Corn Tortillas (page 63) or 24 store-bought,
    warm (see notes on pages 94 and 95)

1 cup minced red onion

1 cup minced cilantro (leaves and tender stems)

2 limes cut into wedges

Place the pork in a 1-gallon zip-top bag; sprinkle the vinegar over the pork and seal the bag. Marinate for 2 hours in the refrigerator.

In the meantime, on a griddle or in a cast-iron skillet over medium-high heat, place the tomatoes, tomatillos, bell pepper, and garlic cloves. Turning them often, roast them until their skins are charred on all sides; some veggies will roast quicker than others, so transfer them to a plate as they become charred, about 10 minutes total. Peel the garlic and add it to the plate. Add the onions to the pan and roast until they're charred; add to the vegetables.

In a small skillet over medium heat, toast the pumpkin seeds until golden, about 2–3 minutes; remove to a plate. Toast the sesame seeds in the same skillet until golden, about 1 minute; add to the pumpkin seeds. Toast the reserved chile seeds for about 20 seconds or until fragrant, add to the seeds; set aside to cool. Place the dried chiles on the same skillet and toast them over medium-high heat until pliable, about 30 seconds on each side.

In a blender, combine the charred vegetables, toasted seeds and chiles, annatto, cinnamon stick, thyme, bay leaf, water, salt, and pepper; blend until smooth.

In a medium saucepan, heat ¼ cup of the oil over medium-high heat; add the vegetable mixture (carefully, as it will splatter) and cook it for 3–4 minutes, stirring constantly with a long-handled spoon. Remove the sauce from the heat and cool completely.

Drain the pork and discard the vinegar. Return the pork to the bag and pour the cooled sauce over it, making sure to coat it well. Marinate for 1–2 days in the refrigerator.

To cook the pork, heat 2 tablespoons of oil in a large skillet over medium-high heat. Cook the pork (which should be coated with a generous amount of the marinade) until it's well done, about 3 minutes per side, adding more oil as needed; discard the excess marinade.

To serve, slice the pork and divide it among the tortillas; top with the onions and cilantro. Serve with lime wedges.

NOTE: Cinnamon is an important ingredient in many Latin American recipes. When blending cinnamon, make sure it's the brittle canela or Ceylon variety only; do not attempt to blend the cassia cinnamon that is most commonly used in the United States or you'll break the motor of your blender; if you can't find canela, substitute each 2½-inch stick with 1 teaspoon of ground cinnamon.

Grilled Beef (Carne Asada) Tacos with Roasted Tomato Sauce

It's easy to re-create the tacos from your favorite taco truck when they're made with succulent beef, marinated in citrus juices and rubbed with spices. All you have to do is grill it until tender and wrap it in supple corn tortillas. My topping of choice is a roasted tomato sauce that enhances the smoky flavors of the grill. If you agree with me that the best tacos hold plenty of filling, then these won't disappoint. In Mexico, you'll also find these garnished with avocado salsas like the ones in this book (see "Condiments, Toppings, and Side Dishes" chapter), along with plenty of chopped onions and cilantro. Select your favorite toppings, but I suggest you serve these with a side of Central American Red Beans and Rice (page 291) and Radish Slaw with Pork Rinds (page 39). My mouth is watering. How about yours?

Makes 12 tacos

> 2–3 sirloin steaks (2 pounds, total)
> ⅓ cup fresh orange juice
> ¼ cup fresh lemon juice
> 1 tablespoon Worcestershire sauce
> 2 bay leaves
> 1 cup sliced yellow onion
> 1 teaspoon salt
> ½ teaspoon freshly ground black pepper
> ½ teaspoon dried thyme
> ½ teaspoon dried Mexican oregano
> ½ teaspoon garlic powder
> ¼ teaspoon ground cumin
> 12 Handmade Corn Tortillas (page 63) or 24 store-bought, warm (see notes on pages 94 and 95)
> 3 cups shredded romaine lettuce
> Roasted Tomato Sauce (page 265)
> 1 cup Mexican crema
> 1 cup Cotija cheese

In a small nonreactive bowl, combine the orange juice, lemon juice, Worcestershire sauce, bay leaves, and onion. Place the steaks in a 1-gallon zip-top bag and pour the marinade over them; marinate in the refrigerator for at least 4 hours (up to overnight).

When ready to cook the steaks, heat a grill to high heat; remove the steaks from the marinade, pat them dry with paper towels, and place them on a large plate; discard the marinade. In a small bowl, whisk together the salt, pepper, thyme, oregano, garlic powder, and cumin; sprinkle the spice mixture all over the steaks. Grill the steaks for 4–5 minutes per side (for medium) or until done to your liking. Let the meat rest for 5–10 minutes before slicing on the bias into thin strips.

To assemble the tacos, place a few slices of beef on each tortilla and top with the lettuce, sauce, crema, and cheese. Serve at once. ❄

Tacos with Pork Carnitas

Carnitas means "little pieces of meat," and here, chopped slow-cooked pork becomes the succulent filling for vibrantly flavored tacos. My carnitas are simmered in milk, which tenderizes an otherwise tough cut of meat, breaking down its fibers until it is fall-off-the-bone moist and luscious. The orange scents the pork with a fruity aroma and the garlic infuses it with delectable flavor. Whenever I make carnitas, I make enough for a crowd. That way, if I want to throw an impromptu get-together—and I'm known for doing that often—or if I want to save some for another weeknight supper, I can do so without having to go to any great lengths to cook a meal. You can make the carnitas the day you plan to eat them, or you can make them a day ahead and reheat them just before serving. Either way, these tacos will satisfy your craving for great street food.

Serves 12

Taco Truck

One 5-pound picnic roast or pork butt (skin removed)
¼ cup lard (or vegetable oil)
3 cups whole milk
2 oranges, unpeeled and quartered
1 small yellow onion, peeled and quartered
8 large garlic cloves, peeled and left whole
½ teaspoon dried thyme
2 bay leaves
1½ teaspoons salt
¼ teaspoon freshly ground black pepper
12 Handmade Corn Tortillas (page 63) or 24 store-bought,
    warm (see notes on pages 94 and 95)
2 cups sliced radishes
1 cup sour cream
1 cup minced cilantro (leaves and tender stems)
Lime wedges

Pat the pork dry using paper towels. Melt the lard in a large Dutch oven over medium-high heat; brown the pork on all sides (about 3–4 minutes per side). Add the milk, oranges, onion, garlic, thyme, bay leaves, salt, and pepper. Bring the liquid to a boil; cover, reduce the heat to low, and simmer pork for 2½–3 hours or until it is tender enough to be shredded with a fork.

Remove the pork from the pot and cut it into 1-inch cubes; discard any bones. Strain the liquid into a large bowl through a sieve to remove all of the solids (discard solids).

Return the pork and cooking liquid to the pot; bring to a rolling boil over medium-high to high heat. Cook, uncovered, stirring occasionally, until all of the liquid has been absorbed, about 10–15 minutes. Remove the pork from the heat and keep warm.

To assemble, top the tortillas with the carnitas, radishes, sour cream, and cilantro, and serve with lime wedges. Leftover carnitas may be frozen for up to 2 months; thaw in the refrigerator and reheat in the microwave or over the stovetop with a little bit of liquid (broth, orange juice, or water) until hot. ❊

Shepherd's-Style Pork and Pineapple Tacos
(Tacos al Pastor)

Shepherd's-Style Pork and Pineapple Tacos (Tacos al Pastor)

These tacos made with bits of chile and annatto-flavored pork are topped with tropical pineapple in a sweet and savory combo like no other. In Mexico, stacks of thinly cut and marinated pork are skewered onto a giant spit, trimmed into a conical shape, book-ended with pineapple chunks, and placed in an upright rotisserie called a *trompo*, where the meat turns and cooks for hours. I call it Mexican gyro. Once the pork is cooked, it's expertly shaved directly onto tortillas. These popular tacos—perhaps the most famous Mexican tacos—are also the hardest to re-create at home because no one I know has a giant upright spit! But worry not: Latin stores carry presliced pork called *milanesas de puerco* or *carne para pastor*, which is already pounded; use this if you can. I can't find it where I live, so I asked butchers at different Latin tiendas to hand-pick their favorite cuts for these tacos. Their choices narrowed it down to pork leg or butt (shoulder). Marinate the pork for at least one hour but no more than four, or the tenderizing enzymes in the pineapple will make the pork mushy. My method may not be the most traditional, but it delivers authentic flavor, and it's easy, so you can enjoy these mouth-watering tacos anytime you want.

Makes 20 tacos

- 1¾ pounds thinly sliced pork butt, pounded to no more than ¼ inch thick
- 6 guajillo chiles
- 1½ ounces annatto (achiote) paste, or about half of a 3½–ounce log (see note)
- 2 canned chipotle chiles in adobo
- 1 garlic clove, minced
- ¼ cup fresh pineapple juice
- ¼ cup white vinegar
- ¼ cup vegetable oil (plus a little more for grilling the pineapple)
- ½ teaspoon dried Mexican oregano
- 1 pineapple, peeled, cored, and sliced
- 1 cup coarsely chopped white onion, soaked in cold water for ½ hour and drained

Salt, to taste

1 cup coarsely chopped cilantro (leaves and tender stems)

Lime wedges

20 Handmade Corn Tortillas (page 63) or 40 store-bought,
    warm (see notes on pages 94 and 95)

Place the chiles in a medium bowl and cover with boiling water (place something heavy on top of them to keep them submerged); soak them for 15 minutes. Drain the chiles, reserving ⅓ cup of the soaking liquid; stem, seed, and devein them.

In a blender, combine the chiles, annatto, chipotles, garlic, juice, vinegar, oil, oregano, and the reserved soaking liquid; blend until smooth (the mixture should have the consistency of ketchup). The marinade can be made up to 24 hours ahead of time, as long as it's covered and kept in the refrigerator.

Place the pork in a large nonreactive bowl; cover it with the marinade, turning to coat the slices on all sides; cover with plastic wrap and chill for 1 hour (up to 4 hours).

When ready to cook the pork, heat an outdoor grill until very hot. Brush the pineapple slices with oil and grill them until they get nice grill marks, about 1 minute on each side. Transfer to a cutting board and chop coarsely; set aside. Working in batches, grill the pork until cooked through, about 1–2 minutes per side. Transfer the pork to a cutting board and chop it into ½-inch pieces; season with salt.

Top warm tortillas with pork, pineapple, onion, and cilantro; serve with the lime wedges.

❊⟩ NOTE: You'll find prepared annatto (achiote) paste, shaped into bars, in Latin stores and some supermarkets.

Red Chilaquiles

I was six years old the first time I tasted this soft and spicy tortilla dish in Mexico City. My nanny Irma took me to the market and we shared breakfast, sitting at a makeshift stall. Taco vendors go through a lot of tortillas, but on occasion they find themselves with leftovers. In Mexico, chilaquiles are traditionally made with day-old corn tortillas. First, they're sliced into strips and fried; then they're cooked in sauce, transforming their consistency from crunchy chips to supple ribbons, very much like pasta. Chances are that your favorite taco trucks also offer chilaquiles on their menu so that nothing goes to waste. They're often topped with eggs, beef, or chicken and sprinkled with exciting toppings. Mexican and Central American cuisine often features charred vegetables to give food a smoky flavor. Guatemalans make a dish called *chilaquilas* made with day-old tortillas filled with cheese, then battered in eggs and fried before they're drenched in sauce. I serve these for brunch with fruit and coffee. I stay in touch with Irma to this day, and every time I eat these I think of her.

Serves 4–6

> 16 store-bought corn tortillas, each cut into 4 triangles or
>   5 thick strips
> 10 plum tomatoes
> 4 jalapeño peppers
> 3 large garlic cloves, unpeeled
> 1 medium white onion, halved (with skins still attached)
> 1¼ cup corn oil, divided
> 2¼ teaspoons salt
> ¼ teaspoon freshly ground black pepper
> 10 large eggs
> Avocado-Tomatillo Taco Truck Sauce (page 270)
> Traditional Mexican Refried Beans (page 286) or canned
>   whole black beans
> Crumbled queso seco
> Mexican crema
> Sliced green onions

Fit 2 large baking pans with metal cooling racks; set aside. In a large skillet with high sides, heat 1 cup of the oil to 360°F (or use a deep fryer according to the manufacturer's directions). Working in batches, fry the tortillas, stirring constantly, until they're crispy and a light golden color (do not let them brown), about 2–3 minutes. Remove the chips to the prepared racks; drain and sprinkle with salt while still hot. (Fry them up to 6 hours ahead of time and keep them wrapped in a paper bag).

Heat a cast-iron skillet or grill over medium-high heat. Working in batches, char the tomatoes, jalapeños, garlic, and onions on all sides (about 8–10 minutes total). Quarter the tomatoes and place them in a blender (along with their juices). Seed and devein two of the jalapeños (or all of them, if less heat is desired) and add all four of them to the blender. Peel the garlic and the onion and chop them coarsely. Add them to the blender, along with the salt and pepper, and blend until smooth.

Heat the remaining oil in a large Dutch oven over medium-high heat; add the sauce all at once (careful, it will splatter), and stir until it comes to a boil; reduce the heat and simmer for 15 minutes. Working in batches, add the fried tortillas to the sauce. Cook, stirring occasionally, for about 5 minutes or until the tortillas soak up most of the sauce and soften. If the sauce is too thick and the tortillas look dry, stir in ¼ cup of water and heat through; keep warm. In the meantime, heat the beans and scramble the eggs. Serve the chilaquiles, drizzled with the avocado sauce and crema; top with cheese and green onions. Serve with a side of beans and eggs. ❖

Red Chilaquiles

LATIN BOWLS

When I was six years old and in elementary school, my class took a field trip to the large market in Guatemala City, called the Mercado Central. My mother gave me a couple of quetzales—in those days equal to two American dollars—and the admonition to spend them wisely. I still remember having enough money to buy one avocado, a bunch of daisies, and one portable bowl of tomato-enriched broth, aromatic with cilantro, and with a few noodles, called *fideos*, swimming in the bottom. I ate the soup on the ride back to school and brought my prized avocado and my flowers home. Ever since that day, I've loved soups.

Almost every meal in my childhood began with a bowl of soup, and to this day, I serve it whenever I can. Soups are easy to make, and since they only include a few ingredients, they are also economical. I love serving them to my family because one hefty bowl is enough to satisfy a hungry appetite. They require such little attention that it allows me to spend time away from the stove, and I use those hours instead to watch classic films with my kids or go out for a walk with my husband.

Soups help to settle the appetite so that when the main component of the meal is served, the palate can truly enjoy the flavors. On the other hand, soup also makes a great meal itself. For me, soups and stews are comfort in a bowl. Not surprisingly, bowls filled to the rim with rich, soothing flavors are among the most popular offerings on the streets of Latin America.

On any given day, you'll see people sitting at makeshift tables or standing on city corners holding cups filled with steamy goodness, embracing the sense of calm and peaceful satisfaction that comes from a warm and filling meal. No matter the weather, people simply gravitate toward soups and stews. If you stroll along the coastal areas of Belize during the summer or walk on a busy street in the high peaks of Bolivia during winter, you'll see people enjoying bowls of something good. People walking through the mist in the middle of a Latin American city on rainy days reach for bowls of soups. Hungry students who can't get home in time to eat one of their mom's stews between classes find reassurance in the bowls that they find on the streets. Every day, and for very little money, day laborers and construction workers can eat reinforcing meals that give them strength for a few more hours of strenuous work.

A great soup, carefully built so that it packs flavor, vitamins, and nutrients, can be a great source of sustenance. Some of these mouth-watering renditions are perfect for everyday meals at home, while others, like the coconut-infused soups found from Guatemala to Brazil, are more suitable for elegant occasions. However, street food vendors offer both varieties. In this chapter, you'll find soups made with fresh ingredients and unadulterated flavors that allow each spoonful to shine. Best of all, none is complicated to make.

Take a bit of water, a few aromatics, and a handful of seasonal vegetables, and you're on your way to building a succulent soup. This is how most recipes start on the streets, where ingredients are often inexpensive and local. From Mexico to Honduras and Panama, you can choose from broth-infused noodle soups called *caldos*, creamy bean porridges, and meatball soups. In South America, you'll find an array of velvety vegetable *locros*, chunky potato *ajíacos*, and meaty *laguas*.

An indigenous woman sells *sancocho* (broth-filled stew) in the Sacred Valley of the Incas, Peru.

Spain's influence on Latin American cuisine is most apparent in the soups offered by street vendors. In the *pucheros* of Argentina and Bolivia, the *ollas* of Costa Rica, the *sancochos* of Colombia, and the *cocidos* of Guatemala and Mexico, you'll find clear associations with Spanish *ollas podridas* and *caldos Gallegos*. All of these dishes are made by boiling large pieces of meat and lots of vegetables in large pots. Each ensuing meal becomes a one-pot wonder that yields bowls of tasty clear broth, sliced meats that can be enjoyed as part of the soup or as a component of other recipes, such as the meat in the cocido that is used to make the Beef and Radish Soft Tacos on page 94, and deliciously flavored vegetables that turn into side dishes, or *contornos*. The Beef and Vegetable Pot in this chapter (page 113) is among the healthiest meals you'll find on the streets. I also included two popular soups from Colombia and Panama that are made with chicken and starchy vegetables that disintegrate while they cook, making the broth creamy.

Boiled meats from soups are often shredded and stirred into sauces. The name of these dishes varies from country to country, but they all originate from the Spanish dish called *ropa vieja* (old clothes). The Central American version is served with scoops of rice. In Venezuela, the shredded beef is served with rice, beans, and plantains—the trio known as the Latin trinity—making up what many Venezuelans consider their national dish, called "Pabellón." I include here a delectable variation of the dish found on Guatemalan streets called *hilachas* that I often prepare at home.

In this chapter, you'll also find a vegetarian soup and some recipes that are neither soups nor stews but fall somewhere in between, including the famous pozoles of Mexico. Street food vendors always have lots of different toppings that customers can sprinkle on their bowls of soup or stew and that offer textural and temperature contrasts. If you love toppings, you'll be happy to know that the selection in this chapter will present you with plenty of opportunities to add them to your heart's content.

Beef and Vegetable Pot (Cocido o Puchero)

Latin America inherited a tradition of boiled meats from Europe. On the streets, for very little money, you can get a large bowl of beef and vegetables filled to the rim with light broth. The classic Central American version is called *cocido*. If you replace the cilantro and the yuca with parsley and butternut squash, it becomes a typical Argentinean *puchero*. This pot provides you with delicious broth, plenty of vegetables, and a prized piece of succulent meat. I like to reserve part of the beef to use as the filling for Costa Rican Tacos Ticos (page 93) or Beef and Radish Soft Tacos (page 94). In fact, you can use any leftover beef in this recipe for any of the dishes in this book that feature shredded beef or pork.

Serves 6–8

> 1 (3–4 pound) bottom round roast or rump roast
> 3 green onions
> 1 bunch cilantro, tied with kitchen twine (for easy retrieval)
> 2 garlic cloves, peeled and left whole
> 1 tablespoon salt, or to taste
> 5 black peppercorns
> 1 bay leaf
> 1 pound yuca, peeled and cut into large chunks
> 1 pound russet potatoes, peeled and quartered
> 4 large carrots, peeled and cut into chunks
> 2–3 ears of corn, cut crosswise into 2-inch-thick slices
> ½ green cabbage (cored and cut into 6 wedges)

Place the beef in a large stockpot over medium-high heat and cover with cold water by 2–3 inches (about 3 quarts, depending on the size of your pot). Bring the water to a boil; reduce the heat and simmer for 15–20 minutes, skimming off (and discarding) the foam that rises to the top. Add the green onions, cilantro, garlic, salt, peppercorns, and bay leaf. Bring the liquid back to a boil; cover, reduce the heat, and simmer for 1½–2 hours or until the juices of the beef run clear when it's pierced with a knife. Add the yuca, potatoes, carrots, corn, and cabbage and continue simmering until the potatoes are tender, about 20–25 minutes. Remove the beef from the broth; season the broth with salt and pepper.

To serve, cut the beef into ¼-inch-thick slices and place on a platter. Transfer the vegetables to a large serving bowl. Serve the broth in bowls and let each person add beef and vegetables, to taste.

❋⟩ NOTE: The leftovers taste great the next day and also freeze well for up to 1 month.

Central American Meatball Soup with Chayote

This aromatic and filling soup is often sold on the streets of Honduras. It's a healthy and popular lunch on the go. I serve it in ceramic mugs called *pocillos* with plenty of warm corn tortillas that have been sprinkled with salt and rolled like a cigar for easy dunking and Jalapeños, Onions, and Carrots in Escabeche (page 266). Chilling the meatballs before cooking helps them retain their shape as they boil, and cooking them in water before adding them to the soup prevents the stock from becoming cloudy. This soup is a perfect one-pot meal, and it freezes beautifully for up to three months.

Serves 8

FOR THE MEATBALLS
¾ pound ground beef
¾ pound ground pork
1 large egg, lightly beaten
½ cup fresh bread crumbs
¼ cup minced flat-leaf or Italian parsley (leaves and tender stems)
¼ cup minced cilantro (leaves and tender stems)
¼ cup minced fresh mint
1 teaspoon ground cumin
1 teaspoon salt
½ teaspoon freshly ground black pepper

2 tablespoons vegetable oil
1 cup minced white onion
1 cup minced red bell pepper
4 garlic cloves, minced
1 bay leaf
2 teaspoons dried thyme
1 cup minced plum tomatoes
1 tablespoon ancho chile powder
2 quarts beef stock
2 cups diced carrots
2 cups peeled and diced Yukon Gold or white potatoes
5 large mint sprigs, tied together with kitchen twine
2 chayote squashes, peeled, seeded, and chopped
Salt and freshly ground black pepper, to taste

In a large bowl, combine the beef, pork, egg, bread crumbs, parsley, cilantro, mint, cumin, salt, and pepper. Form small meatballs (1 tablespoon each), rolling them between your hands and place them on a plate. Chill them for 30 minutes.

In the meantime, heat the oil in a large stockpot over medium-high heat; add the onions, bell peppers, garlic, bay leaf, and thyme and sauté until the onions have softened slightly, about 2 minutes. Add the tomatoes and chile powder; reduce the heat to medium-low and simmer for 15 minutes. Add the stock, carrots, potatoes, and mint and bring to a boil; reduce the heat and simmer, uncovered, for 20 minutes.

In a separate pot, heat 2 quarts of water over medium-high heat to boiling. Working in batches, add the meatballs; cook them until they rise to the surface, about 2–3 minutes; remove them with a slotted spoon and transfer them to the soup. Discard the water.

Add all of the cooked meatballs and the chayote to the soup. Cover and simmer until the chayote is tender, about 10 minutes; season with salt and pepper.

To serve, remove the mint and ladle the soup into bowls. ✳

Red Pozole

This Mexican pork and hominy stew gets its rusty-red color from dried chiles. It's mildly spicy, very filling, and very comforting. Although pozoles are enjoyed all over Mexico, they're said to have originated in the State of Guerrero. They come in the different colors of the Mexican flag: red, green, and white. They can be made with chicken or shrimp, but pork versions are traditional. The toppings for pozole also vary by region. When I was little, my great-aunt Militza lived in Mexico. Her son, Héctor—who loved to remind me of the fact that although he was several years younger than me, he was technically my uncle—spent many summer vacations with my brothers and me. During one of their visits, Tía Militza and my grandmother got together to make pozole and I was allowed to watch. Then they invited all of the kids to eat supper with them. That night, Tía told us that this was the stew to cure all hangovers. Today, I love to start each New Year with bowls of this satisfyingly rich stew.

Serves 8

¼ cup lard (or vegetable oil)
3 pounds pork shoulder or butt, chopped into 1-inch cubes (with fat)
3 cups minced white onion, divided
2 bay leaves
1 teaspoon dried Mexican oregano plus more for the garnish
1 teaspoon dried thyme
2 (29-ounce) cans hominy, drained and rinsed
6 guajillo chiles
6 ancho chiles
2 large garlic cloves, roughly chopped
Salt and freshly ground black pepper, to taste
Shredded romaine lettuce
Sliced radishes
Lime wedges

In a large Dutch oven, melt half of the lard over medium-high heat. Working in batches, sauté the pork until the pieces are browned on all sides, about 8–10 minutes total, adding more lard as needed. Remove the browned pork with a slotted spoon to a plate. Pour off all but 1 tablespoon of the rendered fat in the pot.

Reduce the heat to medium and add half of the onions; sauté until softened and slightly golden, about 3–4 minutes. Add the bay leaves, oregano, and thyme. Return the pork (and any accumulated juices) to the pot, cover with water by 2 inches (about 6–7 cups), and bring the liquid to a boil. Cover, reduce the heat, and simmer until the pork is tender, about 1½–2 hours. Add the hominy; cover and simmer for 15 minutes.

In the meantime, place the chiles in a large bowl and cover with 4 cups of boiling water (put a plate on top of the chiles to keep them submerged) and soak for 10 minutes. Drain the chiles and reserve the soaking liquid.

Remove the stems, seeds, and veins of the chiles and discard; place the chiles in a blender. Add 2 cups of the soaking liquid, the remaining 1½ cups of onion, and the garlic; blend until smooth. Strain the mixture through a sieve, pressing down firmly and add it to the simmering pork; return the strained chiles (left in the strainer) to the blender. Add ½ cup of the reserved soaking liquid and blend again. Strain the mixture again and stir it into the simmering pork (discard the chile residue in the strainer); season the pozole with salt and pepper and simmer for 20 minutes.

To serve, ladle the pozole into bowls and garnish with lettuce, radishes, oregano, and lime wedges. ❊

Green Pozole

Green Pozole

This Mexican pumpkin seed and pork stew is sold in markets and on busy street corners. Pumpkin seeds, or pepitas, thicken the broth; chiles and herbs lend a green color. Although dried hominy (which must be soaked and cooked in order to soften it) is most often used to make traditional pozole, I find that canned hominy works well and is more practical to use. Mayan and Aztec culinary traditions often call for "frying" sauces. Nothing gets the attention of my cooking students faster than the promise of an exciting maneuver and the sound of sizzle. A sauce is fried by adding it to fat (usually lard but sometimes oil) that has been heated in a deep pot. When the sauce hits the fat, it sizzles and splatters. This technique sets the color and deepens the flavor of a sauce in a way that cannot be achieved by merely heating it. Keep in mind that the fat must be very hot. Be sure when you add the sauce to stand at an arm's length from the pot and add it all at once. The sauce will splatter for just a few seconds, and once you reduce the heat and stir it, it will bubble like any other sauce. Use the tallest pot you have, stir the sauce with a long-handled spatula, and arm yourself with a splatter guard. It is important to dry any meat well before adding it to hot fat or it will splatter and then steam instead of browning. To do this, simply dry the pieces of meat with paper towels.

Serves 8

¼ cup lard (or vegetable oil)
3 pounds pork shoulder or butt, cut into 1-inch cubes (with fat)
2 cups minced white onion
1 teaspoon dried Mexican oregano
2 large garlic cloves, minced
2 (29-ounce) cans hominy, drained and rinsed
6–7 medium tomatillos, husks removed, rinsed and quartered
2 serrano chiles (seeded and deveined if less heat is desired)
1 cup chopped cilantro (leaves and tender stems)
½ cup toasted pumpkin seeds (pepitas)
Salt and freshly ground black pepper, to taste
1 cup sliced radishes
2 cups thinly sliced romaine lettuce
Dried Mexican oregano, to taste
Lime wedges

In a large Dutch oven, melt half of the lard over medium-high heat. Working in batches, sauté the pork until the pieces are browned on all sides, about 8–10 minutes total, adding more lard as needed. Remove the browned pork with a slotted spoon to a plate. Pour off all but 1 tablespoon of the rendered fat in the pot; reserve.

Reduce the heat to medium and add the onions; sauté until softened (they will change color as they lift the browned bits left from the pork), about 4–5 minutes. Add the oregano and garlic and cook until fragrant, about 30 seconds. Return the pork (and any accumulated juices) to the pot and cover with water by 2 inches (about 7 cups). Increase the heat to medium-high and bring the liquid to a boil; cover, reduce the heat and simmer until the pork is tender, about 1½–2 hours. Add the hominy; cover and simmer for 15 minutes.

In a blender, combine the tomatillos, chiles, cilantro, pepitas, and ½ cup of water; blend until smooth.

In a medium saucepan over medium-high heat, heat 1 tablespoon of the reserved fat; when the fat is hot, add the blended mixture (careful, it will splatter); reduce the heat and simmer for 5 minutes.

Add the sauce to the pork mixture and stir well; season with salt and pepper. Simmer for 20 minutes.

To serve, ladle the soup into deep bowls; garnish with the radishes, lettuce, oregano, and lime wedges. Leftovers can be frozen for up to 3 months. ✳

Seafood and Coconut Stew (Tapado de Mariscos)

Tapado means "covered," but what makes these creamy chowders so particular to the coastal area of Central America is not only that they're made in covered pots, but that they always feature coconut milk. These creamy stews are served at beach stalls from Belize to El Salvador to Honduras. Tapados can be made with poultry, beef, or pork, but you'll swoon over this seafood version. The classic combination of green plantains and yuca provide the starch of this one-pot meal. You can usually find culantro, the pointy-leafed herb used in the Latin Caribbean that tastes like ubercilantro and retains its bright green color even after it's cooked for a long time, in the produce section of Latin American grocery stores in the United States. If you can't find it, use cilantro instead, but add it toward the very end so it doesn't blacken. Just one spoonful of this soup takes me back to the black sandy beaches and vibrantly orange and deep pink sunsets of my youth. If I close my eyes while I taste this, I can almost hear the sound of the waves crashing on the beach.

Serves 4–6

2 green plantains, unpeeled, cut into 4 chunks each
½ pound yuca, peeled and cut into 8 pieces
2 tablespoons vegetable oil
½ cup chopped white onion
½ cup peeled, seeded, and diced tomatoes
⅓ cup minced red bell pepper
4 large garlic cloves, minced
4 cups fish stock, shrimp stock, or water
1 (8-ounce) jar clam juice
½ pound, deveined shrimp (peels on, if possible)
8 ounces crabmeat, picked for shell fragments (I prefer claw meat)
8 ounces sea bass, cut into ½-inch pieces
½ cup minced culantro leaves or 1 cup minced cilantro
    (leaves and tender stems)
1 (13.6-ounce) can coconut milk
Salt and freshly ground black pepper, to taste

Place the plantains in a large pot and cover with water; bring to a boil. Reduce the heat, cover, and simmer until they're fork-tender, about 15 minutes. Drain, peel, and set them aside.

In the same pot, place the yuca; cover with cold water and bring to a boil. Reduce the heat, cover, and simmer until they're fork-tender, about 10–15 minutes. Drain and set aside.

In a large Dutch oven, heat the oil over medium-high heat; add the onions and sauté until they begin to soften, about 1–2 minutes. Add the tomatoes and bell peppers and cook, stirring often, until softened, about 2 minutes. Add the garlic and cook until fragrant, about 30 seconds. Add the fish stock, clam juice, plantains, and yuca. Bring to a boil; reduce the heat, cover, and simmer for 5 minutes. Stir in the shrimp, crabmeat, fish, and culantro (if using cilantro, add just before serving); simmer for 5 minutes. Add the coconut milk and season with salt and pepper. Simmer for 5 minutes (being careful not to let it boil or it will curdle). Serve immediately. ❈

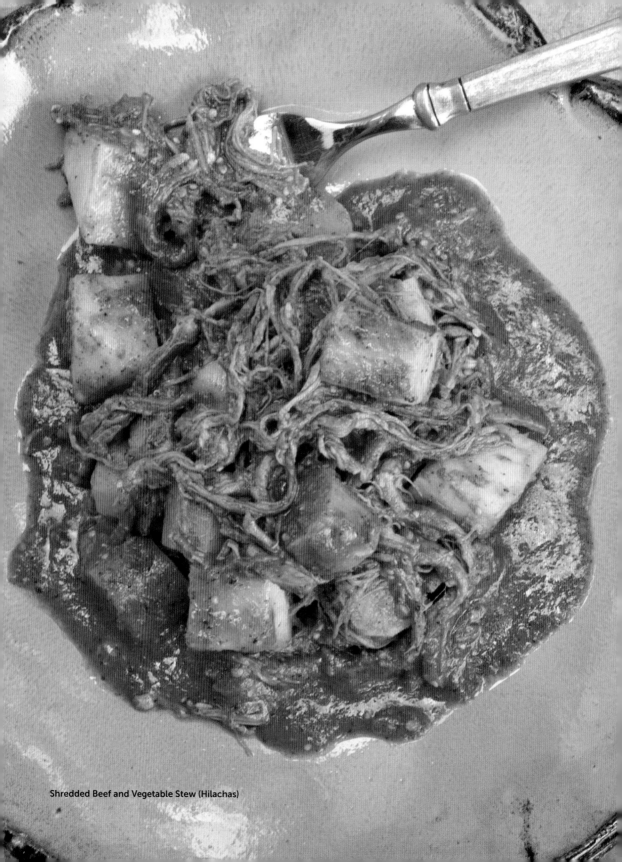

Shredded Beef and Vegetable Stew (Hilachas)

Shredded Beef and Vegetable Stew (Hilachas)

In this mouth-watering stew, beef, potatoes, and carrots simmer in a roasted tomato and annatto sauce with a faint hint of heat, courtesy of a single dried chile. Every Latin country makes a version of shredded beef. Some are thicker than others; the sauce in this one is thickened slightly with masa harina. Cubans make a similar stew called *ropa vieja* (old clothes). In other countries it's known as *carne deshebrada*, and in Guatemala, this dish is simply known as *hilachas* (shreds), and I grew up eating it at home. On any given day in markets throughout Latin America, you'll find slight variations of this stew served with rice and beans. This freezes beautifully, and like many such dishes, it tastes better the next day, after the flavors have been allowed to blend. Here is a delicious way to use an inexpensive cut of beef.

Serves 6

- 1¾–2 pounds of flank steak (or brisket)
- 2 cups roughly chopped white onion, divided
- 1 garlic clove, unpeeled
- 1 bay leaf
- 12 medium tomatillos, husks removed, rinsed and left whole
- 6 plum tomatoes
- 1 guajillo chile
- 1 tablespoon annatto (achiote) paste
- 1 tablespoon masa harina
- 2 tablespoons lard (or vegetable oil)
- 3½ cups peeled and quartered Yukon Gold potatoes
- 3 cups peeled and sliced carrots (slices should be ½ inch thick)
- Salt and freshly ground black pepper, to taste
- 4–6 cups of cooked white rice (optional)

In a large Dutch oven, place the meat, 1 cup of the onions, the garlic, and the bay leaf, and enough water to cover (about 5 cups). Bring the liquid to a boil; reduce the heat and simmer for 15–20 minutes, skimming off (and discarding) the foam that rises to the top. Bring the liquid back to a boil; cover, reduce the heat, and simmer for 1–1½ hours or until the beef shreds easily. Remove the pan from the heat and let the meat cool in the broth for 30 minutes. Remove the beef and strain the liquid, reserving 1 cup to thin the sauce. (The rest can be used in other recipes.) Let the beef rest for 30 minutes or until it's cool to the touch. Shred the meat finely into thin strands (you should have about 4 cups); cover and keep refrigerated until ready to use.

In a dry cast-iron skillet or griddle over medium-high heat, place the tomatillos and the tomatoes. Turning them often, roast them until their skins are charred on all sides and transfer them to a blender. In the same skillet, toast the chile for 20 seconds on each side, or just until pliable. Remove it from the heat; seed, devein, and cut it into 4–5 pieces and add it to the blender. Add the rest of the onion, annatto, masa harina, and half of the reserved liquid to the blender; blend until smooth. (Add more of the reserved liquid to help get the motor started, if needed; discard the rest.)

In a large Dutch oven, melt the lard (or heat the oil) over medium-high heat; when the lard is hot, add the blended sauce all at once (careful, it will splatter) and using a long-handled spatula, stir for 2 minutes. Add the shredded meat, potatoes, and carrots; season with salt and pepper. Stir and bring to a boil; reduce the heat, cover, and simmer until the vegetables are tender, about 20–25 minutes. Serve over rice (if using). ❖

. . . .

Chicken and Root Vegetable Stew (Sancocho Panameño)

On any given day, you'll see Panamanians sitting in front of street stalls enjoying bowls of this comforting and filling stew, traditionally made with hens or free-range chickens. Sancocho is the national dish of Panama, and what distinguishes this from other boiled stews is the addition of *culantro*. Not to be confused with cilantro, which has small, feathery leaves, culantro has pointy leaves that are anywhere from four to eight inches long. Culantro, which is the herb of choice in the Latin Caribbean, tastes like cilantro times a thousand, and, unlike cilantro, it stays vibrantly green even when cooked for long periods of time. Find it in the produce section of Latin American stores. You can substitute cilantro if you can't find it, but don't add it until just before you serve the stew because it will blacken as it cooks. The root vegetable of choice for this stew is called *ñame*. It looks like a giant sweet potato, with a brown, barklike skin and yellow or white flesh; ñame takes longer to cook than potatoes, but it has pretty much the same culinary uses. It breaks down as it cooks, thickening the broth and giving the sancocho the creamy texture it's revered for. If you can't find ñame, use starchy potatoes instead. Sancochos are normally served with steamed white rice.

Serves 10

> 1 free-range chicken, cut into 10 pieces (use neck bone and back bone and any giblets)
> Salt and freshly ground black pepper, to taste
> ¾ cup minced culantro leaves (or 1 cup minced cilantro)
> 1 teaspoon dried oregano
> 1 cup chopped white onion
> 1 teaspoon extra-virgin olive oil
> 1 (3-pound) ñame, peeled, cut into 1-inch cubes, and immersed in cold water (see note)
> 1 small butternut squash, peeled, seeded, and cut into large chunks
> 3 cups cooked white rice (optional)

Place the chicken in a large bowl. Season it well with salt and pepper; add the culantro, oregano, and onions and drizzle with the oil; stir to combine. Marinate the chicken at room temperature for 30 minutes (or up to 8 hours in the refrigerator).

Place the chicken mixture (and any juices that collected) in a large stockpot over medium heat. Cover and cook, stirring once or twice, until the chicken and the onions have begun to sweat, about 6–8 minutes (they should not be allowed to brown). Cover the chicken with cold water by 2 inches and add the ñame. Bring the liquid to a rolling boil; cover, reduce the heat, and simmer for 20 minutes. Add the butternut squash and continue cooking until the vegetables are tender, about 20–25 minutes (if the liquid is evaporating too quickly, add more water as it cooks). Serve hot over rice (if using).

NOTE: Once cut, ñame will oxidize (turn brown) quickly. The cold water will prevent this for up to 30 minutes.

If you want the broth to be creamier, remove the chicken and butternut squash from the soup right before serving and keep it warm; continue cooking the ñame, mashing it down slightly with a potato masher until it has reached the desired consistency. Return the chicken and squash to the broth; stir, heat through, and serve immediately.

Potato, Chicken, and Corn Stew (Ajíaco Bogotano)

When I was in my teens, my family traveled to the island of San Andrés in Colombia. We arrived on a stormy night, only to find that our hotel was overbooked and we had nowhere to stay. There, I was introduced to this most famous soup in Colombia. Its creamy broth and deep chicken flavor soothed our exhaustion on that cool night. Traditionally, ajíaco incorporates a variety of yellow, red, and white potatoes. Andean potatoes, called *papas criollas*, are preferred because they disintegrate while they cook and make the broth creamy. You can sometimes find them in Latin stores, frozen or dried; if you can't find them, use small creamer potatoes like Yukon Gold, which also break apart. Guascas (*Galinsoga parviflora*) is an herb that grows wild throughout Latin America. Also known as Colombian mint, it can be found dried, or fresh in Latin tiendas. It gives this stew the floral taste that defines it. If it's unavailable, use cilantro instead. Historically, ajíaco is served in large, black clay bowls. It's always garnished with avocados, capers, and cream. We ended up finding a place to stay, but what truly made my vacation memorable was the warmth and soothing taste of this classic soup.

Serves 6

¼ cup packed cilantro (leaves and tender stems)
4 green onions
2 large garlic cloves, peeled and left whole
1 celery stalk, halved
1 large bay leaf
2½ pounds whole chicken breasts, with bone
2 teaspoons salt
3 quarts chicken broth
1¼ pounds red potatoes, peeled and cut into thick slices
1 pound small creamer potatoes (such as Yukon Gold), peeled
  (or use canned or frozen papas criollas)
1¼ pounds russet potatoes, peeled, and cut into thick slices
3 ears of corn, cut crosswise into 2-inch-thick slices

1 cup fresh or 1–2 teaspoons dried guascas (or cilantro)
2 Hass avocados
½ cup capers
Mexican crema or sour cream

In a large pot over medium-high heat, place the cilantro, green onions, garlic, celery, bay leaf, chicken breasts, and salt; cover with the broth. Bring the liquid to a boil; reduce the heat to low and simmer for 15 minutes, skimming off (and discarding) the foam that rises to the top. Continue simmering, uncovered, for an additional 15–20 minutes or until the chicken is cooked through. Remove the chicken to a platter; when cool enough to handle, shred it into large pieces; chill until ready to serve.

Strain the broth over a large bowl and discard all of the solids; return the broth to the pot and set it over medium-high heat. Add the creamer potatoes and bring to a boil; cover, reduce the heat, and simmer for 20 minutes. Add the remaining potatoes; cover and simmer until they are fork-tender (about 30 minutes). Add the corn and the guascas and cook for about 25 minutes or until the corn is tender.

Remove 1 cup of the potatoes and mash them until smooth; return them to the soup and stir. Add the chicken and simmer for 5 minutes.

To serve, peel, pit, and slice the avocados. Place a piece of chicken in each bowl; ladle the soup and vegetables on top, and garnish with avocado, capers, and dollops of crema. ❉

Corn Stew with Mayonnaise, Cheese, and Chile Serrano (Esquites)

Corn Stew with Mayonnaise, Cheese, and Chile Serrano (Esquites)

In this Mexican street favorite, corn taken right off the cob is cooked in a spicy and buttery broth. In markets, esquites are served in small glasses and customers add their own toppings. It's the soupy version of Corn on the Cob with Cream and Cheese (page 201) and shares a similar flavor profile. Epazote, or wormseed, is an herb native to Mesoamerica. Its flavor is hard to decipher, but it has a very distinctive aroma that reminds me of a combination of camphor and tarragon. It's sold both fresh and dried in Latin American stores. I prefer using fresh epazote because it's easier to remove after it has done its job flavoring the stew, whereas the dried herb is grassy and impossible to retrieve and can overpower. If you can't find epazote, don't worry: This stew, crowned with creamy toppings, will still be hearty and delicious.

Serves 4–6

- ½ cup (1 stick) unsalted butter or lard
- 6 cups corn kernels (fresh or frozen and thawed)
- 2 cups minced white onion
- 2 serrano chiles, thinly sliced (seed and devein if less heat is desired)
- 2 garlic cloves, minced
- 3 sprigs fresh epazote (optional)
- 2½–3½ cups water (see note)
- Salt, to taste
- ½ cup mayonnaise, or to taste
- ½ cup sour cream or Mexican crema
- ½ cup Cotija cheese or queso seco, or to taste (in a bind, use Parmesan or Pecorino Romano)
- Chipotle or piquín powder
- Lime wedges

In a large Dutch oven, melt the butter over medium-high heat. Add the corn, onions, and chiles. Cook, stirring, until the corn is tender, about 10 minutes. Add the garlic and epazote (if using) and cook until fragrant, about 30 seconds. Add the water and salt. Bring the liquid to a boil; cover, reduce the heat, and simmer for 10 minutes. If you've used the epazote, remove and discard it.

To serve, ladle the stew into mugs and top with a dollop each of mayonnaise and sour cream. Sprinkle with the cheese and chile powder and garnish with a lime wedge.

*⟩ NOTE: The amount of water you use depends on how thick you want your esquites. I prefer it thick, so I usually add only the 2½ cups of water, but use more if you want more broth.

THE SANDWICH MAKER

My mother wasn't a big eater when I was little. She was tiny and elegantly skinny, and as far back as I can remember, she hired cooks to prepare all of the meals in our home. As a dedicated career woman, she was always too busy to cook. She'd often say that she wouldn't find out what was for dinner until she actually sat down at the table; and at that point, she'd only nibble a bit here and there. However, as uninterested as she was in food, my mother—like most of my relatives from her side of the family—was prone to sudden cravings for street foods. This is the one thing she'd indulge in with abandon. I'm happy to say that I often benefited from her gastronomic longings. I can't count the number of times we headed out on a whim to buy stacks of pupusas, bags of shucked corn to eat with lime-scented butter, or meaty chicharrones with vibrantly green chile sauce.

I loved it when we'd scout for hot dogs. Some days she'd take us to the ice cream parlor, called Helados Gloria, at the end of the Avenue of the Americas in Guatemala City for Carolina hot dogs (yes, as in North Carolina–style) filled with creamy slaw. My favorites by far, though, were the hot dogs loaded with sauerkraut and avocado that we'd buy in front of the Catholic boy's school, the Liceo Guatemala. My mother and I'd bring the hot dogs home, and then, along with my brothers, we'd walk to a nearby park; we'd open our paper-wrapped dogs and enjoy them one delicious bite at a time.

Hot dogs are huge in Latin America. In Chile, you'll find *completos*, hot dogs topped with sauerkraut, avocado, and what they call *salsa*

131

A vendor at a choripán stand in Buenos Aires, Argentina.

Americana—a Thousand Island dressing made with carrots, onions, and pickles. They also sell a version called *italianos*, which are dressed with avocados, tomatoes, and mayonnaise, the colors of the Italian flag. In Panama, hot dogs are topped with cheese and strawlike French fries, and in Argentina, you'll find them slathered in *chimichurri*.

There are many different Spanish terms for sandwich. In Peru it's *sanguche*, in Ecuador and Colombia it's *sandúche*, in Guatemala it's *sangüiche* or *panito*, and in Chile it's *sanduich*. In Mexico, it's *emparedado*, *torta*, or *cemita*, depending on what type of bread is used.

In Latin America, sandwiches are much more than just two slices of bread with ham slapped between them. We Latin Americans take our sandwiches very seriously. In fact, some of the most popular sandwiches in Latin America are named after famous people, immortalized between two pieces of bread.

Here in North America, when we see an Elvis sandwich on a menu, we immediately know that it will contain peanut butter, bacon, and bananas because the late singer was fond of that particular combination of ingredients. Similarly, Cubans know that whenever you ask for an Elenita Ruz, you mean turkey, cream cheese, and strawberry jam on white bread, named after the Cuban socialite who created the combination and served it regularly at her famous parties. If you're in Chile and you order a Barros Jarpa, you mean a ham and cheese panini, named after the Chilean minister of the interior in the 1930s. Argentineans know what they'll get if they ask for a Carlitos: a piece of breaded veal, dressed with mayonnaise and ketchup, and served on crusty bread. It's said to have been named after the bartender who first created it in the city of Rosario. And if you're in Venezuela and want a corn cake stuffed with chicken salad, you'll ask for a Reina Pepiada.

Some sandwiches are named after the place where they were invented; others get their name from the ingredients they include, like the Chilean ham and egg sandwich called a York, so called for a kind of ham eaten in York, England. Still others are named for ingredients that never made it

The Sandwich Maker

into the recipe to begin with, such as the famous Uruguayan *chivito* (goat sandwich), named after the meat it's supposedly made of but isn't. In this chapter, you'll even find sandwiches that don't feature any bread at all.

As you can see, sandwiches in Latin America require that you have a sense of humor and a keen sense of adventure. Some of them are quite simple to prepare, while others take some work to assemble. Some are pressed until they are compact, while others are piled with so many toppings that taking a bite is an experience in itself. One thing is for certain, all of the sandwiches in this chapter are highly memorable and very tasty.

The collection of recipes here only scratches the surface of the vast assortment of sandwiches found on the streets, but I tried to give you examples of the most popular ones found from Mexico to Brazil and the Latin Caribbean. Most of the recipes for Latin American sandwiches come from years of dearly held traditions, and many are surrounded by history and lore. I loved recounting these stories for you and hope that you'll enjoy reading them.

I encourage you to have lots of fun making these fabulous Latin American sandwiches. Eat them with a happy spirit, share them with others, and keep the traditions—and the people who inspired them—alive through the generations. All of the sandwiches in this book are good served with a side of fries or a salad. Just please don't blame me if, in the middle of the day, you start getting a sudden urge for one of these amazing street offerings. Blame those cravings on my mother—I always do.

An Arepa con Queso and an Arepa with Chicken and Avocado Salad (Reina Pepiada) (page 136)

Arepas con Queso

Not all Latin Americans eat tortillas; once you cross over into South America, arepas become ubiquitous. Arepas are the corn bread of Venezuela and Colombia, and street vendors sell them, stuffed with a wide array of fillings, for breakfast, lunch, or snack time. Some arepas are sweetened with sugar, flavored with anise, and eaten plain, others are stuffed with eggs and fried until crispy, and others still are flecked with shredded cheese before they are cooked. These are sautéed in a skillet and then finished in the oven before being sliced and filled with soft cheese. The resulting corn cakes are crispy on the outside with soft interiors resembling polenta. I prefer to stuff these arepas with queso blanco, which when heated through, melts and oozes down the sides. Use this recipe (without the cheese) for the other arepa sandwiches in this chapter, like the Arepas with Chicken and Avocado Salad on page 136. However, if you are a grilled cheese aficionado, this will likely be your favorite rendition.

Makes 6 arepas

> 2½ cups white or yellow arepa flour (masarepa or harina pan)
> 1 teaspoon salt
> 1 cup warm (110°–120°F) milk
> 1½–2 cups warm (110°–120°F) water (see note)
> 2 tablespoons unsalted butter
> 2 tablespoons vegetable oil
> 8–10 slices queso blanco (or any good melting cheese)

Fit a large baking pan with a metal rack; set aside. In a medium bowl, combine the arepa flour and salt; slowly add the warm milk and 1½ cups of the water, stirring constantly, and breaking up the lumps in the dough until the dough comes together; the texture should be like mashed potatoes. Cover the bowl with plastic wrap; let it sit at room temperature for 10–15 minutes. (The dough will thicken as it sits, and you should be able to form patties when it's done resting.)

Preheat the oven to 350°F. Line a plate or baking pan with parchment paper. Moisten your hands and divide the dough into six parts (about a generous ½ cup each); shape each into a 3½-inch patty, about ½–¾ inch thick. See note.

In a medium, nonstick skillet, heat the oil and melt the butter over medium heat. Working in batches of three (if you crowd them too much, they'll take a bit longer to cook), slide the arepas into the skillet; cook them until the bottoms begin to turn golden, about 5–6 minutes; flip and cook until the other sides are golden, about 3–3½ minutes. (If they are browning too quickly, reduce the heat—they should just be a rich golden color on each side.) Place the finished arepas on the prepared pan and bake for 10 minutes.

Slice the arepas lengthwise in half; place a slice of cheese between them and return them to the oven for 2 minutes or until the cheese is melted. Serve immediately.

❉⟩ NOTE: Since arepa flour brands are all a little different, the amount of water required to make the dough will vary. Always start with the minimum amount of water called for and then add more water, a few tablespoons at a time, until the dough holds together when pressed between your fingers. Keep your hands moist as you shape the arepas to prevent the dough from sticking to your hands.

You can shape the arepas up to 4 hours before cooking them; simply place them on a baking sheet, cover them with plastic wrap, and refrigerate until ready to cook. Once cooked, arepas can be kept warm (unstuffed) in a 250°F oven for up to 1 hour. Arepas do not freeze well.

If you're using a large skillet, the arepas will take a bit longer to cook (about 1 or 2 extra minutes per side). Reheat leftover arepas in a 350°F oven until warm, about 8 minutes.

Arepas with Chicken and Avocado Salad (Reina Pepiadas)

This is the most famous sandwich in Venezuela, where if you ask for a Reina Pepiada, you'll always get a deliciously crisp corn cake filled with creamy chicken and avocado salad. *Reina* means "queen," and *pepeada* (or *pepiada*, as it's now spelled) meant "sexy" back in the 1950s. The owner of the restaurant where this sandwich was first invented named it after the beauty queen Susana Duijm, Miss Venezuela, when she won the Miss World title in 1955. She is said to have eaten a similar rendition in that establishment. The original version included green peas, but they seem to have been dropped from the dish at some point over the years.

Today you'll find this sandwich sold all over Venezuelan streets. The lime green–tinted chicken salad offers just a hint of avocado and is mouthwatering all on its own. But it never tastes better than when combined with the deep corn flavor of warm and crispy arepas. For a quicker version, use rotisserie chicken.

Serves 6

Arepas con Queso (page 135), without the cheese
6 cups cooked and shredded chicken
2 Hass avocados
1 garlic clove, minced
½ cup mayonnaise
6 ounces cream cheese or Neufchâtel cheese, softened to
    room temperature
¼ cup chopped white onion
¼ cup fresh lime juice (plus extra to brush on avocados)
Salt and freshly ground black pepper, to taste

Place the arepas on a baking sheet and keep warm in a preheated 250°F oven. Place the shredded chicken in a large bowl. Peel, pit, and slice the avocados; brush the slices of one of them with lime juice and set aside. Place the other slices in a blender; add the garlic, mayonnaise, cream cheese, onion, and lime juice. Blend until smooth. Combine the sauce with the chicken and season with salt and pepper.

Slice each arepa lengthwise in half; to make more room for the filling, if desired, remove some of the soft interior. Place 1 cup of the chicken salad on the bottom halves of the arepas; arrange the sliced avocados over the salad, and top it with the remaining halves of the arepas. Serve immediately. ❋

"Goat" Sandwich (Chivito Uruguayo)

"Goat" Sandwich (Chivito Uruguayo)

Chivito means "baby goat," but there is no goat to be found in this assorted meat sandwich. As the story goes, one evening in 1940, Antonio Carbonaro, a restaurant owner from Punta Del Este, Uruguay, welcomed an Argentinean customer who wanted a goat sandwich like one she remembered having nearby. The restaurant didn't have any goat meat. Finding himself in a bind, with an eatery full of people and in the middle of a storm that had cut electricity, the chef sent out a beef and ham sandwich. The customer loved it. Word spread, and before long, this restaurant was selling upwards of a thousand of these sandwiches every day. This towering creation holds everything but the kitchen sink. Mine includes the basic toppings, but other popular condiments include roasted peppers and artichoke hearts. Flavored mayonnaise is always a trademark of this sandwich; don't hold back, it should ooze messily while you eat it. Use the recipe for the flavored mayonnaise here or try my Spicy Mayonnaise (page 276) if you like your sandwiches to have a kick. A meal in and of itself, a chivito is often served with a mound of French fries like the ones on page 175—just in case you're still hungry after eating one.

Serves 8

- 1 cup mayonnaise
- 1 (14-ounce) can hearts of palm, drained and minced
- 2 tablespoons minced capers
- 1 tablespoon extra-virgin olive oil, divided
- 1¼ pound beef tenderloin cut into 8 slices (¼ inch thick) and pounded thinly
- 8 slices Canadian bacon
- 2 cups thinly sliced white onions
- 8 hamburger, Kaiser, or brioche buns, sliced lengthwise and lightly toasted
- 1 pound sliced cooked ham
- 1 pound thinly sliced mozzarella cheese
- 5 hard-boiled eggs, sliced (or 8 fried eggs)
- 8 large iceberg lettuce leaves, washed and dried
- 4 large beefsteak tomatoes, thinly sliced
- 1 cup sliced Manzanilla olives
- Sliced pickled banana peppers (spicy or sweet)

In a small bowl, combine the mayonnaise, hearts of palm, and capers; set aside. In a nonstick skillet, heat half of the oil over medium-high heat; cook the beef for 1–1½ minutes per side (for medium rare), or to desired doneness; remove the beef from the pan and set aside.

In the same pan, cook the bacon on both sides until golden, about 1–2 minutes total; remove the bacon and set it aside. Reduce the heat to medium; add the remaining oil to the pan and sauté the onions until lightly golden, about 3–4 minutes (or leave them raw).

To assemble the sandwiches, spread the bottom of each bun generously with the prepared mayonnaise. Top with a slice of beef, bacon, ham, and mozzarella; set them on a baking pan and place them 1 inch from the broiler for 2–3 minutes or until the cheese is melted and has begun to brown.

Remove the sandwiches from the broiler; top with the lettuce, tomato, hard-boiled eggs, onions, and olives; add peppers and more mayonnaise, to taste. Replace the tops of the buns and serve immediately. ❊

Sliced Pork Sandwiches with Salsa Criolla (Butifarras)

First, pork is lightly seasoned and painted with annatto, which gives it its characteristic yellow tint. Then it's thinly sliced and mounded high onto round buns. Finally, it's topped with a red onion and yellow pepper salad Peruvians call *salsa criolla*. The resulting sandwich is an explosion of contrasts: sour and savory, soft and crunchy. These giant pork sandwiches are sold all over Lima from small, glass-enclosed street carts in parks and on street corners. Traditional *butifarras* are made with large, fresh hams, called *jamones del país*, that are shaved to order while customers watch. I've created a smaller version of these hams for your home kitchen—otherwise, you'd be eating these sandwiches till kingdom come. The trick here is to cook the pork low and slow for a long time, roasting it with the moist heat created by the broth. Allow the cooked pork to cool completely so it can be easily sliced. I like to cook the pork a day in advance, chill it, and then slice it to order.

Serves 6

One 3-pound pork butt or roast, tied with twine to help it
    keep its shape
½–¾ cup chicken broth (or more, if your baking dish is
    larger than the one suggested)
1 tablespoon extra-virgin olive oil
2 teaspoons salt
1 teaspoon annatto (achiote) powder
½ teaspoon garlic powder
¼ teaspoon freshly ground black pepper
8 large, round crusty rolls (or Kaiser rolls)
Peruvian Spicy Onion Salsa (Salsa Criolla) (page 275)

Preheat the oven to 350°F. In a small bowl, combine the oil, salt, annatto,
garlic powder, and pepper; brush this mixture over the entire surface
of the roast. Set the pork in a 9×8×3-inch baking dish; pour the broth
around it. Roast the pork for 1½ hours (or until a meat thermometer
registers 185°F), adding more broth as it evaporates, if needed. Remove
the pork from the oven and cool for 30 minutes at room temperature.
Cover and refrigerate it, if not using immediately.

To make the butifarras, remove the twine from the pork; slice the
pork thinly and pile it up high on each bun. Dress the sandwiches liberally with the Salsa Criolla. Serve at once. ❉

The Cuban Sandwich (Cubano) with Fried Plantains
(Tostones) (page 186)

The Cuban Sandwich (Cubano)

My husband ate his share of these pressed sandwiches as a student living in Miami, and he still loves to eat them today. The *cubano* is one of the trendiest sandwiches in recent years, but this Latin panini-style sandwich has been standard fare for Cuban nationals for decades. The trademark of these sandwiches is layers of roast pork, marinated in *mojo*—a mixture of citrus, garlic, and spices. You'll need to marinate the pork for several hours to obtain the most flavorful meat. Of course, you can also use leftover roast pork you may have on hand from another meal. Unless you live near a Cuban community, the bread used to make these can be hard to come by, but crusty sub rolls, French bread, or Italian buns work great, too. Although Cuban sandwich presses don't have ridges and panini presses do, the latter work just as well in flattening and toasting the bread. If you don't have either, simply grill the sandwiches in a skillet, using another heavy skillet to flatten them. Smaller versions of these sandwiches are called *medianoche* (midnight) and are usually eaten as a late-night snack.

Serves 8

> 2 pork tenderloins (about 1½ pounds each),
>   silver skins removed
> 7 large garlic cloves, minced
> ½ cup fresh orange juice
> ½ cup fresh lime juice
> ¼ cup extra-virgin olive oil
> 2½ teaspoons salt
> 1 teaspoon ground cumin
> 1 teaspoon oregano
> ½ teaspoon ground coriander seed
> Freshly ground black pepper, to taste
> 8 Cuban rolls (or Italian or French rolls)
> Yellow mustard
> 1 pound thinly sliced cooked ham
> ½–¾ pound thinly sliced Swiss cheese
> Sliced bread and butter pickles

In a nonreactive dish (or in a large zip-top bag), place the pork tender-loins. In a small bowl, whisk together the garlic, orange juice, lime juice, oil, salt, cumin, oregano, and coriander; add to the pork and marinate (stirring once in a while to make sure pork is coated on all sides) for 4 hours or overnight.

Preheat the oven to 400°F. Place the pork in a 13×9×2-inch baking dish, season with pepper, and pour the marinade all around it; tent it loosely with foil and roast for 35–40 minutes or until it reaches an internal temperature of 165°F. Remove the pork from the oven and allow it to rest for 20 minutes before slicing it into ¼-inch slices (or chill, well-covered, until ready to use—for up to 3 days); keep the pork moist with the marinade.

To assemble the sandwiches: spread mustard on one side of the bread; top each with sliced pork, ham, cheese, and pickles. Press each sandwich in a panini press until the cheese has melted and the filling is warm (about 4 minutes). ✳

Chilean Steak and Cheese Sandwich (Barros Luco)

Steak and cheese sandwiches may be a commonplace today, but in the 1900s the combination was avant-garde. In Chile, people are so fond of their sandwiches that they give them surnames. This one is named after the Chilean president Ramón Barros Luco (1910–15). The name, which is said to have been coined in the eatery inside the National Congress of Chile—although several eateries now take credit for naming it—stuck like gum to a shoe when customers began to ask for sandwiches like the ones made for the president. Years later, his brother, who was a senator—not one to be left behind—had a ham and grilled cheese sandwich named after him, known as the Barros Jarpa, and that one was coined in the posh Club de la Unión in Santiago. This sandwich makes a great light supper when paired with a simple salad and a glass of wine.

Serves 4

2 teaspoons extra-virgin olive oil

2 teaspoons ají amarillo paste

1 teaspoon ground cumin

1 teaspoon salt

½ teaspoon garlic powder

⅛ teaspoon freshly ground black pepper

1 pound beef tenderloin cut into 8 slices (¼ inch thick)
    and pounded thinly

¾ pound Havarti cheese, thinly sliced

Mayonnaise

4 small ciabatta or French rolls (about 4 × 4 inches),
    sliced in half lengthwise

In a small bowl, combine the oil, ají, cumin, salt, garlic powder, and pepper. Season the beef with this paste (distribute it well) and marinate for 1 hour in the refrigerator.

Heat a griddle over medium-high heat and cook the beef for 1–1½ minutes on each side (for medium), or to desired doneness. Brush the bottom halves of the bread with mayonnaise; top with the beef and cheese. Set the open-faced sandwiches (tops and bottoms) on a baking sheet and place them under the broiler for 3–4 minutes or until the cheese is melted and bubbly and the bread is lightly toasted. Close the sandwiches and serve immediately. ❊

Pork Burgers with Cabbage Slaw (Chimichurris)

In the Dominican Republic, savory and well-seasoned pork patties are first topped with crispy slaw and then drenched in salsa golf, the pink sauce beloved throughout Latin America. While the name of these burgers is the same as the Argentinean herb condiment called *chimichurri*, one has nothing to do with the other. When shaping burgers, I like to make an indentation on the top of them with my thumb, which prevents them from getting that hump that many patties get while cooking. These are easiest cooked on a grill, but if you're using a griddle, I suggest you sear the burgers on both sides first and then ladle a little bit of water around them and quickly cover them with a stainless-steel bowl. The steam created will help to cook the burgers through to the middle. This is particularly important when making these pork burgers, which must be cooked until well-done. This may be a different kind of burger than what you're used to, but it's one that's sure to please over and over again.

Serves 4

> 6 cups thinly sliced green cabbage
> Salt, to taste
> 1 pound ground pork
> ¼ cup minced white onion
> ¼ cup minced cilantro (leaves and tender stems)
> ¼ cup minced flat-leaf or Italian parsley (leaves and tender stems)
> Salt and freshly ground black pepper, to taste
> 4 Kaiser rolls, toasted
> Golf Sauce (page 276)

Place the cabbage in a medium bowl; cover with boiling water and let it sit for exactly one minute. Drain and allow it to cool to room temperature; sprinkle it with salt, cover, and refrigerate until ready to eat.

In a medium bowl, combine the pork, onions, cilantro, and parsley; divide this mixture into four equal portions and shape each into a patty (indenting the center of each patty slightly with your thumb).

Heat a grill (or an indoor grill pan) until very hot; season the burgers on both sides with salt and pepper, and cook (indented side on the top) for 6–8 minutes. Flip and cook for another 6–8 minutes or until cooked through.

To assemble the burgers, place the patty on one side of a bun; top with a generous amount of cabbage and drizzle with a lot of the sauce. Serve immediately, with more sauce on the side. ❈

The Sandwich Maker

Pork Burgers with Cabbage Slaw (Chimichurris)

Sandwiches with Breaded Veal Cutlets (Pan con Milanesa *or* Carlitos)

In South America, you'll very likely encounter these classic sandwiches stuffed with perfectly breaded and crispy veal cutlets called *milanesas*. Executives donning suits and laborers alike grab these huge sandwiches from little kiosks during their lunch breaks on the streets of Buenos Aires. When my family had veal cutlets for dinner when I was a little girl, both my father and I always hoped there'd be leftovers for sandwiches like these. Today, when I prepare milanesas, I make sure to make extras and freeze them to satisfy a sudden craving for these sandwiches. My method includes sautéing the cutlets briefly just until the coating is golden and then baking them just until the veal is cooked through. This method ensures that the coating remains crispy and the meat is tender. My husband and I enjoy these sandwiches—which are just like the ones my dad and I used to eat years ago—with the French fries on page 175, a green salad, and a glass of chilled white wine.

Serves 4

> 6 large veal cutlets (about 1–1½ pounds) pounded to about ¼ inch thick
> Salt and freshly ground black pepper, to taste
> 2 large eggs, lightly beaten with 1 tablespoon water
> Flour for dredging (about ½ cup)
> 1–1¼ cups dry bread crumbs
> ¼ cup unsalted butter
> ½ cup vegetable oil
> 4 large crusty rolls, sliced lengthwise (French rolls, bolillos, and small ciabatta rolls all work well)
> Mayonnaise
> Mustard
> Romaine lettuce leaves
> 1 beefsteak or heirloom tomato, thinly sliced
> Hot sauce (such as Tabasco) (optional)
> Lime wedges (optional)

Preheat the oven to 300°F. Line a large baking pan with a metal rack. Season the veal with salt and pepper on both sides. Place the flour and bread crumbs in 2 separate shallow pans. (For easy clean-up, I spread out a clean garbage bag on the counter and mound the flour directly on one side of the bag and the crumbs on the other). Place the bowl of beaten eggs in the center. Working with one cutlet at a time: dredge them in the flour, shaking off the excess; coat completely with the egg, and transfer to the breadcrumbs, pressing the cutlets into the crumbs so they'll adhere completely. Let the cutlets sit at room temperature for at least 10 minutes and up to 20 minutes so they dry a little bit.

In a heavy 12-inch skillet, melt the butter and oil over medium-high heat. Working in batches, sauté the cutlets on both sides until they are golden brown, about 2–3 minutes per side (reduce the heat if they're browning too quickly). Place the cutlets on the prepared pan and bake until the veal is cooked through, about 12–15 minutes. See note.

To make the sandwiches, spread the bun with a generous amount of mayonnaise and mustard. Place lettuce leaves on the bottom of each bun and top with a cutlet (if the cutlets are much larger than the bread, cut them, to make them fit). Top with the sliced tomatoes and hot sauce (if using). Serve hot, with lime (if using).

NOTE: The baked cutlets can be prepared ahead of time and frozen for later use. Freeze them in a single layer on a baking sheet until solid and then transfer them to zip-top freezer bags. To reheat, place them on a baking sheet in a 350°F oven and bake until heated through, about 8 minutes.

Plantain Sandwich with Shredded Beef in Annatto Sauce (Patacón Pisao con Carne Mechada)

Shredded beef is common all around Latin America, where it's often served with rice and beans. On the streets of Panama and Colombia, though, it's sandwiched between giant, twice-fried plantain halves, called *patacones*, and then topped with delicious condiments. Patacones are prepared much like tostones (page 186), but the plantains for tostones are sliced into coins. For both, though, the first fry creates a crust (which, for the patacones, helps the flattened plantains hold their shape). The second fry makes them crispy. Expect scrumptious juices to drip down your chin as you bite into one of these sandwiches. Of course, if you prefer, you can eat them with a knife and fork. The shredded beef is also great on its own or served over white rice.

Serves 6

One (1½–2 pounds) flank steak, patted dry with paper towels
¼ cup plus 2 teaspoons extra-virgin olive oil (plus more for frying the plantains)
3½ cups water (more to cover)
½ cup dry sherry
1 bay leaf
1 teaspoon annatto (achiote) powder
1½ cups minced plum tomatoes (or canned crushed tomatoes)
1 cup minced white onion
½ cup minced carrots
½ cup minced red bell pepper
3 large garlic cloves, minced
1 teaspoon dried thyme
1 teaspoon ground cumin
Salt and freshly ground black pepper, to taste
6 large green plantains
6 lettuce leaves (iceberg or romaine)
6 slices Monterey Jack cheese, queso blanco, or queso fresco
Mayonnaise
Hot sauce

Heat 2 teaspoons of the oil in a large pot over medium-high heat; sear the steak on both sides until browned, about 6–8 minutes. Add the water, sherry, and bay leaf (the steak should be covered by about ½ inch of liquid; if it isn't add more water). Bring the liquid to a boil; cover, reduce the heat and simmer for 1½–2 hours or until the beef shreds easily with a fork. Cool the beef for 30 minutes; remove it from the cooking liquid, shred it, and return it to the pot.

In a large nonstick pan, heat the remaining ¼ cup of oil; add the achiote powder and stir for 20 seconds. Add the tomatoes, onions, carrots, bell pepper, garlic, thyme, and cumin; cook, stirring, until the mixture has thickened and the carrots are fork-tender, about 15–18 minutes; stir the mixture into the shredded beef and cook, uncovered, over medium-high heat until the sauce has reduced by two-thirds, about 12–15 minutes. Season with salt and pepper, to taste; discard the bay leaf. (The beef can be prepared a day ahead and reheated over the stove or in the microwave).

Fit a large baking pan with a metal cooling rack; set aside. Peel the plantains by cutting the peel lengthwise (being careful not to cut through the flesh). Slide your thumb under the peel up and down the entire length of the plantains until all of the peel comes off. Slice each plantain across in half (each piece should be at least 5 inches long).

Heat ½ inch of oil in a large skillet over medium-high heat. Fry the plantains until they're lightly golden all over, about 2–3 minutes total (see note). Using tongs, transfer the plantains to the racks to drain; remove the skillet from the heat until the patacones are shaped.

Working with one piece of plantain at a time, flatten them between two sheets of parchment paper with a meat mallet (or a heavy skillet) to ¼-inch thickness (they'll be about the size of a slice of bread). When all of the pieces are flattened, set the pan back on medium-high heat; when the oil is hot, fry the plantain slices until golden brown and crispy, about 1–2 minutes per side; transfer them to the prepared racks to drain.

To assemble the sandwiches, place a leaf of lettuce on half of the plantain slices; mound a generous amount of beef over the lettuce and top each with a slice of cheese. Drizzle with hot sauce and mayonnaise and top with another slice of plantain. Serve immediately.

❊} NOTE: Whenever you're frying food and the oil gets too hot, remove the skillet from the heat, let the oil cool a bit, and then return it to the heat; continue frying. Patacones are best when eaten fresh, but they can be kept in a 250°F oven for up to 1 hour.

Hot Dogs with Sauerkraut and Avocado Sauce (Shucos)

Hot Dogs with Sauerkraut and Avocado Sauce (Shucos)

Accounting was my favorite class during my freshman year of university—but not for the reason you might think. I was not interested in the subject matter at all, but every Friday after class our professor would let us out early so we could grab one of these hot dogs from the cart across the street. They're topped with shredded cabbage, slathered with mashed avocado, and then covered with whatever condiments you can manage to add without making the bun collapse in your hands. *Shucos* is Guatemalan slang for "messy," and true to their name, sometimes these can be tricky to maneuver, which is precisely what makes them so much fun to eat! In Chile, similarly dressed hot dogs are called *completos*, and in Venezuela they're known as *chéveres*. Slicing the hot dogs lengthwise allows you to cook them quickly; plus, when you place them—split side up—inside the buns, you have more room for the toppings. It's common to see long lines at the stands of the most reputable vendors of these hot dogs in Guatemala City, sometimes stretching around the block. Some locations, like the one in front of the Universidad de San Carlos, is said to sell upwards of 20,000 of these daily. Luckily, you won't have to wait in a long line to get a bite of one of these. But make sure you have plenty of napkins on hand!

Serves 4–8

8 hot dog buns
8 all-beef hot dogs
2 cups prepared sauerkraut
Avocado Sauce (page 268)
Mustard
Mayonnaise
Ketchup
Hot sauce

Heat a grill (or an indoor grill pan) until very hot. Slice the hot dogs lengthwise in half and place them on the grill, split side down, and cook until you can see the grill marks and the dogs are slightly toasted, about 2–3 minutes; turn and repeat on the other side.

Place the hot dogs in the buns and top with sauerkraut, avocado sauce, mustard, mayonnaise, ketchup, and hot sauce. Serve at once. ✳

Sausage in a Bun (Choripán) with Francisco's Chimichurri

The name of this South American hot dog derives from the melding of the words *chorizo* (sausage) and *pan* (bread). The chorizo in question is a spicy sausage, similar to an Italian sausage. This chorizo has nothing in common with the Spanish pre-cured and paprika-enhanced sausage or with the loose, bulk sausage from Mexico that also go by that name. On the streets of Argentina, Chile, Peru, and Ecuador, the sausages are either grilled or cooked on makeshift griddles. Condiments are usually offered in small bowls on the side of carts. Depending on where you are, the condiments will vary, but in Buenos Aires a bowl of chimichurri is always at hand. My friend Francisco's chimichurri makes a delicious accoutrement for these. Serve these on any crusty sub rolls.

Serves 6

> 6 Italian sausages (hot or mild)
> 1 teaspoon extra-virgin olive oil
> 6 crusty sub rolls, sliced lengthwise
> Francisco's Chimichurri (page 272)

Using a sharp knife, puncture the sausages on all sides. (If you want them to cook faster, slice them lengthwise in half.) Heat a nonstick pan over medium heat; add the oil and swirl. When the oil is hot, add the sausages, cooking and turning to brown on all sides (about 6 minutes). Pour 1 cup of water into the pan; bring the liquid to a boil. Cover, reduce the heat, and simmer the sausages for 8–10 minutes or until cooked through. Remove the cover; increase the heat to medium-high and bring the liquid to a boil, allowing it to evaporate, about 2 minutes. Make sure to stir the sausages to coat with the final glaze that will form in the pan. Remove from the heat.

Toast the buns lightly. Place a sausage in each bun and serve them immediately with a generous amount of the chimichurri. ❊

Sausage in a Bun (Choripán) with
Francisco's Chimichurri

Arepa Sandwiches with Tomato-Enhanced Scrambled Eggs (Arepas con Huevos Perico)

This is the ultimate breakfast sandwich. Creamy eggs studded with the combination of onions, tomatoes, and peppers called *sofrito* or *guiso* are known as *huevos perico*. In Caracas, luscious arepas are filled with this dreamy egg mixture and sold wrapped in paper for an easy-to-tote meal on the run. The arepas can be made ahead of time and kept warm in the oven for up to one hour, or while you make the eggs. The addition of cheese is optional.

Serves 6

Arepas con Queso (page 135), with or without the cheese
2 tablespoons unsalted butter
1 cup minced white onion
2 cups peeled, seeded, and minced plum tomatoes
1 tablespoon minced green bell pepper (or jalapeño pepper, seeded and deveined if less heat is desired)
7 large eggs
Salt and freshly ground black pepper, to taste

Place the arepas on a baking sheet and keep warm in a preheated 250°F oven.

In a large nonstick skillet melt the butter over medium-high heat. Add the onions and sauté until soft, about 3 minutes. Add the tomatoes and bell peppers; sauté until the peppers soften, about 1–2 minutes. In a small bowl, beat the eggs and season with salt and pepper; pour them into the skillet, stirring, to break the eggs into small curds; cook until the eggs are set, about 2–3 minutes. Remove from the heat.

Slice each arepa lengthwise in half; scoop out a bit of the soft interior to make room for the eggs, and fill each with a generous amount of eggs. Top with cheese (if using). Serve immediately. ✳

Brazilian Roast Beef Sandwich (Bauru)

Another steak and cheese combo, the Bauru, features crunchy, tangy pickles and is the most famous sandwich in Brazil. In the 1930s, Casemiro Pinto Neto, a law student from the city of Bauru, asked the line cook at the Ponto Chic, a student hangout, to create the most filling sandwich possible. It's now sold from street carts far and wide—many of which are situated around universities and schools. Recently, the city government of São Paulo instituted official guidelines for how the sandwich can be made and what ingredients can go on it. If a sandwich doesn't meet the guidelines, it can't carry the name. This one is very simple to make; for a quicker version, press the sandwiches on a panini press—but don't tell anyone in São Paulo!

Serves 4

> 4 crusty French rolls or sub rolls, cut in half lengthwise
> and soft interior removed
> 1–1¼ pounds thinly sliced roast beef
> 1–2 large beefsteak or heirloom tomatoes, thinly sliced
> 1 teaspoon oregano
> Salt and freshly ground black pepper, to taste
> 8 long pickle slices (optional)
> ¾ pound mozzarella cheese, cut into 12 slices

Preheat the oven to 400°F. Top half of each bun with roast beef and tomatoes; sprinkle each with ¼ teaspoon oregano; season with salt and pepper. Top each with 2 pickles (if using) and then 3 slices of the mozzarella cheese. Place the open-faced sandwiches on baking sheets and bake just until the cheese has melted (but not browned), about 8–10 minutes. Top with the remaining bun halves and serve immediately. ❊

Poblano and Cheese Quesadillas
(Quesadillas de Rajas)

Poblano and Cheese Quesadillas (Quesadillas de Rajas)

I had to include at least one recipe for the ubiquitous Mexican grilled cheese sandwich that has taken the fast-food world by storm in the last two decades. *Queso* (cheese) gives these stuffed tortillas the gooey characteristic that we all love. Quesadillas can be filled with virtually anything you like (see note), but chiles and cheese are traditional fare in Mexico. Poblanos are long, dark-green peppers. Their skins are quite tough and they're seldom eaten raw. Roasting them makes them easy to peel and softens their flesh; they're not too spicy, although some can be hotter than others. Any melting cheese works well in quesadillas, and if you're lucky to find good Mexican cheese such as Oaxaca, by all means use it. However, my friend Diana Kennedy, who is an authority in Mexican cuisine and a cookbook author, taught me that domestic Muenster melts similarly to the cheeses used in Mexico, so I use it here. Top these with Raw Tomatillo Salsa (page 269), Avocado-Tomatillo Taco Truck Sauce (page 270), or Sweet Dried Chile Sauce (page 278).

Serves 8

- 4 roasted poblano peppers, peeled, seeded, deveined, and sliced into thin strips
- 8 (8-inch) flour tortillas
- 12 ounces Muenster cheese, thinly sliced
- 8 ounces soft goat cheese, crumbled
- ¼ cup thinly sliced green onions (white and green parts)
- Vegetable oil (for brushing on tortillas)
- Mexican crema (optional)

Place the tortillas on a flat surface. Top the bottom half of each tortilla with Muenster cheese, poblano strips, crumbled goat cheese, and green onions. Fold the tortillas in half, to enclose the filling.

Heat a griddle or nonstick pan over medium-high heat; brush the top of the quesadillas with oil and place them on the griddle, oil side down. Cook the quesadillas until one side is golden and crispy, about 1–2 minutes (rotating them as they cook will prevent them from burning before the cheese has a chance to melt); brush the tops with a bit of oil and turn them over to cook on the other side until they're golden and crispy and until the cheese has melted, about 1–2 minutes.

Cut the quesadillas in half; top with your favorite salsa and drizzle with crema (if using). Serve immediately.

❊} NOTE: Possible fillings include any good melting cheese and the chorizo and potato filling for sopes (page 65), Refried Black Beans (page 284), the chicken filling for Tostadas with Spicy Chicken (page 76), or the Beef Picadillo (page 288).

FRIED & TRUE

Going to the fair in my hometown was always an adventure. Once a year, my grandmother would first take us to church, and then off to the fair, where she would buy all sorts of edible goodies that were only found during that festivity. Forget the fact that she was normally shopping with six or seven kids in tow, all of whom wanted to stop to see the man with the jumping beans or the lady with the monkey that danced for money. She was a woman on a mission, and we obediently followed behind as she bartered and bought her prized delicacies.

My favorite reward for being obedient was a bag of crispy chicharrones (pork rinds), still warm from being just fried in a vat of lard. Some even had chewy pieces of meat attached to them. All were salty and primed to be sprinkled with lime juice, which made the pillows of puffy fried pork crackle. If we were well behaved, she'd buy us each a giant rosary made of paper beads; inside each bead hid two oval-shaped sugar drops that dissolved slowly in our mouths as we strolled along. Suffice it to say, I loved going to the fair.

Chances are that, like me, you have already experienced a close encounter with some kind of fried food offering at a fair or outdoor festival. If you haven't, plan on going to the nearest fair next summer so you can discover what most already know: that everything tastes better when it's fried.

In Latin America, fried goodies are available every day on the streets. Pork is so abundant in Latin America that it is not an expensive ingredient. On the streets, the flesh is usually roasted for sandwiches or simmered for soups or stews. But the skins, which most U.S. cooks would throw out, are often fried in lard so that they can become delicious bits to munch on and savor. But "chicharrón" can mean different things depending on where you are in Latin America. In Mexico, for instance, it can mean enormous pieces of skin, first simmered in water and then fried until they're light as feathers, yielding skin so crispy that it's a sin not to bite into it. This chicharrón is salty and usually cut into little rectangles,

A chicharrones stand.

wrapped in paper and eaten on the go or chopped and cooked in sauces. In Mexico, chicharrones also refer to the hardened strips of pork skin that are left behind after rendering lard; these are often simmered in rich sauces to stuff into tacos. Instead of tortilla chips, Central Americans often serve chicharrones alongside avocado or bean dips. They also top refreshing salads or warm bean stews with them to add a little crunch.

The chicharrones in Colombia, on the other hand, are like crispy, chewy bacon, cut into long strips, while some of the chicharrones in Central America have a higher ratio of meat to fat than any other, making them all the chewier. Cubans don't necessarily think of pork when they hear the word "chicharrones" because for them they may very well be fried bits of chicken that are served with a garlicky sauce called *mojo* (which I use as a marinade for the pork in the Cubano sandwiches on page 143). Latin Americans have different words to describe the same thing. In Puerto Rico, for instance, fried pork in all of its forms, whether it is eaten alone, stuffed into sandwiches, or pounded and mixed with plantains, is called *cuchifrito*. In any case, whether you find a street cart

Fried & True

selling chicharrones or cuchifritos, you know they're selling something scrumptious. In Latin America today, few people make chicharrones at home—which is why you won't find a recipe for them in this book. Luckily, they're found in grocery stores all over the United States.

Chicharrones are just one example of the many fried foods you'll discover on a typical day on Latin American streets. The plump and succulent chiles rellenos that you'll find on an average day in Mexico and Guatemala are another. Sometimes they're slathered in sauce, and other times they're stuffed into rolls to make sandwiches or tortas. They're delicious and quite easy to make with my recipe.

There are many categories of fried foods sold by street vendors in Latin America, and I tried to include at least one of each here. Fritters abound, from Brazilian ones made with peas or grains to the Latin Caribbean béchamel-bound pillows called croquetas. You'll find many interpretations of a Latin American favorite, cod fritters—sometimes called *bacalaítos*—along the beaches of the Latin Caribbean, so I included a great recipe here. And if you've never experienced the taste of a Cuban ham croqueta, you're in for a very pleasant surprise. I've also included a recipe for the stuffed potato balls so beloved in Puerto Rico and in Cuba.

You'll also find several recipes that feature plantains, including *bollitos* (or *rellenitos*), fried plantain morsels stuffed with delicious sweetened beans. Of course, I also showcase a recipe for the most famous plantain dish from Puerto Rico—the *mofongo*.

French fries get really interesting interpretations when they find their way onto Latin streets. They can be enjoyed all on their own but usually aren't, and you'll find some amusing new ways of eating them in this book. Potatoes are not the only ingredient fit to make chips, and here you'll find all different types of crispy dippers made with plantains or yuca. From the twice-fried plantain coins called tostones to the paper-thin chips called *mariquitas*, you'll find plenty of new kinds of chips to serve alongside the sandwiches in this book.

And, finally, I would be remiss if I didn't include at least one recipe to represent the many different kinds of fried dough you can buy on the streets of Latin America, so here I offer you a recipe for *yaniqueques*, the little fried crackers found in the Dominican Republic. (And find a recipe for churros, the perfectly fried and sugary strips of dough found all over Latin America, in the "Sweets, Candy, and Ice Cream" chapter.)

Latin Americans have a saying: Una vez al año, no hace daño! (Once a year won't hurt!) The way I see it, it's good to indulge once in a while. Millions of Latin Americans can't be that wrong. Go ahead, make your day!

A NOTE ON FRYING

Always remember that when frying food, it's very important to keep the oil at a constant temperature so that the food becomes crispy without absorbing too much of the fat. If you have a deep fryer with a temperature gage, this will be easy to do; however, keeping the oil at an even temperature in a skillet, pot, or Dutch oven may be trickier. The thickness of the pan you're using and the power of your stove will also play a role, so it's a good idea to get yourself a good-quality frying thermometer to keep tabs on how hot the oil is becoming. The optimal temperature for frying is between 350°F and 375°F, and with a few exceptions, most recipes here will call for a temperature in this range. I tell my students that the oil is "alive and kicking," so you must watch it carefully because it will go up or down in temperature when you least expect it to.

If you don't have a frying thermometer, you'll know the oil is too hot if the food is browning too quickly. Remove the pan from the heat to let the oil cool slightly before continuing to fry. On the other hand, if you let the temperature of the oil drop too low, your food will lose its sear, and instead of frying to a crisp, it will become a soggy and greasy mess. But do not fear! As with anything else, the more you fry food, the easier it will become and you'll be able to trust your instincts.

Finally, remember that you can never be too cautious when you're frying. Keep small children and pets away whenever you fry. Never let even a droplet of water fall in your hot oil or it will splatter and burn you. And never let your oil reach a smoking point or it can catch on fire.

Chiles Rellenos

These stuffed peppers are one of the most beloved and recognized dishes in the Latin culinary repertoire. Here, poblano peppers are lovingly roasted, hollowed out, filled, covered in eggy batter, and fried to perfection. On the streets, they're bathed in tomato sauce like my All-Purpose Tomato Sauce and drizzled generously with crema or stuffed in rolls. The size of the chiles will dictate the amount of filling you'll need, but you'll need large ones here. Choose between two fillings (one is a vegetarian option; see note). When I was growing up, my dad and I were food buddies. On many occasions, I would accompany him to the hospital where I'd wait for him in the waiting room while he made his rounds. After that, we'd often go get a sandwich made with beef-stuffed chiles similar to these.

Serves 8

8 poblano peppers, roasted and peeled
2 tablespoons vegetable oil
½ cup minced yellow onion
1⅓ cups seeded and minced plum tomatoes
1 cup finely diced carrots
1 garlic clove, minced
½ teaspoon dried Mexican oregano
1¾ cup peeled and finely diced russet potatoes
⅔ cup green peas
¾ pound ground pork
¾ pound ground beef (preferably chuck)
½ cup bread crumbs
Salt and freshly ground black pepper, to taste
5 large eggs, separated
1 cup all-purpose flour, divided
Vegetable oil for frying
All-Purpose Tomato Sauce (page 268)
1 cup Mexican crema, or to taste

Carefully make a slit in each roasted pepper starting at the top and ending at the base, being careful not to tear it. Using scissors or kitchen shears, remove as much of the seeds and the pod, as you can but leave the stem attached; set the peppers on a plate, cover, and chill until ready to use.

Heat 1½ tablespoons of the oil in a large skillet over medium-high heat; add the onions, tomatoes, carrots, garlic, and oregano; cook, stirring occasionally, until the carrots are tender, about 5 minutes. Add the potatoes, peas, and 1–1¼ cups of water; cook uncovered, stirring occasionally, until the liquid is completely evaporated and the potatoes are tender, about 8–10 minutes. Transfer the vegetable mixture to a large bowl; set aside.

In the same skillet, heat the remaining oil and brown the pork and beef until no longer pink, about 4 minutes; drain the fat and cool. Add the meat and bread crumbs to the vegetable mixture and stir well; season with salt and pepper and chill for 2 hours. Fill each chile with ¾ cup of filling, packing it well and reshaping the chile into its original shape.

Place the egg whites in a large bowl and whisk until they form soft peaks, about 1 minute (or use an electric mixer on medium speed); add the egg yolks, one at a time, beating well with each addition. Whisk in ¼ cup of the flour until foamy.

Fit a large baking pan with a metal cooling rack; set aside. Place the remaining flour on a large plate. In a large skillet with high sides heat 2 inches of oil to 360°F (or use a deep fryer according to the manufacturer's directions). Working with one chile at a time, dredge it in the flour and then drop it in the batter, turning it with a large spoon to coat all sides. Use a spoon to carefully transfer the pepper to the oil. Repeat the process with each chile, making sure to batter them only when you are ready to drop them in the oil and not to crowd them in the pan. Since the chiles must go directly from batter to the frying pan, fry them in small batches. Fry them until golden, about 4–5 minutes, turning them over halfway through. Using a slotted spoon, transfer them to the prepared rack to drain (see note). Set them on a plate and cover with sauce; drizzle with crema and serve immediately.

NOTE: For the meat-free filling, combine 6½ cups shredded Muenster cheese and ⅔ cup finely chopped yellow onion. Fill each chile with about ¾ cup of the cheese mixture; continue with the recipe as directed above.

Chiles rellenos are best eaten right after frying, but leftovers can be frozen. Reheat them in a 350°F oven for 20–25 minutes or until hot. They can also be filled and frozen before they're battered and fried; thaw them overnight in the refrigerator and continue with the recipe as directed.

Chiles Rellenos

Stuffed Potato Balls (Papas Rellenas)

I've eaten my share of these potato croquettes on the streets of Miami's southwestern area, known colloquially by Cuban Americans as *la sawesera*. Cuban food is flavorful but not spicy-hot; in fact, most Cuban recipes don't feature any heat at all. These spheres are filled with a beef filling called picadillo, flavored with cumin and a hint of oregano. Picadillo comes in many variations, several of which I've included in this book—but the recipe for this one is one of the most straightforward you'll find. It features the clean flavors of sofrito, a mixture of onions, garlic, and peppers cooked in oil, and ground beef. On the streets, papas rellenas are often served in pairs, stuffed into paper bags so you can eat them on the run. These are easiest to shape when both the potato mixture and the filling are chilled well. If you're a meat and potato lover, you'll enjoy these puffy and aromatic fritters as an appetizer or as a light lunch served with a simple salad.

Makes 20 fritters

    1 cup roughly chopped white onion
    1 cup roughly chopped red bell pepper
    2 large garlic cloves, roughly chopped
    2 tablespoons extra-virgin olive oil
    1 pound lean ground beef
    2 tablespoons tomato paste
    1 teaspoon oregano
    1 teaspoon ground cumin
    2 teaspoons salt, divided
    4 pounds Yukon Gold potatoes, cooked until tender,
        peeled, mashed until smooth, and chilled
    ½–¾ cup all-purpose flour
    3–4 large eggs, lightly beaten
    2–2½ cups bread crumbs
    Vegetable oil for frying

Place the onions, bell peppers, and garlic in the bowl of a food processor fitted with a metal blade and process until smooth. In a medium sauté pan with high sides, heat the olive oil over medium-high heat; add the processed mixture and cook until thickened, about 2–3 minutes; add the beef and cook, breaking it down with the back of the spoon, until no longer pink, about 3–4 minutes. Add the tomato paste, oregano, cumin, and 1 teaspoon of the salt and cook for 1–2 minutes. Reduce the heat to low and cook, stirring, for 5 minutes. Cool completely and chill.

Line a baking sheet with parchment paper. Divide the mashed potatoes into 20 equal portions (about ⅓ cup each). Working with one portion at a time, roll the potatoes into a ball; with your fingers, make a large indentation in the center and fill with 1 packed tablespoon of the beef. Roll the potatoes back into a ball, encasing the filling; repeat with the rest of the potatoes, placing them as you go onto the prepared baking sheet. Chill for 1 hour.

Fit a large baking pan with a metal cooling rack. Place the flour and bread crumbs in separate shallow pans. (Or for easy clean-up, spread a clean garbage bag out flat on the counter. Mound the flour on one end of the bag and the bread crumbs on the other and place the bowl of beaten eggs in the center.)

When the balls are chilled, dredge them in the flour, dip them into the eggs, and then coat them with crumbs. In a large skillet with high sides heat 2–3 inches of oil to 360°F (or use a deep fryer according to the manufacturer's directions). Working in batches, carefully slide the balls into the oil and fry, turning to cook them on all sides, until golden, about 2–3 minutes. Using a slotted spoon, transfer them to the prepared rack to drain. Serve immediately or keep warm in a 200°F oven for up to 45 minutes.

The cooked fritters can be frozen for up to 4 months. Freeze them in a single layer until solid and then transfer them to containers. Reheat in a 350°F oven until warm, about 15–18 minutes. ❊

Ham Croquettes (Croquetas de Jamón)

This is perhaps the most famous Cuban croqueta of them all. These cylinders with crispy exteriors are filled with a creamy ham mixture. In fact, these are so decadently creamy that many people spread them on saltine crackers. I have never been to Cuba, but in my youth I was a frequent visitor to Miami, where Cuban street food abounds. Miami was an important hub for my family when I was a student, and we would often meet there for school holidays. Back then, I would enjoy these delicate croquetas as a midmorning breakfast along with a miniature cup of *cafecito cubano*. Today, at home, I serve them for brunch and pair them with eggs or prepare them for a light supper alongside a cup of soup. You can either grind the ham using a food processor or mince it very finely by hand. Serve them warm or at room temperature.

Makes 16 croquetas

> 6 tablespoons unsalted butter
> 1 cup minced yellow onion
> ⅔ cup all-purpose flour
> 1 cup whole milk, warm
> ½ teaspoon salt, or to taste
> ¼ teaspoon freshly grated nutmeg
> ⅛ teaspoon garlic powder
> ⅛ teaspoon freshly ground black pepper
> 1 pound minced or ground Danish or other
>   cooked ham
> 3 large eggs, lightly beaten
> ½–¾ cups all-purpose flour
> 2–3 cups bread crumbs
> Vegetable oil for frying

In a medium, heavy-bottomed saucepan, melt the butter over medium heat; add the onions and cook until soft but not browned, about 2–3 minutes. Reduce the heat to low; add the flour and whisk well, cooking for 1–2 minutes, being careful not to let it turn golden or brown. Remove from the heat; add the milk, whisking vigorously until the mixture is smooth. Return to the heat and continue cooking for 5 minutes, stirring constantly, being careful not to let the sauce burn. The sauce should be the consistency of thick mashed potatoes. Remove from the heat. Stir in the salt, nutmeg, garlic powder, and pepper. When combined, stir in the ham. Transfer to a clean bowl, cover, and refrigerate for at least 3 hours (up to 10 hours).

Line a baking sheet with parchment paper. Divide the ham mixture into 16 equal portions (about ¼ cup each); shape each into a cylinder about 2½ inches long by 1 inch in diameter. Place the flour and bread crumbs in separate shallow pans. (Or for easy clean-up, spread a clean garbage bag out flat on the counter. Mound the flour on one end of the bag and the bread crumbs on the other and place the bowl of beaten eggs in the center.)Dredge the cylinders in the flour, dip them into the eggs, and roll them in the crumbs to coat well. Place them on the prepared sheet and chill for 10–15 minutes.

Fit a large baking pan with a metal cooling rack; set aside. In a large skillet with high sides heat 2–3 inches of oil to 360°F (or use a deep fryer according to the manufacturer's directions). Working in batches, carefully slide the croquetas in the oil and fry, turning to cook them on all sides, until they are golden, about 2–3 minutes. Using a slotted spoon, transfer them to the prepared rack to drain. Serve immediately, or keep them warm in a 200°F oven for up to 1 hour.

You can cook the croquetas ahead of time and freeze them for up to 4 months. They can go right from the freezer to the oven; simply bake them in a 400°F oven for 8–10 minutes or until hot. ❊

Bulgur, Beef, and Pine Nut Fritters (Quibes)

Bulgur, Beef, and Pine Nut Fritters (Quibes)

It may surprise you to find a Lebanese-inspired recipe in this book, but on the streets of modern-day Brazil and the Dominican Republic, you'll find both a raw version and this fried version of this dish. At the start of the twentieth century legions of Lebanese immigrants flocked to Latin America. Their culinary influence stretches from Mexico all the way to Brazil and can be tasted in dishes like *tacos al pastor* and these football-shaped, cracked-wheat fritters (also known as *kibbeh*). Quibes like these are sold on the streets and beachfronts of cities like Rio de Janeiro and São Paolo. They're spicy but not spicy-hot, and they're stuffed with a nutty filling. Quibes are typically served with plain yogurt, but I prefer them with lime wedges and sea salt so they can be sprayed with the sour citrus juice and sprinkled with briny crystals.

Makes 40 fritters

> 2½ cups bulgur wheat (cracked wheat)
> 2 pounds ground sirloin, divided
> 1 tablespoon plus 1 teaspoon extra-virgin olive oil, divided
> ½ cup minced white onion
> 2 large garlic cloves, minced
> ½ cup minced flat-leaf or Italian parsley (leaves and tender stems)
> 1½ teaspoons salt
> ½ teaspoon freshly ground black pepper
> ¾ cup pine nuts, toasted (see note)
> Vegetable oil for frying
> Lime wedges (optional)
> Sea salt (optional)

Line two baking sheets with parchment paper; set aside. In a large bowl, place the bulgur and cover with 2½ cups water; stir and let it sit at room temperature, covered, for 1 hour. Drain and set aside.

In a medium skillet, heat 1 tablespoon of the olive oil over medium-high heat; add the onions and cook until softened, about 1½–2 minutes; remove from the heat and cool slightly.

In the bowl of a food processor fitted with a metal blade, working in batches, combine the bulgur, 1½ pounds of the beef, and the onion, garlic, parsley, salt, and pepper. Pulse for five-second intervals until bits of this mixture pressed between your fingers holds together. If the mixture is too mealy, add some water, a couple of tablespoons at a time, until it holds together. Chill the mixture for 30 minutes.

In the meantime, heat 1 teaspoon of oil in a small skillet and brown the remaining beef until it's no longer pink; transfer to a bowl and stir in the pine nuts.

Divide the bulgur mixture into 40 equal portions (2 heaping tablespoons each) and roll them into balls. Working with one ball at a time, cup it in one hand and make a hole in the center with the forefinger of your other hand, pressing the ball against your hand so it keeps its shape. Fill the hole with 1 teaspoon of the cooked beef mixture, and seal it inside the ball. Press the ball into a football shape and set it on the prepared sheet. Repeat until all are formed. (At this point, the quibes can be frozen for up to 4 months, if properly wrapped to prevent ice crystals, which will cause splattering when the quibes are fried. Freeze in a single layer until solid and then transfer to containers. Don't thaw before frying.)

Fit a large baking pan with a metal cooling rack; set aside. In a large skillet with high sides heat 2–3 inches of oil to 360°F (or use a deep fryer according to the manufacturer's directions). Working in batches, carefully slide the fritters into the oil. Fry them until golden, about 2–3 minutes, turning them over halfway through. Using a slotted spoon, transfer them to the prepared rack to drain. Serve hot with the lime wedges and salt.

✳︎〉 NOTE: To toast pine nuts, place them in a dry skillet over medium heat; toss until golden (about 2–3 minutes), watching them carefully so they don't burn; cool and use as directed.

French Fries (Papitas Fritas)

These are the best fries you'll ever make, bar none. They're fried twice: once to soften the potatoes and the other to sear them to a crisp. These make a perfect accompaniment to any and all of the sandwiches in this book. Ketchup is always optional but in Latin America, they're bound to be topped with Golf Sauce (page 276), Avocado-Tomatillo Taco Truck Sauce (page 270) or Francisco's Chimichurri (page 272).

Serves 4–6

> 4 pounds russet potatoes, peeled
> Vegetable oil for frying
> Sea Salt

Fit two large baking pans with metal cooling racks; set aside. With a sharp knife cut the potatoes into fries 4–5 inches long and ¼ inch thick; place them into a bowl of iced water for 15 minutes. Drain and lay them flat on kitchen towels. Pat them dry and let them air dry for 10 minutes. *It's very important that they be completely dry before beginning the frying process so that they don't spew hot oil.*

In a large pot heat 1½–2 inches of oil to 250°F (or use a deep fryer according to the manufacturer's instructions). Working in batches, cook the potatoes in the oil until they're soft, about 4 minutes (they will not brown). Using a slotted spoon or a small strainer, transfer them to the prepared racks. When all of the fries have gone through the first frying, increase the oil temperature to 360°F and, again working in batches, carefully slide the fries back into the oil; fry them until golden and crisp, about 5–6 minutes. Transfer them to the cooling racks. While they are still hot, sprinkle with a generous amount of salt. Serve immediately or keep them warm on the racks in a 250°F oven for up to 30 minutes before serving. ❊

Black-Eyed Pea Fritters (Acarajés)

These crunchy fritters have a brownish-red exterior that gives way to a dense, creamy, white center. They're made with black-eyed peas that have been peeled—not an easy task but a worthwhile one. The skins are removed by soaking the peas overnight and then rubbing them with a towel. Acarajés are sold at the markets and beaches and on the streets of Salvador da Bahia, Brazil, where they are fried in large vats of *dendé* (red palm oil) in plain view of hungry customers. They get their name from the chant of the women wearing white cotton garb who sell them: "Acará-je!" ("I have acarás!") Acarajés are often split open and stuffed with dried shrimp, stews (*vatapá* or *carurú*), salads, or *malagueta* peppers. I like to serve these as appetizers with Brazilian Hearts of Palm Salad (page 40). Fresh peas are available during summer months, but they can be found frozen year-round. Don't use canned peas, which are too mushy. Whipping the batter is very important. If you've done it correctly, the fritters will float in the oil—a true sign of a great acarajé. Start this recipe one day ahead of time so that you have plenty of time to soak the black-eyed peas.

Makes 6–7 fritters

> 5 cups fresh or frozen black-eyed peas (see note)
> ½ cup grated onion (strained, to remove juices)
> 3 large garlic cloves, grated
> 1 teaspoon salt
> Vegetable oil for frying (see note)

Cover the peas in cold water and soak them overnight; drain them. To remove their skins, rub the peas together in a kitchen towel. Pick out the peas and discard the skins. Place the peas in a bowl of water and soak for 2 hours.

Place the peas in a sturdy blender and add enough water to get the motor running (about 1–1¼ cup); pulse for 5-second intervals until the peas are smooth and feel like soft mashed potatoes (the purée should hold together when pressed between your fingers). If the peas are too watery, drain them through a sieve lined with a kitchen towel. If the mixture is too dry, add a bit more water.

Transfer the puréed peas to a mixer fitted with the paddle attachment. Add the onion, garlic, and salt; whip on medium speed for 2 minutes (or whip them by hand). Whip on low speed for 2 more minutes or until the mixture is light and fluffy (or whip them by hand for 5 minutes).

Fit a large baking pan with a metal cooling rack; set aside. In a medium pan, heat 2–3 inches of oil to 360°F (or use a deep fryer according to the manufacturer's directions). To test the batter, form a tablespoon of the mixture into a football shape (or quenelle) and drop it into the oil. If it falls apart, the batter is too moist; drain again. If it sinks to the bottom and sticks to the pan, whip the rest of the batter for a few more minutes.

To shape the quenelles, scoop up ½ cup of the batter with a large spoon; transfer the batter into a second large spoon, using it to scrape out the batter from the first spoon, yielding a football shape. Carefully, slide the batter into the oil. It should sink briefly and float to the top. Fry the acarajé until it's a reddish brown color, 3½–4½ minutes, turning it over halfway through. Using a slotted spoon, transfer it to the prepared rack to drain. Repeat with the remaining batter.

Split the warm acarajés in half; top with the salad.

NOTE: You can use dried peas, but you'll have to soak them for 3–4 days before their skins will come off.

For a more authentic flavor you can use dendé oil instead of the vegetable oil here. It's very high in saturated fat, so I avoid using it.

You can make these into smaller fritters and serve them as hors d'oeuvres; adjust the cooking time as necessary.

Plantain and Bean Fritters
(Rellenitos *or* Bollitos)

Here, sweet plantains are mashed and stuffed with a very delicate filling made with beans and chocolate. Then they're rolled into granulated
sugar and drenched in crema. The combination of beans and chocolate
sounds strange, but the flavor is sensational. Plantain croquettes are
found in many Latin countries. In Colombia, they're called *bollitos* and
they're stuffed with chicken, but from Mexico to El Salvador, you'll
find similar interpretations to this Guatemalan recipe made with beans.
Shaping the sticky dough is tricky, and at first you may not use up all of
the filling. However, the more experienced you get, the easier this will
become. These are best enjoyed the day you make them, but they can be
frozen for up to 3 months; bring them to room temperature and bake
them at 350°F for 20 minutes or until heated through.

Makes 16–18

> 3½ pounds firm yellow plantains
> 1½ cups Refried Black Beans (page 284)
> 1 cup sugar (plus extra for rolling the fritters in)
> 1 ounce bittersweet chocolate, finely grated
> 2 teaspoons ground cinnamon, divided
> 2 teaspoons vanilla extract, divided
> ⅓ cup flour
> Vegetable oil for frying
> Crema, to taste

Fit a large baking pan with a metal cooling rack; set aside. Place the
whole, unpeeled plantains in a large pot, cover with water, and bring the
water to a boil; cover the pot, reduce the heat, and simmer for 20–25
minutes or until the plantains are easily peeled with a fork (the skins will
split open in the water). Reserve 1½ cups of the cooking water; drain the
plantains and set aside to cool slightly. When cool to the touch, peel and
chop them roughly; set aside.

In a medium bowl combine the beans, sugar, chocolate, 1 teaspoon
of the cinnamon, and 1 teaspoon of the vanilla (you should have about 2
cups). Pour the bean mixture into a nonstick skillet and cook over low

heat until thickened, about 10–12 minutes; set aside to cool (you should have about 1½ cups).

Working in batches, place the plantains in the bowl of a food processor fitted with a metal blade and add ¼–½ cup of the reserved cooking water (to help the motor run); process until they form a thick dough (you can also use a food mill or ricer to mash the plantains). Transfer the dough to a medium bowl and knead in the remaining cinnamon and vanilla.

Before shaping the dough, moisten your hands with water so that the plantains don't stick to them. Roll ¼ cup of the dough into a ball and pat it flat into a 4-inch disk, about ⅛ inch thick. Place about 1¼ tablespoons of the bean mixture in the center. Close the dough over the beans to seal and then roll it between your hands to form a cylinder shape. Repeat with the remaining dough and filling.

In a large nonstick pan with high sides, heat ½ inch of oil to 350°F. Place the flour in a shallow pan. Working in batches, dredge the fritters lightly with flour and fry them until golden on all sides, about 2–4 minutes. (Initially, they'll stick to the bottom of the pan but will release when ready to be turned). Using a slotted spoon, transfer them to the prepared racks to drain. While still warm, roll them into the sugar and return them to the racks. Serve warm or at room temperature (not hot or they'll fall apart) with drizzled crema. ❈

Sausage and French Fry Toss (Salchipapas)

Here, sausages and French fries are all jumbled into one delicious snack. *Salchipapas* are among the most beloved street foods in South America. When chorizos are used, they're called *choripapas*. They're served in baskets, plastic cups, or paper cones, and although you usually get a toothpick or a fork to eat them with, they taste best when you use your fingers. They're topped with as many condiments as you can muster, including Golf Sauce (page 276), pickled onions, and hot sauce. In Peru, they're served with ají crema, a yellow sauce made with ají amarillo and mayonnaise; in Colombia they're sometimes topped with cheese. Because salchipapas are inexpensive, you'll find them sold at street carts strategically located near schools so students can run out to get a quick snack between classes. Go all the way and use any sausages you like: longaniza, bratwurst, kielbasa, and andouille, for example, are delicious here.

Serves 4–6

¼ cup ají amarillo paste or 3 ají amarillos, peeled, seeded,
    and deveined (see note)
½ cup mayonnaise
¼ cup sour cream
2 green onions, thinly sliced (white and light green parts only)
1 tablespoons fresh lime juice, or to taste
Salt and freshly ground black pepper, to taste
French fries (page 175)
10–12 sausages or frankfurters of your choice, fried or grilled
    and sliced
Mustard
Ketchup
Pickle relish

In a blender, combine the ají paste, mayonnaise, sour cream, green onions, and lime juice; blend until smooth. Transfer to a small bowl, season with salt and pepper, and chill until ready to use.

Make the French fries and slice the cooked sausages; toss them together and place them on a large platter (or on individual plates). Serve with the ají amarillo sauce, mustard, ketchup, and pickle relish.

⁑} NOTE: Ají amarillos (whole or as paste) can be found in jars in most Latin American stores. The ají sauce, well covered, will keep for up to 1 week in your refrigerator; it's also delicious on grilled fish and meats or as a sandwich spread (like for the "Goat" Sandwich on page 139).

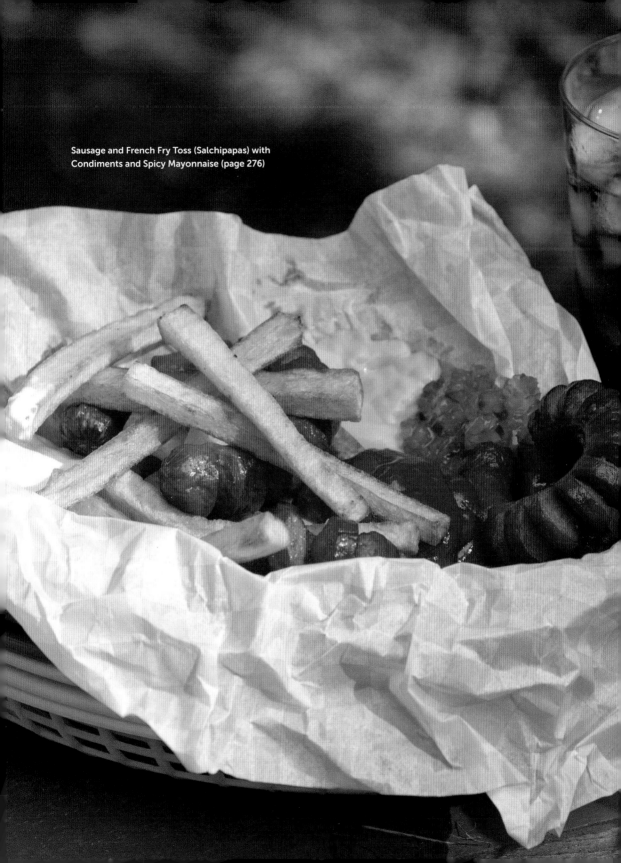

Sausage and French Fry Toss (Salchipapas) with
Condiments and Spicy Mayonnaise (page 276)

Fried Plantain Chips
(Mariquitas, Plataninas, *or* Chifles)

When I was little, my elementary school held a yearly festival to raise funds for the PTA, and sometimes the organization would bring in street vendors to sell food to the attendees. One of my favorite stands sold salty plantain chips like these in small waxed-paper bags. Green plantain chips may have different names throughout Latin America, but they are always crunchy, always salty, and always addictive. In contrast to tostones, the twice-fried plantain coins found in Puerto Rico and Cuba, these chips are paper-thin and fried just once. These are best eaten immediately but will keep for a couple of days, at room temperature, in a paper bag or airtight container.

Serves 8

3 green plantains
Peanut or vegetable oil for frying
Fine sea salt

Fit two large baking pans with metal cooling racks; set aside. Cut off both ends of the plantains with a sharp knife. Score the skin lengthwise (but don't score the flesh) and slide your thumb up and down under the peel until it comes off. Slice the plantains thinly with a mandolin into long strips. In a large pot, heat 1–2 inches of oil to 360°F (or use a deep fryer according to the manufacturer's instructions). Working in batches, fry the plantains until golden and crisp, about 1–1½ minutes (cooking times will vary depending on how thin the plantain slices are, so watch them carefully). Using a slotted spoon, transfer them to the prepared racks to drain; salt while still hot. Serve immediately. ✻

Yuca Fries with Classic Chimichurri

Chimichurri is to yuca what ketchup is to French fries, and once you try this combination, you'll be pressed to make it over and over again. On Latin American streets, potatoes are not the only tubers transformed into fries. Yuca or cassava fries have a meatier texture and a starchier taste than French fries. Chimichurri is traditionally made with parsley, but in my travels I've encountered many different renditions (see, for example, Francisco's Chimichurri on page 272). Some cooks add tomatoes, and others cilantro, but this richly green version stands up to the slightly sweet and earthy taste of yuca very well. Older and larger yuca roots will take longer to cook than younger roots; cook them until they're al dente so that they'll keep their shape as they fry.

Serves 4–6

FOR THE CHIMICHURRI
3 cups coarsely chopped flat-leaf or Italian parsley
    (leaves and tender stems)
1 cup minced yellow onion
2 large garlic cloves, minced
Zest of 1 lemon
2 tablespoons fresh lemon juice
2 tablespoons red wine vinegar
½ teaspoon ground cumin
¼ teaspoon red pepper flakes
¾ cup extra-virgin olive oil
Salt and freshly ground black pepper, to taste

FOR THE YUCA FRIES
3 pounds yuca, peeled and sliced into fries
    (3½ inches long by ½ inch thick)
1 large garlic clove, peeled and left whole
1 bay leaf
1 tablespoon salt
Vegetable oil for frying
Salt, to taste

In a food processor fitted with a metal blade, combine the parsley, onion, garlic, lemon zest, lemon juice, vinegar, cumin, and red pepper flakes. Pulse for ten 1-second intervals or until the mixture is finely chopped. Turn the motor on and slowly add the olive oil through the feed tube, scraping down the sides of the bowl, as needed. Transfer the chimichurri to an airtight container and chill while you make the fries (or for up to 3 days).

Fit a large baking pan with a metal cooling rack; set aside. In a large pot, bring 4 quarts of water to a rolling boil; add the garlic, bay leaf, and salt. When the water returns to a boil, add the yuca and cook it until it's just fork-tender, about 6–8 minutes. With a slotted spoon, transfer them to the prepared rack to dry for at least 15 minutes (or up to 1 hour). *The yuca fries must be very dry before they're fried to prevent the oil from splattering.*

In a large skillet with high sides, heat 2 inches of oil to 360°F (or use a deep fryer according to the manufacturer's instructions). Working in batches, fry the yuca until golden and crispy, about 4–6 minutes. With a slotted spoon transfer them to the prepared rack to drain; season with salt. Serve immediately or keep them warm on the rack in a 250°F oven for up to 45 minutes. Serve the fries with the chimichurri on the side, for dipping. ❉

Yuca Fries with
Classic Chimichurri

Fried Plantains (Tostones) with Guacamole

My husband had a Cuban aunt he used to visit while he was away at college. He recalls the first time he watched her fry tostones with one hand while she chain smoked with the other. He was hoping to eat the fried coins as soon as they came out of the oil, so he was surprised to see her pound them flat against the surface of her 1950s diner–style table, before throwing them back in the oil for a second fry. She knew what she was doing. The first fry was meant to soften the plantains so they could be shaped, and the second was meant to crisp them up. She pounded them with a mallet, but many cooks use a special press called a *tostonera*. Do not confuse tostones with the daintier plantain chips (mariquitas) (page 182); tostones are thicker and much sturdier. Although on the streets they're served with a side of garlicky sauce called mojo or with flavored mayonnaise such as the Spicy Mayonnaise on page 276, my husband loves them best served with smooth guacamole.

Serves 10

FOR THE PLANTAINS
6 green plantains
Canola oil for frying
Salt

FOR THE GUACAMOLE
2 Hass avocados
2 serrano chiles, seeded, deveined, and minced
1 large garlic clove, minced
¼ cup minced cilantro (leaves and tender stems)
Fresh lime juice, to taste
Salt and freshly ground black pepper, to taste
Pinch dried Mexican oregano

Cut off both ends of the plantains with a sharp knife. Score the skin lengthwise (but don't score the flesh) and slide your thumb up and down under the peel until it comes off. Slice the plantains into 1-inch-thick coins (about 8–10 per plantain). Fill a large bowl with cold water and stir in 2 tablespoons of salt. Soak the plantain coins in the salted water for 20 minutes (a very important step done to remove excess starch).

Fit two large baking pans with metal cooling racks. In a large pot, heat 1–2 inches of oil to 330°F (or use a deep fryer according to the manufacturer's instructions). Dry the plantain slices thoroughly with paper towels (*it's very important to dry them well to prevent the oil from splattering*). Working in batches, slide the plantain slices into the oil and fry them until lightly golden and fork-tender, about 1–2 minutes, turning them over halfway through. (If they are browning too quickly, remove the pot from the stove and allow the oil to cool down a bit). Using a slotted spoon, transfer the plantains to the prepared racks; cool for 10 minutes.

Remove them to a cutting board and use a mallet (or a tostonera) to flatten them to ½-inch to ¾-inch thickness. (These may be prepared up to this point and kept at room temperature for up to 1 hour before proceeding with the recipe. If you choose to do this, make sure to remove the oil from the heat).

Heat the oil to 360°F; return the plantain slices to the oil and fry them until crispy and a deep golden color, about 2–3 minutes. Transfer to the prepared racks to drain. While they're still hot, season with salt. Keep the tostones warm on the racks in a 250°F oven for up to 1 hour before serving.

Slice the avocados in half, remove and discard the pits, and remove the flesh to a small bowl; mash it well with a fork. Add the chiles, garlic, and cilantro; mix well. Season with lime juice, salt, and pepper. Sprinkle the guacamole with the oregano and serve with the tostones. ❊

Cod Croquettes (Bacalaítos)

Salty cod fritters with creamy centers like these are famous all over the Latin Caribbean and in Brazil. Dried, salted cod is available in most Latin grocery stores, particularly around the Lenten season, when fish becomes a mainstay of religious observations. Start this recipe a day in advance because it must be soaked in water and the water changed periodically to remove the saltiness in the cod. I recommend soaking it in warm water for the first hour to help it release the outer shell of salt faster; then soak it in the refrigerator for up to twenty-four hours. Other than the fact that this step takes time, cod is an easy ingredient to use. My grandmother swore that soaking cod in milk made the flavor milder, but that's a luxury most of us can't afford! Serve these croquettes with lime wedges and a cold cerveza (beer).

Makes 36 bacalaítos

12 ounces skinless and boneless, salted, and dried cod
1 cup whole milk, warm
2 teaspoons annatto (achiote) paste
6 tablespoons unsalted butter
⅔ cup all-purpose flour
⅛ teaspoon garlic powder
⅛ teaspoon freshly ground black pepper
2–3 large eggs, lightly beaten
½–¾ cups all-purpose flour, for dredging
2–3 cups bread crumbs
Lime wedges (optional)

Place the cod in a large bowl and cover in warm (100°F) water. Let it sit for 30 minutes and then drain. Cover it again with warm water, let it sit 30 more minutes, and drain. Cover the cod in cold tap water and place it in the refrigerator. For at least 12 hours, every 1 hour, drain it and cover it again in cold water. After the soaking period is over, drain the cod, pat it dry with paper towels, and chop it very finely (with a sharp knife or in a food processor).

In a medium bowl, combine the milk and annatto paste; stir until the paste is dissolved; set aside.

In a medium, heavy-bottomed saucepan, melt the butter over low heat; add the flour and whisk well. Cook for 1–2 minutes, being careful not to let it turn golden or brown. Remove from the heat; add the milk. Whisk vigorously until the sauce is smooth and uniformly tinted orange. Return it to the heat and continue cooking for 2–3 minutes, stirring constantly, until it's the consistency of thick mashed potatoes, being careful not to let it burn. Remove from the heat and stir in the garlic powder and pepper, and then stir in the cod. Transfer to a clean bowl; cover and refrigerate for at least 3 hours (up to overnight).

Line a baking sheet with parchment paper. Divide the mixture into 36 equal portions (about 1 tablespoon each) and shape them into balls. Dredge them in flour, dip them into the eggs, and roll them in the crumbs until they are well-coated, placing them on the prepared sheet as you go (at this point you should chill them for at least 10 minutes or up to 30 minutes to help them keep their shape as they fry).

Fit a large baking pan with a metal cooling rack; set aside. In a large skillet with high sides heat 1–2 inches of oil to 360°F (or use a deep fryer according to the manufacturer's directions). Working in batches, carefully place the croquetas in the oil, and fry, turning to cook them on all sides, until golden, about 2–3 minutes. Using a slotted spoon, transfer them to the prepared rack to drain. Serve immediately or keep them warm on the racks in a 200°F oven for up to 1 hour. Serve with lime wedges, if using. ❊

Citrus and Garlic–Infused Plantain and Pork Rinds (Mofongo)

Salty, sweet, and sour flavors join forces and make up one of Puerto Rico's most famous street foods, often sold at beachfront stalls. It combines the gutsy taste of chicharrones with the piquant flavor of garlic and citrus-infused plantains. Some cooks boil the plantains for this dish, but frying them is the more traditional (and the quickest) way to prepare them. The mofongo ingredients are pounded together in a wooden mortar and pestle called a *pilón*; individual portions are then pressed back into the pilón and then unmolded. They're then filled with a lemony sauce called *mojito*, with seafood salads, or with ceviches. This version is simple to make at home, even if you don't have a mortar and pestle.

Serves 8

> 3 green plantains, peeled and cut into 1-inch slices
> Vegetable oil for frying
> 1 cup roughly chopped onion
> 2 large garlic cloves, roughly chopped
> 1 cup packed cilantro (leaves and tender stems),
>   roughly chopped
> ⅓ cup fresh lime juice
> 1 teaspoon oregano
> 1 teaspoon salt
> 1 teaspoon freshly ground black pepper
> 1 cup extra-virgin olive oil
> 4 cups coarsely chopped fried pork rinds

Fit a large baking pan with a metal rack. In a large skillet with high sides, heat 2 inches of oil to 360°F (or use a deep fryer according to the manufacturer's instructions); working in batches, slide the plantains into the oil and fry until golden, about 5–6 minutes total, turning to cook on all sides. Remove them with a slotted spoon and place them on the prepared rack to drain.

To make the mojito, place the onion, garlic, cilantro, lime juice, oregano, salt, pepper, and oil in a blender and blend until smooth; set aside. Oil eight ½-cup ramekins; set aside (see note).

Working in batches, pound together a third of the plantains, a third of the pork rinds, and a quarter of the mojito in a large, sturdy bowl (or a mortar and pestle) until the mixture holds together when pressed between two fingers; repeat with another third of the ingredients and then the rest. Divide the pounded mixture into 8 (⅓-cup) portions and press each into the bottom and sides of the prepared ramekins; shape them into cups; turn them over and unmold. Turn the cups over and fill them with the remaining mojito and serve.

✳⟩ NOTE: Mofongo can also be shaped into balls (⅓ cup for large ones or 2 tablespoons for appetizer size) and served with the remaining mojito on the side.

Fried Bread (Yaniqueques)

These salty, light, and airy flatbreads are sold on the beaches of the Dominican Republic and are said to have arrived with cooks from neighboring English-speaking islands—along with their name, which sounds very much like "Johnny cakes." The dough is easy to make, and it needs only a few minutes rest before it's ready to roll and cut. You can make it in a food processor or by hand, and I give instructions for how to do both. The former makes smoother dough, but they fry the same. If you want them to puff up and remain soft (like small pita bread loaves), roll them a bit thicker; but, if like me, you like them to resemble crackers, roll the dough thinly and prick the cut rounds with the tines of a fork before you fry them. I like to serve these alone or with my Scallops with Creamy Yellow Ají Sauce (page 46) or Shrimp Cocktail (page 56). They're also delicious with any of the ceviches in this book.

Makes 20–24

> 2 cups all-purpose flour
> ½ teaspoon baking soda
> Pinch salt, plus more for sprinkling
> ¾ cup iced water
> Vegetable oil for frying

In a bowl of a food processor fitted with a metal blade, combine the flour, baking soda, and the salt; pulse for 20 seconds to combine. Slowly, while pulsing, add the water, 1 tablespoon at a time, through the feed tube until the dough comes together into a ball. Place the dough in a bowl and cover with a damp towel; let it rest for 10 minutes.

To make the dough by hand, in a medium bowl, whisk together the flour, soda, and salt; using your hands, incorporate the water, 1 tablespoon at a time, kneading the dough until it comes together into a ball and is smooth to the touch. (If the dough becomes too sticky, add more flour; if it's too dry, add more water; see note). Cover the dough with a damp towel and let it rest for 20 minutes (see note).

Roll the dough out on a clean, lightly floured surface to a thickness of ⅛ inch (for puffy and soft ones) or 1/16 inch (for crispier ones). Use a 3-inch round cutter and cut it into circles. (Try to get all of the rounds cut in the first roll; if you don't succeed; cover the scraps and let them rest for 10 minutes before rerolling. You should end up with 20–24 rounds.) For crispy flatbread, prick the rounds a few times with the tines of a fork.

Fit a large baking pan with a metal cooling rack; set aside. In a large skillet with high sides heat 2–3 inches of oil to 360°F (or use a deep fryer according to the manufacturer's directions). Working in batches, carefully slide a few of the rounds in the oil. Fry them until lightly golden, about 1–1½ minutes, turning them over halfway through. Using a slotted spoon or tongs, transfer them to the prepared rack to drain; while still hot, sprinkle with salt. Serve immediately.

❋⟩ NOTE: If you're kneading the dough by hand, you may need a bit more water (about 2–3 teaspoons) than you need for the machine-made dough. Be sure to let the dough rest for *20 minutes* so it will roll well (activated gluten in the flour will cause the dough to shrink back as you roll it, yielding fewer rounds).

FOOD ON A STICK

An apple is just an apple, unless you put it on a stick and cover it with caramel, and then it achieves a new level of culinary heights. How something so ordinary can become extraordinary just by making it portable is fascinating to me.

My all time favorite street foods anywhere in the world are the fun and original renditions of corn on the cob served in Mexico and Guatemala. Some are buttered and then doused with lime juice; others are grilled until the kernels are charred and then sprinkled with spicy salt. Then there are those that are slathered generously with mayonnaise, sprinkled with crumbly cheese, and rolled in spicy chile powder. Mercy! I have stood in line waiting my turn to purchase one of these *elotes locos* many times in my life, and it never gets old. Part of what makes waiting to eat them so much fun is watching other people around me trying to eat theirs. Let's just say that there is a lot of contorting and neck-bending that goes along with eating any of these decadent treatments of corn on the cob. The smiling faces of contented eaters, however, make it clear that these are worth the wait, the gymnastics required to eat them, and the mess.

On one of his voyages to the Americas, Christopher Columbus found the Taíno people of the New World cooking food on sticks over fire. They called it *barbacoa*, and today meat is cooked on sticks all over Latin America. Mostly, you'll find kabobs, or *pinchos*, sold at stands near soccer fields, sports stadiums, beachfronts, and markets in Panama and South American cities. What makes Latin American kabobs most different from many you'll eat in the United States is the fact that they are usually composed of only one ingredient at a time, that is, if you order a meat kabob, just meat is what you get. Likewise, if it's a chicken kabob you want, you won't find anything else threaded on the skewer with it.

Elotes (grilled corn) sold from a makeshift grill.

Perhaps the most famous—or infamous, depending who you ask—of all Latin kabobs are the *anticuchos* that are sold late in the evenings on the streets of Lima. I say infamous because very few people outside of Peru know that the skewered meat that they're eating is beef's heart, and many would drop the stick at the mere mention of it. Before you decide to skip this chapter, know that if I've included a recipe here calling for beef's heart, it's because heart is completely succulent, but if you have any doubt, you can always use steak. Either way, you ought to try them and see what the big deal is. Soon you'll discover why they're so renowned.

When it comes to cooking kabobs, I prefer to use flat bamboo skewers that have an area wide enough to hold the meat in place. Whenever you cook with wooden sticks, be sure they've been soaked overnight in cold water so they don't burn during the cooking process. There is no food on a stick more disappointing than the kind that ends up broken into charred pieces on the ground because the wood burned. You can always protect the ends of the sticks by wrapping them in aluminum foil. If you can find metal skewers, by all means use those. Just remember that they'll remain hot long after the food is removed from them. And never, ever bite off pieces of food from a metal skewer. I'm just sayin' . . .

The most famous food on a stick is cotton candy, known as *algodón*, and I remember going to many birthday parties as a child where *algodoneros* had been invited to make the spun sugar confection of different colors in front of our very eyes. The smell of hot sugar always makes me think of cotton candy. I recall being able to select among many differ-

Food on a Stick

ent colored sugars. There was ballerina pink, parrot green, alabaster blue, egg yolk yellow, and grape-colored purple. I always chose pink. I know, it's boring, but what can I tell you, other than little girls usually love pink. I remember clearly how the person making the candy would throw a plastic tablespoonful of the sugar of our choice into the drum of the machine. Then, if you stood quietly, you could hear the tiny grains of sugar hitting the revolving basin. They would make a tick, tick, tick sound that you could hear long before you could smell any sugar and long before any strands of cotton even began to take shape.

The excitement at the promise of the sweetness to come was hard to contain. All of a sudden, just like magic, little strands of sugar and thin wisps of candy would begin to appear. It never ceased to amaze me how that could happen. Then the aroma of sweet sugar would envelop my nostrils and the wad of cotton would begin to grow. Finally, the candy-maker would hold a stick to the inside of the drum, spinning and twisting it until a cloud as large as my head would envelop the stick. Every time I saw this, it made me think of the coiffed hair of little old ladies who tinted their gray hair funny shades of pastel colors. I don't know why, but the image never failed to appear. To this day, I love the feeling of grabbing cotton candy between my fingers and taking it to my mouth, where it stays cottony for only a second or two before it melts into warm, sweet juice.

There are a few desserts on sticks that can rival cotton candy in Latin America, but if I had to choose one, chocolate covered bananas would top that list. The flavor of ripe, frozen bananas, coated with dark chocolate is a classic, and in Latin America you'll find them further embellished with toppings such as crushed nuts, coconut, chocolate candies, or colorful sprinkles. You'll find a very easy recipe for this treat in this chapter.

Though it might not rival cotton candy, the most famous dessert on a stick in Latin America is the *paleta*. This multicolored popsicle can be found all the way from Mexico down to Central America and comes in so many flavors that including them all in a book is impossible. However, I've put together an easy formula that works with many different flavors. I hope you'll be inspired to go out and buy some popsicle makers so you can fill your freezer with these frozen sensations.

Food on a stick can still make me feel like a little girl. It makes me laugh, and it makes me happy. Get in touch with your inner child—you'll be glad you did.

Chocolate-Covered Bananas (Chocobananos)

Chocolate-Covered Bananas (Chocobananos)

Many Latin American kids have experienced the pleasure of eating a perfectly frozen banana, coated in silky chocolate, and sprinkled with toppings. As a child, I could buy them from ice cream trucks. I made these often when my kids were little; now that they are all grow up, I still make them for myself. It's important to freeze the bananas very well so that they're sturdy when you dunk them into the chocolate; if they aren't frozen solid, they'll break into pieces. Once frozen, work swiftly—the chocolate sets quickly after they're dipped. I'm told these keep well in the freezer for a few months, but I wouldn't know because, in my home, they're devoured immediately.

Serves 8

> 4 ripe but firm bananas, peeled and cut in half crosswise
> 8 popsicle sticks
> 12 ounces semisweet chocolate, chopped
> 1 cup flaked coconut
> 1 cup finely chopped unsalted roasted peanuts

Line a baking sheet with parchment paper. Insert a popsicle stick into each banana half; place them on the prepared sheet (so they aren't touching each other). Freeze them until solid (for at least 3 hours up to 3 days).

Melt the chocolate on top of a double boiler over very low heat, stirring until smooth. Dip the frozen bananas into the chocolate; working quickly (or the chocolate will set), sprinkle one side of the banana with coconut and the other side with peanuts. Place the bananas back on the prepared sheet and freeze them again for 10–20 minutes before serving. Once frozen solid, these will keep well in a freezer-safe container or bag for up to 3 months. ✳

Latin American Popsicles (Paletas)

Paletas, or Latin American popsicles, have taken the culinary scene by storm in the last decade. Some are made with fruit juices, others use frozen fruit pulps, and still others are made with mixtures similar to smoothies. In Latin America, popular beverages such as horchata and cinnamon iced tea are also transformed into popsicles. Paletas are sold all over the streets of Mexico and Central America, and they come in all sorts of flavors; mango and chile, chocolate and peanut, and lime and coconut are a few of my favorites. You'll also find them in all colors of the rainbow. These are so simple to make that giving you a recipe feels a bit silly, so consider this more a set of guidelines than a recipe. The only equipment you'll need is a blender and store-bought popsicle containers. Tropical fruit concentrates such as *guanábana* (soursop), mango, and tamarind make great popsicles. Puréed fruits also make delicious popsicles. For example, strawberries can be puréed, mixed with sugar, and strained through a sieve to remove any seeds before being frozen. My Pineapple Smoothies (page 327), Orangeade (page 332), Anise-Scented Limeade (page 329), Rice and Almond Milk Smoothies (page 323), Cinnamon Iced Tea (page 330), and Hibiscus Iced Tea (page 331) all can be turned into these luscious frozen treats. Be forewarned, though: once you start making paletas, you may not be able to stop!

Makes 6–8 popsicles

> 1 cup fruit concentrate or pulp (available frozen
>   in Latin tiendas)
> 1 cup water
> Sugar, to taste
> 2 teaspoons fresh lime juice

In a blender, combine the fruit concentrate, water, sugar, and lime juice. Blend until smooth and pour into popsicles containers. Freeze until solid. ❖

Food on a Stick

Latin American Popsicles (Paletas)

Corn on the Cob with Cream and Cheese
(Elotes Locos)

Corn on the Cob with Cream and Cheese (Elotes Locos)

Here, fire-roasted corn on the cob takes a bath in creamy sauce before it's rolled in cheese and sprinkled with chile. Corn fixed this way is definitely the most famous food on a stick sold in Mexico and Central America. It's called "crazy corn" because it's drive-you-crazy delicious. Crazy corn is great fun to serve at parties and barbecues. Find sturdy skewers and offer plenty of napkins. Latin stores sell thick wooden sticks ideal for skewering through corn. Cotija cheese is the Parmesan cheese of Mexico, and it's very easy to find in most American supermarkets; if you wish, you can use grated Parmesan or Pecorino Romano cheese instead. Buy corn at the top of the season when it's fresh enough to eat raw. I briefly boil the corn first so it quickly chars before the sticks start to burn. You can grill the corn all the way if you prefer; just forgo the sticks and leave the stalk—nature's stick—at the bottom of each cob. Wrap the stalks in aluminum foil to ensure that they don't burn. Either way, this recipe is sensational and bound to drive you locos with its deliciousness. It's impossible not to have fun while eating these. Make plenty for seconds; chances are, you won't be able to stop at one.

Serves 12

> 12 ears (very fresh) corn on the cob (husked and stalks removed)
> 12 sturdy wooden skewers
> 1 cup Mexican crema or crème fraîche
> 1 cup mayonnaise
> 2 cups crumbled Cotija cheese (or Parmesan)
> Ancho chile powder

Cook the corn in a large pot of boiling water for 3–4 minutes; remove from the heat, drain, and set aside. When cool enough to handle, insert a skewer in the bottom of each cob (see note).

Heat a grill (or indoor grill pan) until moderately hot. Grill the corn, turning the cobs often, until they are tender and slightly charred all over, about 4–6 minutes. In a large measuring cup, combine the crema and mayonnaise; set aside. Place the cheese in a shallow plate; set aside.

Wrap the bottom fourth of the cobs plus the skewers in aluminum foil so they're easier to hold. Dip them into the crema mixture, coating them well, then roll in the cheese and top with chile powder (see note). Serve immediately.

❄} NOTE: If you're preparing these for a large crowd, you can blanch the corn and insert the skewers ahead of time. Cover and refrigerate for up to 8 hours. Heat the grill and continue with the recipe right before you serve them. Keep in mind that they may take a bit longer to char.

To make them easier to coat with the sauce, fill a tall glass half full with the dipping sauce and then let the guests dip and roll their own cobs, as they please. Place the chile powder in a jar with a sprinkle top.

Beef Skewers Bathed in Annatto and Orange (Carne en Palito)

These kabobs feature tender beef redolent of citrus and spices. In city streets, you'll see them mounded on shiny trays—sometimes tented under aluminum foil—all lined-up, waiting to be cooked on makeshift grills built over barrels. *Carne en palito* literally means "meat on a stick," and these truly mouth-watering kabobs are often sold during religious festivals and fairs. They're sold by the beaches of Ecuador and outside the sports stadiums all over Panama City, where vendors compete for customers by offering delicious versions of these skewers. For less than a dollar each, you can go cart to cart, and sample them all. Wrapped in warm corn tortillas, these make spectacular appetizers, and they make a filling meal when paired with the Latin trinity: white rice, beans, and plantains.

Serves 8 as an appetizer or 4 as a main course

1 (1½–1¾-pound) flank steak, sliced on the bias into
    ⅛-inch-thick strips
1 tablespoon finely grated orange zest
1 cup fresh orange juice
¼ cup extra-virgin olive oil
5 large garlic cloves, minced
2 teaspoons annatto (achiote) powder or paste
1½ teaspoons ground cumin
8 (12-inch) bamboo skewers, soaked overnight in cold water
Salt and freshly ground black pepper, to taste

Food on a Stick

In a large nonreactive bowl, whisk together the orange zest, orange juice, oil, garlic, annatto, and cumin. Add the beef and stir, making sure to coat it on all sides; transfer it to the refrigerator and marinate for at least 40 minutes (but no longer than 2 hours or the citrus will break down the beef, turning it mushy). Thread two to three slices of beef on each skewer; brush them with a bit of the marinade and discard the rest of the marinade. Heat a grill (or an indoor grill pan) until very hot. Grill the kabobs for 3–4 minutes per side or until well-done but still moist. (Latin Americans eat these well-done, but you can cook them for less time if you desire.) ❊

Beef Kabobs in Beer Marinade (Chuzos de Carne)

Chuzo stands are abundant on the streets of Colombia, particularly around sports stadiums and during festivals. These kabobs offer deeply flavored beef that sizzles as soon as it comes into contact with hot grills. They're usually grilled directly over makeshift coal fires. Although the kabobs in other cuisines feature different ingredients skewered between the pieces of meat, chuzos are all about the meat. The marinade helps to tenderize the beef while also infusing it with luscious flavor. On the streets of Guayaquil, small arepas are often speared at the end of each chuzo, collecting the juices that drip off the meat. At home, we love to eat these over a bed of Central American Red Beans and Rice (page 291) and dressed with a generous amount of Colombian Hot Sauce (page 279).

Serves 4

1½ pounds beef tenderloin or flat iron steak, cut into 1-inch cubes
1 cup dark beer
⅓ cup extra-virgin olive oil
1 lemon, quartered
½ cup roughly chopped white onion
2 large garlic cloves, thinly sliced
2 bay leaves
1½ teaspoon ground cumin
½ teaspoon dried thyme
Salt and freshly ground black pepper, to taste
8 (12-inch) bamboo skewers, soaked overnight in cold water

In a nonreactive bowl, combine the beef, beer, oil, lemon, onions, garlic, bay leaves, cumin, and thyme. Cover and refrigerate for at least 8 hours or overnight. Remove the beef from the marinade and pat it dry with paper towels; thread the pieces through the skewers (see note). Discard the marinade and season the beef with salt and pepper.

Heat an outdoor grill (or indoor grill pan) until very hot; cook the kabobs, turning them once in a while, until done to your liking (about 8–10 minutes for medium). Serve at once. See note.

✳⟩ NOTE: If you don't have skewers, dry the beef well and heat 1 teaspoon of oil in a nonstick pan over medium-high heat; stir-fry the beef until it's done to your liking (about 4 minutes for medium).

Chuzos make great party fare because they can be put together hours ahead of time and grilled at the last minute. After I discard the marinade and skewer the meat (or chicken), I cover and refrigerate the kabobs (this can be done 2–3 hours ahead of a party). When I entertain big crowds, I'll triple or quadruple this recipe and grill the chuzos while my guests graze on appetizers. These go so well with a wide variety of the sauces in this book that I like to prepare an assortment of them. I present the multicolored sauces all lined up in little bowls so my guests can try them all.

Beef Kabob in Beer Marinade (Chuzo de Carne) with a Grilled White Corn Arepa (Arepa Blanca) (page 82) and Colombian Hot Sauce (Ají Colombiano) page 279)

Grilled Heart or Steak Kabobs (Anticuchos)

Late in the evenings on Lima's streets, vendors begin to set up makeshift grills and signal the sale of these spicy and savory beef kabobs called *anticuchos*. They are traditionally made with beef's heart and are served with a fun assortment of colorful sauces. Beef's heart is flavorful, succulent meat, but finding it may prove difficult because American grocery stores don't carry it, and in the Latin tiendas that do carry them, they sell out quickly. If you can, befriend your local farmers and ask them to save you one whenever they can. If, try as you may, you still can't find the prized heart, make anticuchos with steak. The acidic marinade in this recipe breaks down the flesh of the heart, rendering it tender. If you use steak instead, marinate it only for a fraction of the time or it will become too soft. Anticuchos are often served with salsa criolla and spicy mayonnaise. The ají panca, a reddish-brown chile from Peru, can be found already ground to a paste in most Latin grocery stores. If you can't find it, substitute equal amounts of Sriracha sauce. Serve these kabobs the way they do on the streets of Peru: with a generous amount of boiled yellow potatoes.

Serves 8

 2–2½ pounds beef heart or flat iron steak
 ½ cup red wine vinegar
 2 teaspoons ají panca paste (or Sriracha sauce)
 2 tablespoons minced garlic
 1 teaspoon annatto (achiote) powder
 1 teaspoon ground cumin
 1 teaspoon salt
 ½ teaspoon freshly ground black pepper
 ½ teaspoon oregano
 ¼ cup vegetable oil
 8 (12-inch) bamboo skewers, soaked overnight in cold water
 Peruvian Spicy Onion Salsa (page 275)
 Spicy Mayonnaise (page 276)
 2 pounds baby potatoes, boiled and halved

Clean the heart, if using, by slicing it in half and removing any visible nerves and fat (or trim the steak). Slice the meat on the bias into ¼-inch strips.

In a large nonreactive bowl, combine the vinegar, ají paste, garlic, achiote powder, cumin, salt, pepper, oregano, and vegetable oil. Add the meat, turning and tossing until well coated; marinate it for 8 hours (if using steak, marinate for 2 hours).

Thread the meat onto skewers and discard the marinade. Heat a grill (or indoor grill pan) until very hot. Grill the kabobs for 2–3 minutes per side (for medium-rare) or until the meat is done to your liking; top the meat with the Peruvian Spicy Onion Salsa and Spicy Mayonnaise; serve with the potatoes on the side. ❊

Chicken on a Stick (Chuzos de Pollo)

Here, tender chicken is marinated in a mixture of herbs and spices before it's threaded through skewers and grilled to perfection. You'll find chicken kabobs sold on the streets in Colombia, Panama, and Ecuador. Depending on where you are, chuzos will be accompanied by salted potatoes called *papas saladas* or bowls of white rice. My favorite way to eat them, though, is with deliciously plump corn arepas. Using uniformly cut pieces of chicken allows these kabobs to grill evenly. Chicken breasts can sometimes taste dry, so I marinate them for a few hours before assembling the skewers so that the chicken can absorb the goodness of the flavors and remain moist as it cooks.

Serves 4

> 1½ pounds chicken breasts, cut into 1-inch pieces
> ½ cup extra-virgin olive oil
> ⅓ cup fresh lime juice
> 2 large garlic cloves, minced
> 2 tablespoons minced flat-leaf or Italian parsley
>   (leaves and tender stems)
> 1 teaspoon dried thyme
> 1 teaspoon ground cumin
> 2 bay leaves
> Salt and freshly ground black pepper, to taste
> 8–10 (12-inch) bamboo skewers, soaked overnight in cold water
> Grilled White Corn Arepas (page 82)

In a medium nonreactive bowl, combine the chicken, oil, lime juice, garlic, parsley, thyme, cumin, and bay leaves. Cover and chill for at least 2 hours (but no longer than 4 or the citrus will break down the flesh of the chicken, turning it mushy). Remove the chicken from the marinade and thread the pieces through the skewers. Discard the marinade and season the chicken with salt and pepper.

Heat an outdoor grill (or indoor grill pan) until very hot; cook the kabobs, turning them once in a while, until the chicken is cooked through on all sides, about 10–12 minutes (or until the chicken is no longer pink). Place an arepa at one end of each skewer. Serve at once. ❊

EMPANADA EMPORIUM

Empanadas are a very popular street food because they're easy to tote. Every day millions of people buy little handheld pies on the streets of Latin America and then go on with their business. Many people buy them by the dozen to take home. *Empanar* means "to encase in bread," and there are all sorts of ingredients used to surround the many flavorful fillings of empanadas. Among the casings, you'll find puff pastry, butter pastry, bread dough, masa, precooked cornmeal, mashed tubers, and plantain dough.

Methods for cooking empanadas are also varied; some are baked, others are grilled, and yet others are fried. Although most empanadas are shaped like half-moons, some resemble miniature pies and others are triangular. Some are large enough to make an entire meal, but most are snack size. Some are paired with succulent sauces, usually housed in squirt bottles lined up at one end of an empanada kiosk. To me, there is nothing better than biting into a perfectly crisp empanada, exposing a savory filling, and squirting a bit of hot sauce on it.

What fascinates me most about empanadas is that each variation is a window into the culinary influences that have shaped local cuisines. In Buenos Aires, for example, you'll find Middle Eastern influences on the empanadas stuffed with beef, olives, and raisins, and Italian influences on those filled with ricotta and Swiss chard. You can also taste the Spanish influence on those stuffed with quince, and the French and Guaraní influences on those filled with corn and béchamel, called *empanadas de choclo*. And that's just a sample of what is served in a single Argentinean city. Imagine the scope of the offerings across Latin America. The possibilities are endless.

In fact, there are so many fillings for empanadas that they boggle the mind. Some of the most recognizable classics include chorizo, beef,

A woman makes empanadas on a street in Ilobasco, El Salvador.

beans, seafood, vegetables, or cheese. However, street vendors are always at the vanguard, creating new versions every day. In Peru, for instance, the latest rage is empanadas filled with *lomo saltado*—stir-fried beef, onions, tomatoes, and potatoes. And modern interpretations of empanadas in Argentina, are stuffed with blue cheese and walnuts. In Mexico, you'll find them filled with squash blossoms and *requesón* (a ricotta-like cheese), and in Central America you'll find empanadas encased in dough made entirely of yuca. Some empanadas have dry fillings, while others are so soupy that they drip down to your elbows when you bite into them. Some are savory and some are sweet, but since Latin Americans often combine elements of both flavors, you'll find those, too—for example, Guatemalans are known for their pork and raisin empanadas and the Ecuadorians are known for their onion and cheese empanadas that are first fried and then rolled in sugar; they're so light that they're called *empanadas de viento* (air). The collection of strictly sweet fillings for empanadas is also never-ending, and includes fruit pastes, nuts, chocolate, milk custards, caramelized milk, or chopped fruits. When it comes to empanadas, there is something for every taste.

The most difficult empanada dough to master is the one that must be cut while the pastry is still warm. With this in mind, I developed two different master recipes that will help you out. Each will walk you through every step so you can make beautiful empanadas. Some empanadas can be sealed with egg wash, while others require the pinch and fold method called *repulgue*, which seals them with ropelike edges (see page 218). The technique can be frustrating at first, but once you get the hang of it, you'll be folding and pinching in no time. My daughters and I love to spend afternoons shaping empanadas by the dozens and talking our hearts out. Of course, you can buy empanada disks in the frozen section of many stores (see "Sources for Ingredients") and crimp their edges tightly with the tines of a fork.

A long time ago, I created a recipe for a simple butter-based pastry for my novice students (see Speedy Pastry for Empanadas, page 216). I always use this one whenever I want to make empanadas on a whim and don't have a lot of time. Made with the aid of a food processor, it can be used with any of the empanada fillings in this chapter.

I selected a group of empanadas that covers the range of flavors that you'll find in Latin America: sweet, savory, fried, and baked. I also showcase many different kinds of casings and a great variety of succulent fillings. I hope you'll find the tips I share on how to freeze and store them for later helpful, so you can shape them one day and enjoy them for many more.

I teach cooking classes on many subjects, sometimes to dozens of students at a time, but by far my favorite classes are the more intimate ones where I can demonstrate new techniques and then invite my students to practice them with me. There is nothing I find more rewarding than to see them at their individual moments of epiphany and to watch them first master the proper way to make a recipe. Some of my most requested hands-on cooking classes are on the subject of empanadas.

Once when I had to give a presentation for a crowd, I had to shape hundreds of empanadas in a matter of two hours so that they could be served during class. None of my cooking assistants that day had ever made an empanada. Armed with the tips that I share with you here, we filled, shaped, and cooked over five hundred of them. People say hindsight is twenty-twenty. Looking back, I should have just hired them all and started a business. Luckily, you likely won't ever find yourself in that predicament, but with my tips and secrets you, too, will master the art of the empanada.

Master Dough for South American Empanadas

This dough is truly in a category of its own. When baked, it develops a tender breadlike texture that's thicker than pastry, but when it's fried, it's transformed into crispy and flaky dough. It's the traditional casing for empanadas in Argentina, Chile, Uruguay, and Bolivia. If you can make pie dough, you'll have no trouble making this. The one difference—and it is a big difference—is that while pastry for pie needs to remain cold, this one, made with hot water, must be kept warm until cut. This dough cannot be rerolled, so make sure to cut out as many rounds as possible from each rolled-out piece. Once it's been cut, the disks can cool to room temperature and even be refrigerated for later use (see note). I learned to make this dough from an Argentinean woman I met years ago, and although she never gave me a set recipe—her style was to add a pinch here and another there—I've taken her tips and secrets to heart. I share them with you here.

Makes 24 empanada disks

   4 cups all-purpose flour
   1½ teaspoons salt
   1½ teaspoons baking powder
   ⅓ cup vegetable shortening or lard
   3 tablespoons unsalted butter
   1 large egg, lightly beaten
   ¾ cup warm (110°–120°F) water

In the bowl of a food processor fitted with a metal blade, combine the flour, salt, and baking powder; pulse to combine. Add the shortening and butter; pulse until the mixture resembles coarse sand, about 1 minute. Add the egg. Gradually add the water through the feed tube, pulsing for 5-second intervals, until the dough holds together and begins to form a ball (you may not need all the water). Turn the dough out onto a clean surface and knead until smooth, about 1 minute. Cover it with a clean towel and let it rest for 15 minutes. The dough should be rolled out while still slightly warm to the touch.

Working with a third of the dough at a time (keeping the rest covered), roll it out to ⅛-inch thickness. Using a 4¼-inch cutter, cut out rounds; repeat with the remaining dough. You should end up with 24 rounds. Fill and seal using the repulgue method (page 218) and bake as directed in each recipe.

✳⟩ NOTE: If you're filling the dough within the hour, the disks can be kept at room temperature, covered. If you aren't, keep them covered and refrigerated (for up to 4 hours). This dough is best made fresh each time. Since, generally, the fillings should be chilled before using, it's best if you have the filling made before making the dough. I recommend starting the dough 1 hour before you intend to fill and bake the empanadas.

· ·

Pastry Dough for Salteñas

This pastry has a vibrant, orange hue and the texture of bread dough. Use it for the Bolivian empanadas, or *salteñas*, on page 221. The technique used to make this dough is similar to that used for the pastry for the South American Empanadas, but this one allows you to knead scraps back together after cutting it and reroll. It's painted orange with annatto and contains a touch of sugar. At first, the dough can be a bit tricky to handle. As you roll it, sprinkle a generous amount of flour to the working surface so that the moist dough—which tends to break when it's first rolled—can absorb it a little bit at a time. Each time you roll it, add more flour to your work surface. How much flour is required will depend on how much humidity is in the air and on how deft you are at handling the dough. Beginners may need a bit more flour than advanced bakers will. It may seem counterintuitive to make the dough so moist at first, but it's important to start it that way so that by the time the rolling and cutting are finished, you haven't made the dough too tough to work with by adding too much flour. Made this way, the dough will cut easily and the disks will stretch well without tearing when filled. This dough is best made fresh each time. Always chill the filling for the salteñas thoroughly before you make this dough.

Makes 24–26 (4½-inch) salteña disks

1 tablespoon annatto (achiote) paste
4–5½ cups all-purpose flour, divided
1½ teaspoons salt
1½ teaspoons baking powder
½ cup vegetable shortening or lard
¼ cup unsalted butter, diced
½ cup sugar
1 large egg, lightly beaten
5–6 tablespoons warm (110°–120°F) water

In a small bowl, combine the annatto with 2 tablespoons of boiling water. Stir, breaking up the annatto, until smooth; set aside to cool.

In a bowl of a food processor fitted with a metal blade, combine 4 cups of the flour (reserve the rest for when you roll the dough), salt, and baking powder; pulse to combine. Add the shortening and butter; pulse until the mixture resembles coarse sand, about 1 minute. Add the sugar and pulse until combined, about 20 seconds. Stir the egg into the annatto, add it through the feed tube, and begin adding the water, one tablespoon at a time, pulsing for 5-second intervals, until the dough holds together (you may not need all the water). Turn the dough onto a clean, generously floured surface and knead it until smooth, about 2 minutes, adding more of the reserved flour to the surface so the dough doesn't stick. Cover the dough with a clean towel and let it rest for 15 minutes.

Flour the work surface well and flour a rolling pin. Working with a third of the dough at a time (keeping the rest covered), roll it out to ⅛-inch thickness. If the edges break, use the side of your hand to press them back together. Using a 4¼-inch cutter, cut out rounds (knead the scraps together and let them rest, covered, for 10 minutes before rolling them out again). Keeping the rounds covered, repeat with the rest of the dough, cutting a total of 24–26 rounds. If you're filling the dough within the hour, the rounds can be kept at room temperature, covered. They can also be wrapped and refrigerated for up to 4 hours before using them. Fill the salteñas as directed. ✳

Pasta Frolla

This egg-based pastry is used in countries like Argentina, Uruguay, Bolivia, Chile and Brazil. I love it because it's easy to work with and rerolls easily. It's the base for my Brazilian Hearts of Palm Pies (page 224) and Miniature Quince Empanadas (page 235), but any filling works. I make this in bulk (always one recipe at a time) and freeze it to have it on hand when I need it.

Makes dough for 12 Brazilian empadas, 40 empanadinhas,
or 1 recipe for empanadas

> 3 cups all-purpose flour
> 2 tablespoons sugar
> 1 teaspoon salt
> 1 cup (2 sticks) unsalted butter, chilled and cut into ½-inch cubes
> 1 teaspoon white vinegar
> 2 large egg yolks
> 5–6 tablespoons iced water

In the bowl of a food processor fitted with a metal blade, combine the flour, sugar, and salt; pulse for 20 seconds. Add the butter and pulse until the mixture resembles coarse sand. Add the vinegar and pulse for 10 seconds. Add the egg yolks, and gradually add the iced water through the feed tube, pulsing for 5-second intervals between additions, until the dough begins to hold together, stopping once to scrape down the sides of the bowl. Press some of the dough between your fingers; if it holds together, it's ready. If it doesn't, add a bit more water and pulse for a few more seconds. Turn the dough out onto a clean surface and divide it in half. Press each half into a disk and wrap tightly in plastic wrap; chill for at least 30 minutes (or up to overnight).

❋〉 NOTE: The dough can also be frozen for up to 3 months. Thaw it in the refrigerator overnight. For easier rolling, let it sit at room temperature for 20–25 minutes.

Speedy Pastry for Empanadas

This is the easy pastry I reach for when I don't have time to make the others in this book. It works with savory and sweet flavors and bakes to flaky and golden perfection. Empanadas using this pastry can be shaped, frozen, and then baked to order. The one thing you can't do with this pastry, however, is fry it. You'll need to make a double batch for the empanada recipes here, or you'll have leftover filling. When my girls were little, I'd fill rounds of this pastry with ham and cheese so that when their friends came over, I could quickly bake a batch of mess-free, portable goodies. Try it with the picadillo on page 288 and the chorizo and potato filling for the sopes on page 65.

Makes 40 small or 30 medium empanada disks

> 3 cups all-purpose flour
> 1 teaspoon salt
> 1 cup (2 sticks) unsalted butter, chilled and cut into ½-inch cubes
> 2 teaspoons white vinegar
> 4–6 tablespoons iced water

In the bowl of a food processor fitted with a metal blade, combine the flour and salt; pulse for 20 seconds. Add the butter and pulse for 5-second intervals until the mixture resembles coarse sand. Add the vinegar and pulse for 10 seconds. Gradually add the iced water through the feed tube, pulsing for 5-second intervals between additions, until the dough begins to hold together. Press some of the dough between your fingers; if it holds together, it's ready. If it doesn't, add a bit more water and pulse for a few more seconds. Turn the dough out onto a clean surface and divide it in half. Press each half into a disk and wrap tightly in plastic wrap; chill for at least 30 minutes (or up to overnight) or freeze for up to 2 months. Thaw in the refrigerator overnight; roll, cut, fill, and bake. ✳

South American Beef Empanadas (Empanaditas de Pino)

You'll find many versions of pastry succulently filled with raisin and olive-laced beef in South America. This is the recipe I developed over a decade ago for my cooking classes, and to date, it's still one of the most requested by my cooking students. The resulting pastry pockets are savory and sweet at the same time. In Chile, the beef is traditionally minced by hand, but good-quality ground beef works just as well. Make the filling at least two hours before shaping the empanadas, and chill it thoroughly. Since the dough must be shaped while it's still warm, plan on making it one hour before filling the empanadas. Don't drain the ground beef after browning it; the fat in the recipe helps keep the filling moist as the empanadas bake. The baked empanadas can be frozen and stored for up to 4 months. Freeze them in a single layer until solid and then transfer to freezer-safe containers or zip-top bags. Reheat them in a 350°F oven until hot, about 15 minutes.

Makes 24 empanadas

    2 tablespoons extra-virgin olive oil
    1 cup minced yellow onion
    2 large garlic cloves, minced
    ½ pound ground chuck
    ½ teaspoon ground cumin
    ½ teaspoon oregano
    ¼ teaspoon cayenne pepper
    ¾ cup raisins
    1 cup finely chopped Manzanilla olives
    Salt and freshly ground black pepper, to taste
    2 hard-boiled eggs, finely chopped
    Master Dough for South American Empanadas (page 212)
    Egg wash made of 1 large egg beaten with 1 teaspoon olive oil

In a medium skillet, heat the oil over medium-high heat. Add the onion and cook until softened, about 2–3 minutes. Add the garlic and cook until fragrant, about 20 seconds. Add the beef, cumin, oregano, and cayenne; cook until the meat is evenly browned, about 3 minutes. Add the raisins and olives and season with salt and pepper. Stir well; reduce the heat to low and cook for 3–4 minutes. Remove from the heat and let it cool for 30 minutes; stir in the chopped egg, cover, and refrigerate for at least 2 hours (or up to overnight).

One hour before baking the empanadas, make the dough. Preheat the oven to 350°F. Line two baking sheets with parchment paper. Working with a third of the dough at a time (keeping the rest covered), roll it out to ⅛-inch thickness. Using a 4¼-inch cutter, cut out 8 disks; repeat with the remaining dough (you'll have 24 disks, total).

Place 2 tablespoons of the filling in the middle of each disk. Bring the edges of the pastry together to enclose the filling, forming a half-moon shape; pinch or press the cut edges together tightly to seal. Stretch out the edges to form a ½-inch rim; pinch and fold the rim to seal using the repulgue method to create a ropelike design (see note). Place the empanadas on the prepared pans; brush the tops with the egg wash. Bake until golden, about 30–35 minutes. Serve hot or at room temperature.

NOTE: The repulgue method: Deft hands can shape the edges of the dough to resemble ropes by folding and pinching the seams over each other. This is called the *repulgue* method because the thumb, or *pulgar*, leads the action. Depending on what dough you use, the instructions will call for you to either press the dough into a rim, or stretch it into a rim. Cradle the empanada in one hand. Starting at one corner of the empanada, use your thumb and index finger to fold a tiny triangle of dough on the sealed edge. Fold it over itself and pinch it tightly. Fold down a small piece of the edge again, overlapping slightly on the first fold and roll and pinch it tightly. Repeat this rolling and pinching of small pieces all along the edge, and soon you'll see a ropelike design taking shape. The smaller the sections you pinch, the more detailed the rope design will be. If your edges look more like crimped pie dough than ropes, you're leaving too much space between sections; the pinches should overlap slightly.

South American Beef Empanadas
(Empanaditas de Pino)

Bolivian Chicken Empanadas
(Salteñas de Pollo Bolivianas)

Bolivian Chicken Empanadas (Salteñas de Pollo Bolivianas)

In Bolivia, there's a festival that celebrates these empanadas, called *Feria de las Salteñas*, where vendors compete for the coveted title of best salteña baker. The sweet dough is tinted with annatto—which Bolivians call *urucú*—until it's a very bright orange, and the filling is made with aromatic chicken stew. Salteñas have flat bottoms; they're plump and hold a lot of filling. A great salteña is judged not only by the way it tastes but also by the color of its crimped rims, which should develop a dark-brown, almost black hue as it bakes. The filling must always remain moist. Some cooks fill them with beef and chiles, while others add olives and hard-boiled eggs, but a true salteña always includes minced potatoes. At first, it may be hard to use up all of the filling in this recipe—the dough truly stretches out enough to use it all—but with practice, you'll succeed. Chilling these salteñas before baking them will help them keep their shape. A salteña is supposed to be very large—a meal in and of itself—but these are about half the size and easier to eat. Bolivians eat them with hot sauce and a squirt of lime.

Makes 24–26 salteñas

> 2 tablespoons vegetable oil
> 1 cup minced red bell pepper
> 1 cup minced white onion
> 1 tablespoon annatto (achiote) paste
> 2–2½ cups chicken broth
> 1¾ cups chopped Yukon Gold potatoes (the pieces should be
> the size of peas)
> 2 cups cooked and shredded chicken
> 1 cup green peas
> 1 bay leaf
> 1 teaspoon thyme
> 1½ teaspoons ground cumin
> ½ cup minced flat-leaf or Italian parsley (leaves and tender stems)
> Salt and freshly ground black pepper, to taste
> Pastry Dough for Salteñas (page 213), cut into 24–26
> (4½-inch) disks
> Egg wash made of 1 large egg beaten with 1 tablespoon water

Heat the oil in a large skillet over medium-high heat. Add the bell pepper and onion and cook until softened, about 3–4 minutes; add the annatto and 2 cups of the broth, breaking up the annatto until dissolved. Add the potatoes, chicken, peas, bay leaf, thyme, cumin, and parsley; bring the liquid to a boil and cook, uncovered, until the potatoes are tender and most of the liquid has evaporated, about 10 minutes. (It should still be a bit moist. If the potatoes haven't cooked through, add the remaining broth and cook until they are.) Season with salt and pepper; cool, cover, and chill until ready to use (chilling will solidify moist filling, making it easier to fill the empanadas; the filling will become moist again as it bakes inside the pastry).

Place 1–1½ heaping tablespoons of the filling in the middle of the prepared pastry disks; bring the edges of the pastry together to enclose the filling (it will help to press the filling down with your forefinger to compact it). Form a half moon and stand the salteña on its bottom, flattening it so it can stand without toppling. Pinch the edges tightly, and press to form a small rim, about ¼-inch wide. Then, with your fingers, pinch and fold the rim decoratively, making pleats (as you would a dumpling or a piecrust). Stand the salteñas on the prepared pans and chill them for at least 20 minutes (up to 2 hours).

Preheat the oven to 350°F. Brush the salteñas with the egg wash. Bake until golden, about 30–35 minutes. Serve hot or at room temperature.

❊⟩ NOTE: The baked salteñas can be stored frozen for up to 4 months. Freeze them in a single layer until solid and then transfer to freezer-safe containers or zip-top bags. Reheat them in a 350°F oven until hot, about 15 minutes. Leftover filling can be heated and enjoyed as is.

Tuna Empanadas (Empanadas de Atún)

There are few things I love to do more than to curl up on a sofa with a blanket, a great book, and a delicious snack. Sometimes the book is so good that I don't want to put it down. On these occasions, a handheld empanada is the perfect snack because I can eat with one hand and hold my book with the other. In this version, breadlike pastry surrounds a filling made with tuna, sofrito, and potatoes in my rendition of an Argentinean fish hand pie. South Americans often mix fish and potatoes, and the combination is actually quite exquisite. Sofrito is a Latin American flavor base made with cooked onions, bell peppers, and oil. Some countries add other ingredients to sofrito, such as tomatoes, garlic, or annatto. In Argentina, it's not unusual to find sofrito studded with herbs and spices. Here, oregano adds a very Mediterranean flair to these empanadas. Make a batch of these and freeze them so that the next time you're reading a book you just can't put down, you'll be prepared! Make the dough one hour before filling the empanadas.

Makes 24–26 empanadas

> 2 tablespoons vegetable oil
> ½ cup minced white onion
> ½ cup minced red bell pepper
> 1 cup seeded and minced tomatoes
> 2 cups peeled and chopped Yukon Gold potatoes
>   (the pieces should be the size of peas)
> 1 teaspoon oregano
> 1 (12-ounce) can tuna (packed in oil or water), drained
> ½ cup minced flat-leaf or Italian parsley (leaves and tender stems)
> Salt and freshly ground black pepper, to taste
> 2 hard-boiled eggs, minced and chilled until ready to use
> Master Dough for South American Empanadas (page 212)
> Egg wash made with one large egg and one tablespoon of water

Heat the oil in a medium skillet over medium-high heat. Add the onions, peppers, and tomatoes and cook until softened, about 2–3 minutes. Add the potatoes, oregano, and 1 cup of water and bring to a boil. Cook, stirring, until the potatoes are tender and most of the liquid has evaporated, about 8–10 minutes (if the potatoes are not yet fork-tender at this point, add ½ cup more water and continue to cook until they are). Remove from heat. Stir in the tuna and parsley; season with salt and pepper. Cool slightly; cover and chill for at least 30 minutes (up to overnight).

Preheat the oven to 350°F and line two baking sheets with parchment paper. Add the hard-boiled eggs to the filling. Place 2 tablespoons of the filling in the center of the prepared disks. Bring the edges of the pastry together, enclosing the filling to form a half-moon shape; pinch the edges tightly to seal. Stretch out the edges to form a ½-inch rim; pinch and fold the rim to seal (see note on the repulgue method on page 218). Place the empanadas on the prepared pans; brush the tops with egg wash. Bake until golden, about 30–35 minutes; serve hot or at room temperature.

*} NOTE: The baked empanadas can be frozen for up to 4 months. Freeze them in a single layer on baking sheets until solid and transfer to freezer bins or zip-top bags. To reheat, bake at 350°F for 15–20 minutes or until hot.

Hearts of Palm Pies (Empadas de Palmito)

Miniature handheld pies like these are called *empadas* in Brazil. Smaller versions are known as *empanadinhas*. The vegetarian filling is a bit tangy, very creamy, and absolutely addictive. Unlike most of the empanadas found in the rest of Latin America, which are folded into half-moons, these are round or oval and look like miniature pies. Sometimes they're intricately decorated with designs made with pastry remnants. Brazilians use special molds to make these small pies, but I use my nonstick muffin tins instead (they're a bit tricky to unmold, but they work). For appetizer-sized empanadinhas, you can use mini-muffin tins (see note), but I like to use the standard-size ones and serve these at luncheons with crispy green salad that's been scantily dressed with lemon juice and olive oil.

Makes 16 empadas or 40 empanadinhas

Assorted Hearts of Palm Pies
(Empadas de Palmito)

6 tablespoons unsalted butter
1 cup minced white onion
⅔ cup all-purpose flour
1¾ cups whole milk
2 teaspoons salt
½ teaspoon freshly ground nutmeg
¼ teaspoon freshly ground black pepper
1 (14-ounce can) hearts of palm, drained and finely chopped
¾ cup peeled, seeded, and finely chopped plum tomatoes
⅔ cup minced black olives
Pasta Frolla (page 215)
Egg wash made of 1 large egg beaten with 2 teaspoons heavy cream

Melt the butter in a medium saucepan over medium-low heat; add the onions and cook until soft, about 3–4 minutes, stirring often so they don't brown. Add the flour and whisk well; cook for 1–2 minutes, being careful not to let it take any color. Remove the pan from the heat and add all the milk, whisking well. Return the pan to the heat and continue cooking, stirring constantly, for 2 minutes, or until it's the consistency of mashed potatoes. Remove the pan from the heat and stir in the salt, nutmeg, and pepper. Transfer the mixture to a large bowl and stir in the hearts of palm, tomatoes, and olives. Cover and chill for at least 1 hour (or up to overnight).

Remove the pastry dough from the refrigerator and let it sit at room temperature for 15–20 minutes so that it's easy to roll. Roll it out until it is about ⅛ inch thick (like you would a piecrust); cut out 16 (4½-inch) circles, and 16 (3-inch) circles, kneading the scraps together and rerolling the dough as needed.

Press the large circles into a standard-sized muffin tin, leaving a bit of overhang. Divide the filling among the tins (not quite ⅓ cup each). Top the filling with the small pastry circles and pinch the edges of the pastry together to seal the crust. (If desired, reroll the dough scraps and cut them into decorative shapes—like leaves—and attach them to the tops of the pies using the prepared egg wash.) Brush the tops of the pies with egg wash and chill them for 30 minutes.

Preheat the oven to 350°F. Bake the empadas for 25–30 minutes or until the tops are golden. Cool in the tins for 5 minutes; turn onto cooling racks and serve warm.

Empanada Emporium

After baking, the empadas can be frozen for up to 4 months. Freeze them in a single layer on baking sheets until solid and transfer them to freezer bins or zip-top bags. Bake them at 400°F for 10-20 minutes (depending on their size) or until hot.

❋} NOTE: For mini-muffin tins, you'll have a bit of leftover filling; use 2-inch and 2½-inch cutters and 1 heaping teaspoon of the filling. Bake for 22–25 minutes.

Fried Tomato, Basil, and Mozzarella Empanadas (Empanadas Caprese)

In Argentina, empanadas are sometimes baked and sometimes fried. Flaky pastry pockets like these filled with melted goodness can be purchased in brown paper bags, straight out of the fryer. The filling is a classic, and it's not surprising to find plenty of Italian-inspired foods on the streets of Argentina. During the twentieth century, a large number of Italian immigrants descended upon this South American country, changing its culinary landscape for good. These empanadas are a little bit like calzones—but with a twist. Here, the same Master Dough for South American Empanadas that bakes so beautifully with a breadlike texture turns flaky and puffy when fried. You won't believe it's the same dough! Blanching and shocking the basil before it's added to the filling helps it stay vibrantly green. Learn how to pinch and roll the edges of these empanadas (see note on the repulgue method on page 218) to ensure that they are properly sealed or they'll burst while they fry and the filling will escape. To cut the acidity of the tomatoes, I love to serve these with a glass of a well-bodied Argentinean red wine.

Makes 24 empanadas

⅓ cup packed basil leaves
2¼ cups shredded mozzarella cheese
1½ cups packed seeded and minced plum tomatoes
1 tablespoon extra-virgin olive oil
¼ teaspoon freshly ground black pepper
Master Dough for South American Empanadas (page 212),
    cut into 24 (4¼-inch) disks
Vegetable oil for frying
Salt (optional)

Fill a small bowl with iced water; set aside. In a small saucepan, bring 2 cups of water to a rolling boil. Drop the basil into the water and boil for 20 seconds. Remove promptly and drop it into the iced water. Drain the basil and pat it dry with paper towels; chop finely.

In a medium bowl, stir together the basil, cheese, tomatoes, olive oil, and pepper; set aside.

Line a large baking sheet with parchment paper. Place 1 generous tablespoon of the filling in the middle of the prepared empanada disks. Bring the edges of the pastry together, enclosing the filling to form a half-moon shape; pinch the edges tightly to seal. Stretch out the edges to form a ½-inch rim; pinch and fold the rim to seal using the repulgue method to create a ropelike design (see note on the repulgue method on page 218). Set them on the prepared sheet.

Fit a large baking pan with a metal cooling rack; set aside. In a large skillet with high sides heat 2–3 inches of oil to 360°F (or use a deep fryer according to the manufacturer's directions); working in small batches, carefully slide the empanadas into the oil. Fry them until golden, about 1½–2 minutes, turning them over halfway through. Using a slotted spoon, transfer them to the prepared rack to drain.

While they're still warm, sprinkle lightly with salt (if using). Let them cool for 2 minutes and serve.

❊⟩ NOTE: You can keep the fried empanadas warm in a 250°F oven for up to 30 minutes before serving. These can be frozen after frying for up to 2 months. To reheat bake at 400°F until warm, about 8 minutes. You can also freeze them raw for up to 2 months and fry them right from the freezer (no need to thaw) until golden and hot, about 2–2½ minutes or until the filling is hot.

Beef and Potato Empanadas (Empanadas de Parroquia)

These Colombian meat turnovers, often sold on the streets near *parro-quias* (church parishes) after Sunday Mass, are flavored with *guiso*, a mixture of onions, tomatoes, and garlic. These empanadas are made with precooked cornmeal, which is also used to make arepas. Here, it's treated more like pastry dough: rolled thinly, filled, and fried. My friend Luisa Fernanda Rios, a fabulous private chef who now lives in Vancouver, recalls eating empanadas made by her grandmother that were similar to these. She taught me that in Colombian cuisine, green onions reign supreme over all others; thus, they're prominently displayed in this recipe. Luisa suggests serving these with ají (see my recipe for Colombian Hot Sauce on page 279), or with squirts of lime.

Makes 20 empanadas

  1 pound beef brisket
  2 tablespoons vegetable oil
  ½ cup minced white onion
  ½ cup minced plum tomatoes
  ½ cup minced green bell pepper
  2 large garlic cloves, minced
  1 teaspoon ground cumin
  ½ teaspoon annatto (achiote) powder
  2 cups peeled and chopped Yukon Gold potatoes
     (the pieces should be the size of peas)
  3 teaspoons salt, divided
  ⅓ cup very thinly sliced green onions (light and dark parts)
  3 cups precooked yellow cornmeal (harina pan or masarepa)
  3 cups of hot tap water (not boiling)

Place the brisket in a pot of salted water set over medium-high heat and bring it to a boil. (Remove any foam that rises to the surface and discard.) Cover, reduce the heat, and simmer for 1–1½ hours or until it shreds easily. Cool in the broth for 30 minutes. Remove the brisket and reserve 1¼ cups of broth (save the rest for soups). Shred the beef and then chop it finely.

In a medium skillet, heat the oil over medium-high heat. Add the white onions, tomatoes, bell peppers, garlic, cumin, and annatto and cook until the onions have begun to soften, about 2–3 minutes. Add the potatoes, 2 teaspoons of the salt, and the reserved broth and cook, stirring often, until the potatoes are tender and the liquid has evaporated, about 8–10 minutes. Transfer to a bowl and combine with the beef; add the green onions and stir. Chill for at least 15 minutes (or up to overnight).

In a large bowl, whisk together the cornmeal and the remaining salt. Slowly add the water, kneading the mixture with your hands until it comes together into a ball. Turn it onto a clean surface and knead until smooth, about 1 minute. Cover and let it rest for 5 minutes.

Line a tortilla press with a plastic sandwich bag that has been cut down the sides and opened flat. Divide the dough into 20 pieces (about ¼ cup each); roll each into a ball, keeping the completed balls covered as you work. Working with one ball at a time, place the dough in the center of the press and flatten it into a 5-inch disk, about ⅛ inch thick. Place 2 heaping tablespoons of the filling in the middle of the disk. Using the plastic to aid you, fold the disk in half over the filling and seal the edges well. Repeat with the rest of the dough, keeping the empanadas covered as you go. Fry them immediately.

Fit a large baking pan with a metal cooling rack; set aside. In a large Dutch oven heat 2–3 inches of oil to 360°F (or use a deep fryer according to the manufacturer's directions); working in batches, carefully slide the empanadas in the oil. Fry them until golden, about 3–4 minutes, turning them over halfway through. Using a slotted spoon, transfer them to the prepared rack to drain. Keep them warm in a 250°F oven for up to 1 hour before serving.

❋⟩ NOTE: These can be frozen for up to 3 months. Freeze them in a single layer on baking sheets until solid and transfer to freezer bins or zip-top bags. Reheat at 350°F for 12–15 minutes or until hot.

Shrimp and Masa Empanadas (Empanadas de Camarón)

Inside these crispy turnovers, which are similar to those found in the Yucatán Peninsula, is a spicy mélange of shrimp and sofrito. These empanadas are fried, so the resulting crust is both crunchy and meaty. When working with masa, the amount of water required will vary slightly depending on the brand of masa harina. If the edges of the shaped masa crack, for example, you'll need to add a bit more water to the masa, and always keep it covered as you work so it doesn't dry out. Serve these empanadas with the Avocado Sauce on page 268 or the Corn and Avocado Salsa on page 277 and dress them with refreshing garnishes, a drizzle of tangy crema, and a squeeze of lime. For extra color, crunch, and tanginess, top them with the pickled onions on page 281.

Makes 12 empanadas

1 tablespoon vegetable oil
3 large garlic cloves, minced
1 (14.5-ounce) can crushed fire-roasted tomatoes
1 medium chipotle chile in adobo, minced (about 2 teaspoons)
1 teaspoon adobo sauce (from the canned chipotles)
1 tablespoon annatto (achiote) paste
1 pound cooked and minced shrimp (about 2 cups)
Salt and freshly ground black pepper, to taste
3 cups masa harina
3–3½ cups warm water (or more, as needed)
Vegetable oil for frying
Shredded lettuce (optional)
Chopped tomatoes (optional)
Mexican crema or crème fraîche (optional)
Lime wedges (optional)

In a medium skillet over medium-high heat, cook the garlic until fragrant, about 10–20 seconds; add the tomatoes, chipotle, adobo sauce, and annatto. Stir well, breaking up the annatto, until smooth (add a couple of tablespoons of water if the annatto is too hard). Reduce the heat to low and cook the sauce, stirring, until the it thickens to a paste, about 10–15 minutes; season with salt and pepper. Remove from the heat and cool. Stir the shrimp into the sauce and chill for 1 hour (up to 8 hours; chilling makes the filling easier to work with).

Place the masa harina in a large bowl; gradually add 3 cups of the warm water to form dough with the consistency of playdough; cover and let it rest for 10 minutes. To determine whether the dough is the proper consistency, shape ⅓ cup of it into a ball and press it flat; if the edges crack, return it to the remaining masa, knead in a bit more water (a few tablespoons at a time) until you can form tortillas that do not crack.

Line a baking sheet with parchment paper and line a tortilla press with a zip-top freezer bag cut open along the sides (so it opens like a book). Divide the masa into 12 equal portions (about ⅓ cup each); roll each into a ball, keeping them covered with a damp kitchen towel as you work. Line a tortilla press with a zip-top freezer bag cut open along the sides (so it opens like a book).

Working with one empanada at a time, place a ball of masa in the middle of the tortilla press and flatten it into a 5½-inch disk about ⅛ inch thick. Place 2 heaping tablespoons of the filling in the middle of the tortilla, leaving a small rim; use the bag to fold the masa over the filling, forming a half moon; press the edges together with your fingers to seal. Transfer the empanada to the prepared sheet. Repeat with the rest of the dough, keeping the empanadas covered as you go. The empanadas can be shaped and filled up to 1 hour before frying; keep them covered and refrigerated until ready to fry.

Fit a large baking pan with a metal cooling rack; set aside. In a large skillet with high sides, heat 1–2 inches of oil to 360°F (or use a deep fryer according to the manufacturer's directions). Working in batches, carefully slide the empanadas in the oil. Fry them until golden, about 4–6 minutes, turning them over halfway through. (The oil may get hotter as you fry; lower the temperature if they're browning too quickly; cool the oil slightly before frying any more.) Using a slotted spoon, transfer them to the prepared rack to drain.

Serve immediately or keep them warm on the rack in a 250°F oven for up to 1 hour before serving. To serve, place the empanadas on a platter and garnish with lettuce, tomatoes, and crema (if using); offer limes on the side.

※} NOTE: These can be frozen after frying for up to 2 months. Freeze them on a baking sheet in a single layer until solid and then transfer them to containers. Bake them directly from the freezer in a 400°F oven for 10–15 minutes or until hot.

Spinach Turnovers (Empanadas de Espinaca)

Flaky pastry hides a vegetarian treasure of creamy spinach and béchamel in these traditional Cuban street empanadas. Empanadas are often sold from push-carts or from carts attached to bicycles. The beautifully crafted morsels on display in glass cases entice passersby to stop and taste. On my last visit to Miami for a book fair, I couldn't resist purchasing some of the flaky pastries offered by vendors on the street corner. Store-bought puff pastry and frozen spinach make these a cinch to make. When my girls were little, they'd take these to school in their lunch boxes. Now, I pair them with my favorite white wine and enjoy them as an elegant first course.

Makes 18 empanadas

6 tablespoons unsalted butter
½ cup minced yellow onion
⅔ cup all-purpose flour
1½ cup whole milk, warm
½ teaspoon salt, or to taste
¼ teaspoon freshly grated nutmeg
1 pound frozen spinach, thawed and squeezed dry
1 cup shredded queso blanco (or mozzarella cheese)
2 ready-to-bake puff pastry sheets (1.1-pound package),
   thawed according to package directions
Egg wash made of 1 large egg beaten with 1 tablespoon water

In a medium, heavy-bottomed saucepan, melt the butter over medium heat; add the onions and cook for 1–2 minutes or until soft but not browned. Reduce the heat to low; add the flour and whisk well, cooking for 1–2 minutes, being careful not to let it turn golden or brown. Remove from the heat; add the milk, whisking vigorously, until the mixture is smooth. Return to the heat and continue cooking, stirring constantly, until the sauce is the consistency of soft mashed potatoes, about 3 minutes, being careful not to let it burn. Remove from the heat. Stir in the salt, nutmeg, spinach, and cheese; set aside to cool for 10 minutes.

Preheat the oven to 400°F. Line two baking sheets with parchment paper. On a clean, lightly floured surface, roll out one puff pastry sheet to form a 12-inch square; using a sharp knife or pastry wheel, cut it into 9 (4×4-inch) squares.

Place about a ¼ cup of the spinach mixture on the center of each square; brush the edges of the pastry with egg wash and fold the pastry over the filling to form a triangle. Use the tines of a fork to crimp the edges decoratively to seal. Place the pastry triangles on the prepared baking sheets. Repeat with the second puff pastry sheet.

Brush the tops of the empanadas with the egg wash and bake until golden, about 15–20 minutes. Serve warm or at room temperature.

NOTE: The unbaked empanadas can be frozen for up to 2 months. Freeze them in a single layer until solid and then transfer them to containers. Don't thaw before baking; simply add about 5–8 more minutes to the baking time or bake until they're golden.

Guava and Cream Cheese Empanadas (Empanadas de Queso y Guayaba)

In this classic Cuban turnover, nectarous guava paste meets tangy cream cheese and flaky puff pastry. Guava paste has a consistency similar to softened gumdrops—a bit pasty, very thick, and truly luscious when it melts. In a pinch, use the more readily available guava jelly. Make these pastries ahead of time and freeze them before you bake them; there is no need to thaw them. If in the middle of the afternoon you're secretly craving one (or two or three!) of these decadent empanadas, simply throw them in a toaster oven, bake, and eat them to your heart's content. It will be our little secret.

Makes 18 empanadas

- 2 ready-to-bake puff pastry sheets (1.1-pound package), thawed according to package directions
- 10–12 ounces guava paste, sliced into 2-inch-long by ¼-inch-thick rectangles (see note)
- 10 ounces cream cheese, sliced into 2-inch-long by ¼-inch-thick rectangles
- Egg wash made of 1 large egg beaten with 1 tablespoon water

Line two baking sheets with parchment paper. Preheat the oven to 400°F. On a clean, lightly floured surface, roll out one puff pastry sheet to form a 12-inch square; using a sharp knife or pastry wheel, cut it into 9 (4×4-inch) squares.

Brush a pastry square with egg wash. Place one piece of the cream cheese on top of a guava paste rectangle and place the stack on the diagonal in the center of the pastry square. Bring the two opposite corners of the pastry together to form a triangle; seal the edges with your fingers and then crimp the edges decoratively using the tines of a fork. Repeat with the rest of the ingredients.

Place the filled empanadas on the prepared sheets and brush the tops with egg wash. Bake until golden, about 15–20 minutes. Serve them warm or at room temperature. (To freeze the unbaked empanadas, see note on page 233.)

❉⟩ NOTE: If you're using guava jelly, you'll need 1 tablespoon for each empanada.

Miniature Quince Empanadas
(Empanaditas de Membrillo)

These delicate quince hand pies are found in southern Argentina, sometimes called *pasteles* or *masitas*. Quince preserves are known as *dulce de
membrillo*, and they taste a bit like lemon-scented apples—a bit tangy
and plenty sweet. These are a smaller version of the kinds of empanadas you'll find sold in parks and cafes with outdoor seating. Find quince
paste in gourmet markets and in some grocery stores. At home, I serve
these as part of a cheese course, with a glass of ice wine. Whether you're
enjoying them on a park bench while sipping coffee from a take-out cup
or during a candle-lit dinner while savoring champagne from a crystal
flute, you'll find that these empanaditas are always delightful and always
sweet.

Makes 4–4 ½ dozen empanadas

> Pasta Frolla (page 215)
> 10 ounces quince paste
> Egg wash made of 1 large egg beaten with 2 teaspoons heavy cream

Preheat the oven to 350°F. Line two baking sheets with parchment paper;
set aside. On a floured surface, roll the pastry to ⅛-inch thickness (as you
would a piecrust). Using a 2½-inch round cutter, cut out 4–4½ dozen
disks. Place one teaspoon of quince paste in the middle of each disk. Fold
the pastry over the filling to form a half moon. Seal the edges decoratively
with a fork. Set the finished empanadas in the prepared sheets, brush the
tops with the egg wash and bake until golden, about 12–15 minutes.

NOTE: These can be frozen unbaked for up to 3 months. Freeze them in a
single layer until solid and then transfer to containers. Bake them directly
from the freezer (no need to thaw them) until golden, about 15–20 minutes.

Chocolate and Peanut Empanadas

These sweet handheld pies filled with chocolate paste are my answer to chocolate cravings. The pastry yields softly to the tooth, and silky chocolate and peanut sauce takes them over the edge. Mine are smaller than those sold on the streets, but you can make them as large as you wish.

Makes 30 empanadas

FOR THE DOUGH
2 cups all-purpose flour
2 tablespoons cocoa powder
¼ teaspoon salt
8 ounces cream cheese, chilled and cubed
½ cup (1 stick) unsalted butter, chilled and cubed
1 teaspoon apple cider vinegar

FOR THE FILLING
1 (14-ounce) can sweetened condensed milk
½ cup cocoa powder
¼ cup half and half
3 ounces chopped milk chocolate
3 ounces chopped semisweet chocolate
1½ cups roasted peanuts
Egg wash made of 1 large egg beaten with 1 tablespoon water
⅓ cup turbinado or raw sugar

FOR THE SAUCE
Reserved filling
¾ cup half and half
2 ounces chopped milk chocolate

In the bowl of a food processor fitted with a metal blade, combine the flour, cocoa powder, and salt; pulse 2–3 times to combine. Add the cream cheese, butter, and vinegar; pulse on and off until it forms a wet, sticky dough. Divide the dough in half and press each half into a disk. Wrap each in plastic and chill for at least 1 hour (up to overnight).

Meanwhile, make the filling. In a medium pot, stir together the condensed milk, cocoa, and half and half over medium heat. Bring to a boil; remove from heat. In a double boiler (a bowl over barely simmering water), melt 3 ounces of the milk chocolate and all of the semisweet chocolate, stirring, until smooth; set aside for 5 minutes.

In a food processor fitted with a metal blade, pulse the peanuts until they are finely ground (about 30 seconds). Add the melted chocolate and process until smooth, scraping down the sides of the work bowl occasionally. Add the condensed milk mixture and pulse until combined. Reserve 1 cup of the filling for the sauce; set aside.

Preheat the oven to 400°F. Line 2 large baking sheets with parchment paper. Dust a clean surface with flour; roll out the pastry to ⅛ inch thick (as you would a piecrust). Using a 3-inch round cookie cutter, cut out rounds; continue rolling (rerolling the scraps when necessary) to make 30 rounds. Working with a few pastry rounds at a time, moisten the edges with egg wash; place 1 scant tablespoon of filling in the center of each round; press the filling down into the center and fold the pastry over to form half-moon shapes. Seal the edges with your fingers, and set the empanadas on the prepared baking sheets. Brush the tops with egg wash and sprinkle with sugar. Bake for 15–20 minutes or until slightly golden (some will burst slightly). Remove them from the oven and transfer to wire racks to cool slightly.

For the sauce, in a medium pot, combine the reserved cup of filling with the half and half over medium-low heat, stirring until smooth. Remove from the heat; add the chocolate and stir until the chocolate has melted.

Serve the empanadas drizzled with a bit of sauce.

❊⟩ NOTE: These are best eaten fresh but will keep in an airtight container up to 24 hours. They may be frozen raw (without egg wash and sugar) or after baking. Freeze in a single layer until solid and then transfer to zip-top bags. Freeze for up to 2 months. There is no need to thaw the raw empanadas before baking. Brush with egg wash and sprinkle with sugar and bake as directed. Thaw the baked empanadas at room temperature and reheat until warm in a 300°F oven (about 4 minutes).

Cornmeal and Milk Pudding Empanadas (Empanadas de Manjar Blanco)

These sweet and tender empanadas are sold in Guatemalan streets only during the Lenten season, which, when I was a child, meant I had to wait a very long year before I could eat them again. Annatto paints them a bright orange color and the creamy custard filling, called *manjar blanco*, is good all on its own. It took me years to develop this recipe because *harina de salpor*, the corn flour used to make them, is not easily found outside Guatemala. I made it work with white cornmeal and some tweaking. These are only good for a day or two after they're made because the moist custard will make them soggy. However, they freeze well; thaw them at room temperature before eating. Now I can enjoy them all year round, and so can you.

Makes 10 empanadas

> 2 teaspoons annatto (achiote) paste
> 1¾ cups finely ground white cornmeal
> 1 cup all-purpose flour
> 1½ teaspoons baking powder
> Pinch salt
> ⅓ cup vegetable shortening
> 1⅓ cups sugar, divided
> 3 large egg yolks, divided
> 5–6 tablespoons iced water
> 1½ cups milk
> 1 stick Mexican cinnamon (canela)
> ¼ cup cornstarch

In a small bowl, combine the annatto with 1 tablespoon of boiling water; stir to form a smooth paste and set aside to cool.

In a large bowl, sift together the cornmeal, flour, baking powder, and salt. Cut the shortening into the flour mixture with a pastry cutter until the mixture resembles small peas. Stir in 1 cup of the sugar; set aside.

Stir 2 of the egg yolks into the cooled annatto mixture and stir this into the flour mixture with a fork (it will get lumpy). Use your hands to knead in 5 tablespoons of the water until the dough comes together into a ball. If it's too dry, add one more tablespoon of water, kneading well, until it holds together; cover and let it sit for 45 minutes (the dough will be very moist).

In a medium pot, heat the milk and cinnamon stick over medium heat until it comes to a slow simmer (don't let it boil); remove from the heat and cool for 5 minutes. Discard the cinnamon stick; stir in the remaining sugar.

In a small bowl, combine ¼ cup of cold water with the cornstarch and the remaining egg yolk; stir this into the warm milk mixture and return to the stove. Cook and stir over medium-low heat until the custard thickens and comes to a boil, about 4 minutes, being very careful not to burn it. As soon as it reaches a boil, remove it from the heat and cool, stirring often, for 15 minutes.

Preheat the oven to 350°F. Line two baking sheets with parchment paper. Divide the dough into 10 equal portions (about ¼ cup each) and roll each into a ball, keeping them covered with a damp kitchen towel as you work. Line a tortilla press with a plastic bag that has been cut along two sides (so it opens like a book). Make one empanada at a time. Place a dough ball in the middle of the bag and press to flatten into a 5-inch round about ⅛ inch thick. Place 1 heaping tablespoon of custard in the middle of the round, leaving a small rim; use the bag to fold the dough over the filling, forming a half-moon shape; seal the edges by pressing them together. Place empanadas on the prepared sheet; bake for 20–22 minutes or until edges are golden. Cool on racks.

NOTE: These can be kept frozen for up to 2 months. Freeze them in a single layer until solid and then transfer them to freezer containers or zip-top bags. Thaw to room temperature. They're not suitable for reheating.

TAMALE TRAIN

I like to say that Latin America's backbone is made of corn and cassava and at its heart is a deep respect for the soil that gave the world chocolate, chiles, potatoes, squash, nuts, tomatoes, and so many other precious ingredients. If you really want to taste the spirit of the Americas, you must first discover the vast world of tamales. All of the ingredients native to the New World play a key role in crafting these dumplings, which date back to the pre-Columbian era. Many people think that all Latin Americans eat tortillas, but it's really tamales that truly connect us, from Mexico all the way to Patagonia. So jump on the tamale train and bring your appetite for an adventure filled with facts, fun, and flavor.

When the Spanish conquerors arrived in the New World, they found that the indigenous peoples had already developed hundreds of varieties of corn, known in Mesoamerica as *maíz* and in South America as *choclo*. Bernal Diaz del Castillo, who was among those traveling with Hernán Cortés, described tamales as uncooked corn dough, plastered on husks, spread with fillings and then folded like envelopes. In essence, the same description still applies to the myriad tamales prepared today all over Latin America—except that not all of them are made with corn; some are made with plantains or root vegetables like cassava, malanga, potato, or ñame; and others are made with rice.

The word "tamal" comes from the Nahuatl word *tamalli*, but each country has its own name for tamales and its own special way of making them. Among the myriad tamales you'll find, are *pamonhas* in Brazil, *humitas* in Bolivia, *pasteles* in Puerto Rico, and *chuchitos* in Guatemala. In Nicaragua, if they include meat, they're called *nacatamales*, and in Mexico, tamales shaped into cones and filled with cheese and vegetables are called *corundas*. Even when tamales have the same components, such as those made with fresh corn and cheese, they'll go by different names, depending on where you find them.

Tamales are always available on the streets, sold from baskets, coolers, or giant steaming pots over wood fires. People buy them mostly because they're tasty and satisfying but also because they're portable. I chose a variety of recipes here for tamales, from those served every day to the ones usually reserved for celebrations. You'll notice that most of these recipes will yield at least a dozen tamales. The good thing is that all of them freeze beautifully and are easy to reheat. My recipes will tell you how.

Since tamales can take a long time to assemble, it has long been a tradition in many Latin homes to hold *tamaladas*, or tamale-making parties, in which cooks gather to prepare them. It's a fun way to spend an afternoon, and it helps to expedite the process. Carve out a few hours in your day to make tamales, or do what Latin Americans do and invite a few friends to help you make a party out of it!

Tamales come in all sorts of shapes: round, rectangular, square, conical, and triangular. They're also wrapped in different kinds of leaves. The recipes I've included here call for corn husks (both dried and fresh) and banana leaves because they're the easiest wrappers to find. If you can't find either, don't worry. You can wrap tamales in parchment paper and then aluminum foil to seal them; they won't taste the same but they'll still be delicious.

Every Christmas Eve, my family gathers around the table to eat traditional tamales. The aroma of banana leaves, chiles, and pork reminds us of past holidays in Guatemala, where carpets made of fresh pine needles dressed the tiled floors and wreaths made out of stringed white cherry fruit called *nances* hung from the ceiling. Wherever there are tamales, there is a fiesta. I hope you'll experience the joy of opening each one of these little edible gifts and traveling through centuries of flavor.

PREPARING CORN HUSKS AND BANANA LEAVES FOR TAMALES

Before you get started on any recipe for tamales, you'll need to prepare the corn husks or banana leaves.

Venezuelan tamales, or hallacas, and ingredients for the filling.

Corn Husks

To prepare dried corn husks, soak them in warm water for at least an hour, then separate the husks. Remove any silk and discard. Keep the husks submerged in water as you work so that they don't dry out (use a heavy plate to keep them under water). Tear ⅛-inch strips following the natural ridges of the husks to use for ties (make them thicker, if the husks are too brittle). Use the largest husks for wrapping the tamales and use the small ones to line the pot you'll steam them in. Store any leftover dry husks in plastic bags in a dark place for up to two years. Any leftover soaked husks can be dried again. Shake the excess water off and spread them out on towels on your kitchen counter to dry for several days. Don't dry them in the oven because they could catch on fire. Once dried, they can be stored as indicated above.

The size of the corn husks will dictate how long the strips you make for tying the tamales will be. The ideal corn husks are at least 8 inches wide and 10 inches long. If the corn husks are on the smaller side, you may have to use kitchen twine to tie the tamales. If the corn husks are too small and you're having trouble shaping the tamales, just slightly overlap two husks so you can encase the filling. All tamales resemble packages but traditionally, most tamales resemble envelopes, with the edges of the corn husks cleanly meeting in the middle and tied in the center. Some are left open on the top and others are tied on both ends like a candy wrapper.

Banana Leaves

Banana leaves come whole and furled into bundles. If they are frozen, thaw them at room temperature for at least two hours. To prepare them for cooking, unfurl the leaves on a long counter. With scissors, cut away the tough outer vein from the two sides of the leaves and discard. Cut the leaves to the size indicated in the recipe. At this point, they must be flamed over a gas stove or, if you don't have a gas stove, simmered in boiling water to make them pliable and to remove their sticky, bitter sap. To do this on a gas stove, turn the burner on to medium-high and, working with one leaf at a time, pass it quickly back and forth directly over the flame just until it turns bright green and becomes pliable. To cook the leaves on an electric stove, bring a large pot of water to a boil over medium-high heat and place the leaves in the pot; simmer until they turn an olive green color, about 2 minutes. Remove them from the water and cool completely. Do not eat the banana leaves!

AN IMPORTANT NOTE ABOUT WORKING WITH MASA

Not all masa is created equal. Depending on what you're making, the consistency of the masa will vary: sometimes it should feel like soft mashed potatoes, sometimes stiff cookie dough, and sometimes smooth playdough. Read the recipes carefully, so you know what the masa should feel like for each dish. Sometimes the masa will have to be precooked, while other times it will simply need to be mixed with water.

Finally, some of the tamales in this book will be steamed and others will be boiled. When steaming tamales, it will be important for you to keep the water at a constant simmer. If you need to replenish the water as it evaporates, use boiling water so the temperature doesn't drop suddenly and you lose the steam. Likewise, if a recipe calls for boiling the tamales, add only boiling water if you need to replenish it. Be sure to keep the water at a *rolling boil* to prevent the tamales at the bottom of the pot from burning. Tamales should never be microwaved.

Venezuelan Tamales (Hallacas)

These are the traditional Christmas tamales of Venezuela, where many busy cooks purchase them from street vendors and take them home. The filling is made out of the same precooked cornmeal used to make arepas. The resulting tamales are very different from those made with the nixtamalized corn masa used in Mesoamerica. The masa is topped with a vegetable mixture called *guiso*; then it's studded with meats (chicken, pork, or beef), raisins, and olives. Traditional hallacas are intricately wrapped in three different shaped banana leaves, but I use an easier method using a combination of banana leaves and aluminum foil. Like many South American tamales, these are boiled, not steamed, so be sure to wrap these as directed to ensure they don't get waterlogged. Hallacas can be frozen after they're cooked and cooled; before serving, they must be boiled or steamed until hot.

Makes 8

¾ cup melted lard, vegetable shortening, or chicken fat
2 tablespoons annatto (achiote) seeds
1 cup minced leeks (white and light green parts only)
1 cup minced white onions
1 cup minced plum tomatoes
¾ cup minced red bell pepper
7 cups chicken broth
1½ teaspoons salt, divided
5 cups precooked cornmeal (masarepa or harina pan), divided
2 cups cooked and shredded chicken, chilled
2 bacon slices, each cut into 4 pieces
16 Manzanilla olives
24 large capers, rinsed
24 raisins
1–2 tablespoons slivered almonds
1 pound banana leaves, prepared as directed on pages 242–43
    and cut into 9½×12½-inch sheets
8 (12×20-inch) sheets aluminum foil

In a small saucepan, melt the lard over medium heat; add the annatto seeds, reduce the heat to medium-low, and gently simmer the lard for 45 seconds to 1 minute, being careful not to burn the seeds. Remove the pan from the heat and steep the seeds for 10 minutes. Strain the seeds and discard; reserve the lard.

Heat ¼ cup of the reserved lard in a medium skillet over medium-high heat. Add the leeks, onions, tomatoes, and bell peppers and cook, stirring often, until soft, about 10 minutes. Add 1 cup of broth and continue cooking until most of the broth has evaporated, about 5–6 minutes. Remove from the heat.

In a large bowl, combine 4 cups of the masarepa, the remaining lard, and the remaining broth; stir with a wooden spoon until the mixture is smooth and the texture of soft mashed potatoes. Gradually add the remaining 1 cup of masarepa, kneading it into the dough for 2–3 minutes or until it's the consistency of playdough. (If it's too stiff, add a bit more broth; if too wet, add a bit more masarepa). Divide the dough into 8 equal portions (about 1 cup each).

To assemble: Making one hallaca at a time, center a banana leaf on a sheet of the aluminum foil lengthwise, with the long side toward you. Spread a portion of the prepared dough in the center of the banana leaf, shaping it into a 6 × 4½-inch rectangle. Spread 2 tablespoons of the vegetable mixture and ¼ cup of the chicken over the dough. Arrange a piece of bacon, two olives, three capers, three raisins, and ½ teaspoon almonds on top. Fold the long sides of the banana leaf over the filling and then fold the sides of the leaves in to make a package. Place the hallaca seam-side down on the foil and wrap it tightly in the foil to seal. Repeat with the rest of the ingredients.

Bring a large pot of water to a boil. Drop the hallacas into the pot, cover, and boil for 30 minutes. Drain them in a colander over the sink for 10 minutes. Remove the foil and slide the hallacas from the banana leaves onto a plate; discard the leaves.

*}{ NOTE: To freeze hallacas, cool them completely (still wrapped) and freeze in a single layer until solid. Transfer to freezer bins or zip-top bags and freeze for up to 3 months; to reheat, boil (without thawing beforehand) until hot, about 30 minutes.

Guatemalan Christmas Tamales (Tamales Colorados)

In my home, it's not Christmas until the kitchen is filled with the aroma of these banana leaf–wrapped tamales filled with pork that has been deliciously bathed in a terracotta-colored sauce called *recado*. Inside each striking package is a white dumpling dressed with the colors of the holiday season. Every year in Guatemala, people line up to purchase tamales from their favorite *tamaleras*, so they can take them home to eat them on Christmas Eve. Some cooks add potatoes or rice to the filling, but this is the way we make them at home. My husband, our daughters, and I get into the holiday spirit by making these tamales together every year. Many times we've enlisted friends to help and after breaking bread together at our table, send them home with some of these edible gifts. The sauce can be made two days before the tamales are assembled. Serve these tamales the way they're meant to be served: with plenty of lime wedges and crusty French bread. In place of pork, you may use chicken or turkey.

Makes 15 tamales

- 2 pounds boneless pork butt
- 5 cups chopped plum tomatoes
- 12–15 medium tomatillos, husks removed, rinsed and chopped
- 1 chopped red bell pepper
- ⅓ cup minced white onion
- 2 large garlic cloves, peeled and left whole
- 1 ancho or pasilla chile, seeded and deveined (reserve the seeds)
- 1 guajillo chile, seeded and deveined (reserve the seeds)
- 1 (5-inch) stick Mexican cinnamon (canela)
- ½ teaspoon ground cloves
- 2 tablespoons annatto (achiote) paste
- ½ cup sesame seeds
- ½ cup raw pumpkin seeds (pepitas)
- 1 tablespoon plus 1 teaspoon salt, divided
- ¼ teaspoon freshly ground black pepper

8 cups masa harina

Reserved pork cooking broth plus enough water to make 11 cups

2 cups lard (or vegetable shortening)

2½–3 pounds fresh banana leaves, prepared as directed on
    pages 242–43 and cut into 15 (roughly 12×13-inch) and
    15 (roughly 8×9-inch) rectangles; reserve the scraps

15 large capers, rinsed

15 Manzanilla olives

1 (2-ounce) jar sliced pimientos

Kitchen twine cut into 15 (30-inch) pieces

Lime wedges

Place the pork in a large pot, cover with water, and bring it to a boil. Cover, reduce the heat, and simmer until fully cooked, about 50–55 minutes. Cool the pork in the broth. When cool, strain the broth and chill it until ready to use. Cut the pork into 15 chunks (about 1½ inches each); cover the pork and chill until ready to use.

In a large pot over medium-high heat, combine the tomatoes, tomatillos, bell peppers, onions, garlic, chiles, cinnamon, cloves, and annatto. Cook, covered, for 10 minutes. Reduce the heat to low and simmer for 10 minutes; remove from the heat and cool slightly.

In the meantime, toast the sesame seeds in a dry skillet over medium heat until golden, about 4 minutes; remove to a plate. Place the pumpkin seeds in the skillet and toast until golden and puffed, about 1–2 minutes; combine with the sesame seeds. Toast the reserved chile seeds for 10 seconds; add to the other seeds and cool them completely.

In a blender, combine the cooked vegetables, and the seeds; blend until smooth. Add 1 teaspoon of the salt and the pepper.

In a large pot, using a wooden spoon, mix the masa harina with enough broth to make it the consistency of soft mashed potatoes (add the liquid gradually until it reaches the desired consistency; if you need more liquid, add water). Set the pot over medium heat and add the lard and the tablespoon of salt; stir until the lard has melted and is well distributed. The masa will thicken and reach the consistency of mashed potatoes—if it's too thick, add more liquid. Continue stirring until it begins to pull away from the sides and bottom of the pot, about 3–4 minutes; remove from the heat, cover the pot with a towel, and let the masa cool for 30 minutes.

To assemble the tamales: Place one large banana leaf rectangle before you, long side toward you and shiny side down; place a smaller piece in the center. Place a cup of masa in the center of the small leaf. Shape it into a 3½ × 4-inch rectangle. Indent the center slightly and top with ¼ cup of the sauce. Set a piece of pork, an olive, a caper, and a pimiento strip on the tamal. Fold the bottom part of the banana leaves over the filling; with the sides of your hands press the leaves down to mark the perimeter of the tamal. Fold the sides of the leaves over the filling (as if you were making an egg roll). Roll the tamale upward and over to finish wrapping it. Tie the tamale with twine in crisscross fashion (as you would a present). Repeat with the remaining ingredients.

To steam the tamales: Place a wire rack or steamer basket in the bottom of a pot. Arrange some of the leftover banana leaves on the steamer. Layer the tamales over the leaves, snuggly. Fill the pot with 2–3 inches of boiling water and keep it at a boil over medium-high heat; cover the pot, reduce the heat to a simmer, and steam the tamales for 2 hours, adding more water as it evaporates. Turn the heat off, uncover the pot, and leave the tamales there to cool for 30 minutes before eating.

✻} NOTE: Once cooked and cooled, the tamales can be refrigerated for up to 24 hours. To reheat, steam until hot, about 20–30 minutes. To store them longer, you'll need to freeze them. To do so, cool completely (still wrapped) and freeze in a single layer until solid. Transfer to zip-top bags and freeze for up to 3 months; to reheat, steam (without thawing beforehand) until hot, about 45 minutes to 1 hour.

Peruvian Tamales

These comforting dumplings are highly seasoned with a bright and spicy sofrito that contains annatto, which tints the dough a golden color. The combination of corn and rice flours makes a sturdy meal with truly delectable texture, yielding dense and meaty dumplings. These tamales represent the coming together of the Incan, Spanish, and African cultures that helped shape Peruvian cuisine. These tamales—like many South American types—are boiled rather than steamed. They're typically served with salsa criolla, which is filled with the sour and spicy flavors of lime and chiles. The salsa livens up the tamales further, taking them to yet another level of tastiness. The red and spicy hot rocoto is one of Peru's most valued chiles. You can purchase them frozen or in jars or cans in most Latin stores; if you can't find them, use jalapeños instead.

Makes 18 tamales

- ¼ cup extra-virgin olive oil
- 1 cup minced white onion
- ½ cup minced red bell pepper
- ¼ cup tomato paste
- ¼ cup annatto (achiote) paste
- 2 teaspoons ground cumin
- 1 teaspoon garlic powder
- 6 cups warm chicken broth, divided
- 4 cups masa harina
- 2 cups rice flour
- 2 tablespoons salt
- 1 cup melted lard (or melted vegetable shortening or vegetable oil)
- 18 green olives
- 18 roasted peanuts (salted or unsalted)
- 2 rocoto peppers (or 4 jalapeños) seeded, deveined, and thinly sliced
- 2–3 cooked chicken breasts, shredded into 18 pieces
- 18 banana leaves, prepared as directed on pages 242–43 and cut into 9×9-inch sheets
- 18 (12×15-inch) sheets aluminum foil
- Peruvian Spicy Onion Salsa (Salsa Criolla) (page 275)

Heat the oil in a medium skillet over medium heat; cook the onions and bell peppers until softened, about 4–5 minutes. Add the tomato paste, annatto, cumin, garlic powder, and 2 cups of the broth. Using the back of a spoon, break up the annatto until dissolved, and cook the mixture until slightly thickened, about 20–25 minutes; set aside to cool for 10 minutes.

In a large bowl, combine the masa harina, rice flour, and salt. Gradually add the remaining broth, stirring the dough with a wooden spoon until it resembles thick mashed potatoes. Stir in the cooled mixture and the lard until they're thoroughly incorporated (the dough will look a bit fluffy). Cover with a towel and let it rest for 20 minutes.

To assemble the tamales: place one sheet of aluminum foil on the counter, long side toward you; center a banana leaf in the middle of the foil. Place ½ cup of the masa in the center of the banana leaf, and using a spatula, shape it into a 5×2-inch rectangle. Place one olive, one peanut, a slice of pepper, and one piece of chicken on the masa. Bring the long sides of the aluminum foil together (grabbing onto the banana leaf when you do so), so that the filling stays inside. Keep folding the foil until you reach the filling. With the sides of your hands, press down on the ends of the tamal to form a rectangle; flatten out the aluminum foil on each end of the tamal and fold over both ends several times until you reach the tamal. It should look like a little package. Repeat with the rest of the tamales.

Stack the tamales in a large pot (or use two, if needed). Fill the pot with hot water, completely submerging the tamales. Bring the water to a boil over medium-high heat; cover, reduce the heat, and simmer for 2 hours. Remove the tamales from the pot and cool for 20 minutes.

Unwrap the tamales and discard the wrappers (don't eat the banana leaves). Serve each tamal topped with the salsa.

❋⟩ NOTE: Once cooked and cooled, the tamales (still wrapped) can be refrigerated for up to 24 hours. To reheat, boil until hot, about 20–30 minutes. To store them longer, you'll need to freeze them. To do so, cool completely (still wrapped) and freeze in a single layer until solid. Transfer to zip-top bags and freeze for up to 4 months; to reheat, boil (without thawing beforehand) until hot, about 30–40 minutes.

Peruvian Tamales with Peruvian Spicy Onion Salsa (Salsa Criolla)

Guatemalan Christmas Tamales (Tamales Colorados) (left) (page 246),
Pork and Roasted Tomato Tamales (Chuchitos) (lower right), and
Green Chicken Tamales (Tamales Verdes) (page 255)

Pork and Roasted Tomato Tamales (Chuchitos)

When I was a teenager, I didn't like eating breakfast on school days because it meant I had to get up earlier than usual. It was a small price to pay for a few more precious minutes of sleep, even if that meant I often went to school with an empty stomach. These hominy and pork tamales, popular on the streets, made a great handheld breakfast that I could buy at school during recess. In Guatemala, they're known as *chuchitos* (puppies), and they're among the easiest tamales to make. Dried corn husks are submerged in warm water to make them soft and pliable. Chuchitos freeze well after they're steamed and cooled. There's no need to thaw or unwrap them; simply steam them again for 30 minutes or until heated through. Never microwave a tamal—it will fall apart into a crumbly mess! In order to whip air into this masa, you'll need the lard to be chilled until it's solid; in a pinch, use vegetable shortening instead.

Makes 24 small tamales

> 50 dried corn husks (plus more to cut into strips to tie the tamales), soaked in warm water as directed on pages 241–42
> 1½ pounds boneless pork butt
> 5 black peppercorns
> 6 cups masa harina
> 1 tablespoon salt
> 1½ cups chilled lard or vegetable shortening
> Roasted Tomato Sauce (page 265)

Place the pork and peppercorns in a medium pot; add water to cover. Bring to a boil, skimming off the foam that rises to the surface during the first few minutes; reduce the heat, cover, and simmer for about 45 minutes or until cooked through. Remove the pork from the broth and set aside to cool. Strain the broth into a bowl; add enough water to make 4¼ cups and set aside. When the pork is cool enough to handle, chop it into 24 roughly 1-inch pieces. Chill the pork and broth until needed.

In a large bowl, whisk together the masa harina and salt. Gradually add 4–4½ cups broth, kneading the dough with your hands and adding liquid until the dough comes together into a ball. The dough should be smooth and not sticky. Using an electric mixer, whip the lard at medium-high speed for 30 seconds–1 minute or until fluffy. With the motor running at medium speed, add the dough by large pieces until all has been incorporated; continue beating until the dough has the consistency of thick mashed potatoes and is no longer sticky. Cover the dough; let it rest for 20 minutes.

Working with one corn husk at a time, place it on a clean surface and wipe it dry. Using an offset spatula, spread ⅓ cup of masa onto the middle of the husk, shaping it into a roughly 3×3-inch square, leaving at least a 1½ inch border on all sides (the size of the husk will determine how much of a border you'll have). Place 1 piece of pork and a heaping tablespoon of sauce in the center. Roll the left side of the husk lengthwise over the filling to cover it. Fold the right side so that it overlaps the other side of the husk, encasing the filling completely. Twist the ends of the corn husk (like a candy wrapper) and tie the ends with the prepared corn husk strips. Repeat with the rest of the masa and the filling until all of the tamales are made.

Fit a large pot with a steamer basket and line the basket with a few corn husks; fill the pot with 2–3 inches of water. Layer the tamales flat in the basket. Cover the pot and bring the water to a boil over high heat; reduce the heat to a simmer and steam the tamales for 45 minutes (replenishing the water as needed). Turn off the heat and let them cool in the pot for 30 minutes.

To serve, remove the ties and slide each one of the tamales out of their husks; discard the husks. Heat the remaining sauce in a small pot; place each serving on a plate and ladle the sauce over the tamales. ❖

Green Chicken Tamales (Tamales Verdes)

Early in the morning and late in the evening in Mexico City, tamales like these are sold in streets to hungry passersby looking for a quick and warm bite to eat. I recall buying these with my great aunt from a lady on a street corner who sold them warm from huge aluminum vats. My aunt served them with dollops of smooth crema and a sprinkling of salty cheese, but they were just as delicious without the embellishments. Many grown-ups think kids don't pay attention to what they eat, but some of my most beloved food memories are from my childhood. Today, a bite of one of these tender and satisfying tamales stuffed with chicken in a vivid green tomatillo sauce, can take me back to that one Christmas I spent in Mexico City long ago with relatives who are now long gone. These tamales are mildly spicy; seed the chiles if you want to remove the heat, but I encourage you to try them once as they are meant to be. Cotija is a salty, crumbly Mexican cheese and it's widely available in the United States, but if you can't find it, substitute feta or Pecorino Romano cheese.

Makes 25 small tamales

> 5 serrano chiles, left whole, stems removed
> 10 medium tomatillos, husks removed, rinsed and left whole
> ¾ cup chicken broth (or water)
> ½ cup roughly chopped white onion
> 2 large garlic cloves, peeled and left whole
> ¾ cup packed cilantro (leaves and tender stems)
> 2 tablespoons vegetable oil
> 1 tablespoon, plus 1 teaspoon salt, or to taste, divided
> 2 cups cooked and shredded chicken
> 4 cups masa harina
> 4 cups warm water (or chicken broth)
> ½ cup melted lard
> 30 dried corn husks (plus more to cut into strips to tie the tamales),
>   soaked in warm water as directed on pages 241–42
> Mexican crema, to taste
> Cotija cheese, to taste

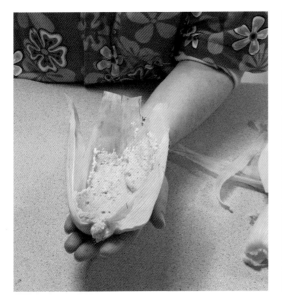

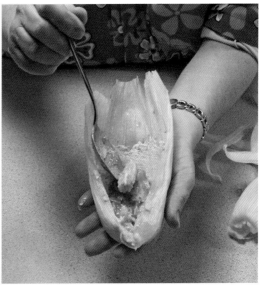

To assemble tamales in corn husks: Spread the masa in the center of the corn husk.

Place the filling in the center of the masa.

In a medium saucepan, combine the chiles, tomatillos, and broth and bring to a boil; cover and simmer over medium heat for 10 minutes or until the tomatillos begin to pop. Remove from the heat, cool, and transfer to a blender. Add the onions, garlic, and cilantro and purée until smooth.

Heat the oil in a medium saucepan over medium-high heat; when hot, add the blended sauce (careful, it will splatter) and stir. Reduce the heat to low; partially cover, and cook until slightly thickened, about 8 minutes. Add the shredded chicken and 1 teaspoon of the salt, or to taste, and cool; chill until ready to use.

In a large bowl, combine the masa harina and the remaining salt. Gradually, add the warm water, kneading until the dough reaches the consistency of thick mashed potatoes (or playdough); pour the lard into the masa and continue kneading until smooth. Cover the masa and let it rest for 10 minutes.

Working with one corn husk at a time, place it on a clean surface and wipe it dry. Using an offset spatula, spread ¼ cup of masa onto the husk, shaping it into a roughly 3×3½-inch rectangle, leaving a roughly 1½-inch border on the long sides and a roughly 2-inch border on the short sides (the size of the husk will determine how much border you'll have).

Tamale Train

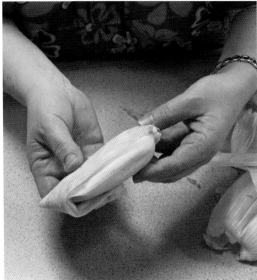

Fold the edges of the husk over the masa and filling.   Fold down the top part of the husk.

Spread about 1 heaping tablespoon of the chicken over the masa; turn the tamale so it's facing you lengthwise. Fold the long ends of the husk over the masa so that they meet in the middle. Bring the narrow tip of the husk over to the center of the tamal. Tie a husk strip around the center (where the tip meets the seam) of the tamal to secure it (but not too tight; it shouldn't have a "waist"). When you're done folding the tamal, the top end will not be sealed and you should be able to peek into the filling.

Fit a large Dutch oven with a steamer basket; stand the tamales (open side up) in the basket. Add 2–3 inches of boiling water to the pan; cover and bring to a boil over high heat. Lower the heat to a simmer and steam the tamales for 1 hour; remove from heat. Allow them to cool in the pot, covered, for 30 minutes.

Remove the husks and discard; serve tamales with crema and cheese.

✺} NOTE: Once cooked and cooled, the tamales (still wrapped) can be refrigerated for up to 24 hours. To reheat, steam until hot, about 20 minutes. To store them longer, you'll need to freeze them. To do so, cool them completely (still wrapped) and freeze in a single layer until solid. Transfer to zip-top bags and freeze for up to 3 months. To reheat, steam (without thawing beforehand) until hot, about 30–40 minutes.

Chipilín Tamales

Corn dumplings like these, with an earthy flavor and dressed with speckles of herbs, are commonly sold in Central American streets. As a little girl I'd watch in awe as the *tamaleras* (ladies who sell tamales) walked by balancing giant baskets filled to the rim on their heads without using their hands. Today, whenever I see this balancing act, I still wonder how they do it. This kind of tamal is often served in place of bread to sop up sauces from stews, such as *pepianes* (Guatemalan stews enriched with seeds and or nuts), or as an accoutrement to soups. Making tamales requires practice, but the experience can be tremendously rewarding. Children can easily get involved in making these. Once steamed, freeze the tamales for up to 3 months. To reheat, simply steam them until hot, and serve. Chipilín is a fragrant herb native to Central America and sold frozen or in jars in Latin American stores. If you can't find it substitute cooked spinach or kale.

Makes about 2 ½ dozen small tamales.

> 6 cups masa harina
> 2 teaspoons salt
> 5–5 ½ cups warm water (or vegetable broth)
> 1 ½ cups chilled lard or vegetable shortening
> 2 cups chipilín leaves, hard stems removed, pressed dry,
>   and roughly chopped
> 1 cup grated queso seco or Cotija cheese
> 30 corn husks (plus more to cut into strips to tie the tamales),
>   soaked in warm water as directed on pages 241–42

In a large bowl, combine the masa harina and salt. Gradually add the warm water, kneading with your hands, until the dough comes together into a ball and has the consistency of cookie dough. It should be smooth and not sticky.

Using an electric mixer, whip the lard at medium-high speed for 30 seconds to 1 minute or until fluffy. With the motor running at medium speed, add the dough by large pieces until all has been incorporated; continue beating until the dough has the consistency of thick mashed potatoes and is no longer sticky.

Transfer the masa to a large bowl. Add the chipilín and the cheese to the masa and knead it until all are combined. Cover the masa and let it rest for 10 minutes.

Working with one corn husk at a time, place it on a clean surface and wipe it dry. Using an offset spatula, spread roughly ⅓ cup of the masa in the center of the husk, shaping it into a roughly 3×1½-inch rectangle. With the short sides of the tamal facing you, leave a 2-inch border at the bottom and a 1-inch border at the top. Following the natural bend of the husk, fold the sides over the masa and then fold the bottom part of the husk over. Tie loosely with a corn husk strip to hold it together. (The top of the tamal will be open).

Fit a large stockpot or Dutch oven with a steamer basket; stand the tamales (open side up) in the basket. Add 2–3 inches of boiling water to the pot; cover and bring to a boil over high heat. Lower the heat to a simmer and steam the tamales for 45 minutes. Allow them to cool for 20 minutes before serving; remove the husks and serve hot.

NOTE: Once cooked and cooled, the tamales (still wrapped) can be refrigerated for up to 24 hours. To reheat, steam until hot, about 20 minutes. To store them longer, you'll need to freeze them. To do so, cool them completely (still wrapped) and freeze in a single layer until solid. Transfer to zip-top bags and freeze for up to 3 months. To reheat, steam (without thawing beforehand) until hot, about 30–40 minutes.

Corn and Cinnamon Tamales with Raisins and Cheese (Humintas *or* Tamalitos de Elote)

Sweet corn dough meets savory cheese, transforming dainty tamales into portable corn puddings. Sweet tamales speckled with fruit and sweet spices are found throughout Latin America. The real star here is the corn and not the masa, which is only used as a binding agent. Unlike other tamales, these are enclosed in fresh corn husks. The tender leaves furl up to hug the dumplings as they steam. For my eighteenth birthday—my last in Guatemala—my university classmates arrived at my parents' home at dawn with a mariachi band and a whole lot of firecrackers that awoke our neighbors. My mother, who had been warned of the planned *serenata*, invited them all to a breakfast that included *huevos rancheros*, tamales like these, and hot chocolate (page 324).

Makes 24 small tamales

> 12–13 ears of corn (to yield 6 cups fresh corn kernels),
>   husks reserved (see note)
> 1 cup lard or vegetable shortening (do not use butter)
> 1¼ cups sugar
> 1½ cups grated queso seco or Cotija cheese
>   (or Parmesan, in a pinch)
> 1 teaspoon ground cinnamon (see note)
> Pinch salt
> 1½ cups masa harina (a bit more or less depending on
>   moisture content of the fresh corn)
> ½ cup raisins

Select 5 or 6 corn husks to cut into 24 strips (long enough to tie around each tamal); keep them submerged in cold water and set them aside.

With a sharp knife, cut the corn kernels from the ears of corn and place them in the bowl of a food processor fitted with a metal blade. Pulse for eight, five-second intervals or until the corn is mashed but still retains texture. (If you overprocess, you'll have corn juice, so easy does it! The kernels must be finely chopped but some tiny pieces should be discernible for texture.)

With an electric mixer, cream the lard and sugar together until fluffy. Add the corn, cheese, cinnamon, and salt; blend at low speed until they are incorporated. Gradually add the masa until the dough holds together when pressed between your fingers. It'll feel like thick mashed potatoes (if it's too wet, add more masa harina). Stir in the raisins just until combined. Cover with plastic and let rest at room temperature for 20 minutes.

Drain the husks and dry them between paper towels—just enough to remove excess water. Place roughly ¼ cup of the prepared dough in the center of a husk, shaping it into a long log with your fingers, leaving ⅓ of the corn husk free of dough at the bottom and at least 1 inch free at the top. Wrap the masa in the husk—the husk will embrace it as if it were still hugging the cob. Fold the bottom tip of the husk up to where the seams meet in the center of the tamal (the top part of the tamal will be open); tie it securely with a strip of corn husk (not too tight; it shouldn't have a "waist" or it'll explode while it cooks). Repeat with the remaining corn husks and dough.

Fit a large stock pot with a steamer basket. Stand the tamales (open side up) in the basket. Add 2-3 inches of boiling water to the pot; cover, and bring the water to a boil over medium-high heat; reduce the heat to a simmer and steam the tamales for 1 hour, replenishing the water, as needed. Remove the pot from the heat and allow the tamales to rest, covered, for 30 minutes. Serve warm.

✻} NOTE: To remove the husks from the fresh corn, slice off the bottom of the corn stalks. Unfurl them one at a time—being careful not to rip them. Soak the husks in cold water for at least 1 hour (up to 3 hours).

For a more authentic flavor, use Mexican cinnamon sticks (canela). To grind, use a coffee grinder or a mortar and pestle.

These tamales are best eaten fresh but can be frozen after they're cooked (still wrapped) for up to 3 months. Steam them again until they are hot, about 20–25 minutes.

CONDIMENTS, TOPPINGS, & SIDE DISHES

At the first thought of street food, my mind is filled with visions of colorful, vibrant, and texturally interesting food. For me, an integral aspect of street food and what makes it so exciting to eat is the vast collection of condiments, toppings, and side dishes that are available for the taking.

Take the humblest of all tacos: a tortilla simply filled with a piece of grilled chicken and sprinkled with salt. It's okay, but if we're honest, it's not that exciting. However, pile it up with shredded lettuce, chopped red onions, and some minced tomatoes, and I bet your mouth will start watering. Of course, if we truly wanted to elevate it to another level, we could add a dollop of crema here, a squirt of lime there, a drizzle of avocado salsa over the top, and a splash of hot sauce for good measure. Now we're talking!

Condiments and toppings are all about raising the bar just a bit, kicking it up a good notch, and jazzing up a humble recipe so it can become a gastronomic masterpiece. Every day, there are countless options of extras that we can slather, pile, sprinkle, and drizzle on an equally dizzying array of possible street offerings. The combinations are endless.

But toppings don't just take a dish to a new level of deliciousness; they're also a means of self-expression. I can say with some certainty that the condiments you choose to put on your taco will look and taste completely different from those I, or anyone else for that matter, choose. Street food brings the cook out of the passerby—regardless of culinary prowess—at the precise moment when that person embellishes a dish with a condiment.

The way I see it, garnishing dishes gives customers the ability to participate in the crafting of their food and to make it taste exactly the way they like it. This is what distinguishes the street food movement from any other culinary trend. It makes eaters active participants in creating a dish that they don't have to cook themselves.

In my opinion, one of the few requirements for a great topping—even if it's just one ingredient—is that it packs a punch, so even if you add only a little bit of any one topping, its flavor will always be noticeable. Condiments and toppings must also complement all of the other ingredients in a particular dish, and they must also play nice with each other. On the streets, garnishes are not used just as a decorative accent; they're there for their taste. Yes, street foods are composed of a lot of visual contrasts, but the ingredients must always work in unison to create better flavor. When it comes to toppings and condiments, the word to think of is "balance."

To help you create exciting new dishes, I've come up with a select compendium of recipes that will come in handy whenever you're putting together the street foods you'll find in this book. And in each recipe, I'll suggest the dishes that the toppings and condiments will best complement, so that you can customize each recipe to your palate.

Street food vendors also offer lots of side dishes. From Mexico all the way to Brazil, many platters are embellished with rice, beans, and plantains, which together make up what is widely known as the Latin trilogy. Side dishes are usually not very elaborate because they're meant to complement each other and not to compete with the main component

A woman with her baby in tow sells bread in Laja, La Paz, Bolivia.

of a meal. On the streets of Peru, a side dish can be comprised simply of a few boiled potatoes; in Colombia, it can be a small arepa; in Bolivia, it can be a homemade roll; and in Mexico, it can be as humble an offering as a corn tortilla sprinkled with salt and rolled up or a whole serrano chile.

Sometimes a side salad consisting of shredded lettuce, onions, and tomatoes will be added to a luncheon platter. Most often, a couple of slices of avocado or a mélange of pickled peppers and vegetables will become a garnish. French fries and fried yuca and plantain chips are always a common sight on the streets (find those recipes in my "Fried and True" chapter).

On very rare occasions, you'll find more complex side dishes. Among them are *llapingachos*, the little potato cakes so beloved in Ecuador, that are served on breakfast platters alongside eggs and sausages, as well as on lunch plates featuring grilled meats.

In this chapter, you'll find recipes for both simple and complex side dishes. Included here is one of my favorite rice dishes sold on Mexican streets. I also included two very different bean recipes that are classics on the streets of Mesoamerica. My ground beef picadillo here, chock full of vegetables, is similar to the one I used to get at my favorite pupusa cart in Guatemala City, where it was always served as a side, along with mounds of cabbage slaw. You'll be able to use that recipe for picadillo also as a component for many of the other recipes in this book.

The condiments and toppings people choose to put on their food can say a lot about them: whether they're daring or cautious, fun loving or tentative, or open to new possibilities or set in their ways, and whether they're neat-freaks or whether they delight in making a mess. Me, I'm a little bit of all of these, depending on what day of the week you catch me ladling, sprinkling, and drizzling toppings on some of my favorite things. Discover more about yourself as you taste your way through the condiments, toppings, and side dishes in this chapter.

Roasted Tomato Sauce

Charring vegetables prior to making sauces imparts a smoky flavor that was ubiquitous in the foods of ancient Mesoamerican civilizations and is still present in the flavor profile of indigenous foods today. This step imparts simple ingredients with a rich and exotic flavor. Most cooks have been taught not to burn garlic, but in Latin cuisines, charring it is desired for depth of flavor. Because the garlic is roasted while it's still unpeeled, it develops a smoky and sweet flavor without turning bitter. This only goes to show that no one way is the absolute right way and that it all depends on the school of thought you follow. This is a great sauce to have on hand for incorporating into recipes like the Guatemalan tamales called chuchitos (page 253) and Grilled Beef Tacos (page 101). This sauce keeps in the refrigerator for up to four days. It also freezes well, although it will turn a bit watery, so after you thaw it, cook it over high heat for about 5 minutes. I love it on tacos and on tostadas, ladled over eggs, or stirred into soups.

Makes 3 cups

- 12 plum tomatoes
- 1 large red bell pepper
- 2 large garlic cloves, unpeeled
- 1½ cups roughly chopped onion
- 3 guajillo, pasilla, or Nuevo Mexico dried chiles, seeded and chopped
- ¼ cup vegetable oil
- Salt and freshly ground black pepper, to taste

Place the tomatoes, bell pepper, and garlic on a dry skillet over high heat (or on a hot grill). Turn them until their skins are charred and blackened, about 4–5 minutes. Remove the garlic and peel it.

In a blender with a good motor, and working in batches, combine the charred vegetables, onions, and chiles. Blend until smooth.

In a large pot, heat the oil over medium-high heat. Pour the sauce into the hot oil so that it sizzles; stir vigorously until it stops splattering and continue stirring for 5 minutes. Reduce the heat and simmer the sauce for 30 minutes or until it has begun to thicken; season with salt and pepper. Allow it to cool and refrigerate until ready to use. ❊

Jalapeños, Onions, and Carrots in Escabeche

In the summertime when my jalapeño plants get heavy with plump chiles, I pickle them in large quantities. Most markets in Mesoamerica feature chiles like these and exhibit them in huge glass containers. These chiles are to tacos what pickles are to sandwiches, and that's why many street vendors favor serving them as a condiment. Once chilled, if properly covered, they'll keep in the refrigerator for up to three months.

Makes 12 servings

¾ cup extra-virgin olive oil
3 cups thinly sliced white onion
2 cups peeled and thinly sliced carrots (see note)
24 large whole jalapeños, washed and dried
3 large garlic cloves, peeled and left whole
4 sprigs fresh thyme (or 1 teaspoon dry)
2 bay leaves
5 black peppercorns
1¼ cups white vinegar

In a large pot, combine the oil, onions, and carrots, over medium heat. Cook, stirring, until the onions are softened but have not changed color, about 2–3 minutes. Add the jalapeños, garlic, thyme, bay leaves, and peppercorns; cook, stirring, for 2–3 minutes. Add the vinegar and bring to a boil; cover, reduce the heat, and simmer, stirring occasionally, just until the jalapeños have softened, about 15 minutes. Remove from the heat; cool to room temperature. Transfer to a clean glass container; cover and chill.

❉〕 NOTE: Other vegetables, for example cauliflower florets and diced zucchini, lend themselves nicely to this treatment. Add a cup of each when you add the carrots.

Jalapeños, Onions, and Carrots in Escabeche

All-Purpose Tomato Sauce (Salsa Casera)

With a clean and straightforward tomato flavor, this is an all-purpose sauce. Serve it over pupusas (pages 68 and 71), or use it to top Tricolor Tostadas (page 79) or Beet Salad Tostadas (page 81). Ladle it over poached eggs or grilled vegetables, or use it in place of the sauce in the chilaquiles recipes in this book. Every cook should have at least one basic tomato sauce recipe in their repertoire. This one will serve you well. It can be frozen for up to two months.

Makes 1 ½ cups

   1 (14-ounce) can whole tomatoes
   2 garlic cloves, roughly chopped
   1 teaspoon salt
   ¼ teaspoon freshly ground black pepper
   2 tablespoons vegetable oil

In a blender, combine the tomatoes, garlic, salt, pepper and oil; blend until smooth. Transfer the sauce to a medium saucepan and bring it to a boil over medium-high heat. Cover, reduce the heat, and simmer for 15 minutes. (If you prefer a thicker sauce, remove the cover and cook for a few minutes more or until it has reduced to your liking.) Keep warm and covered until ready to use or refrigerate for up to 4 days; reheat when ready to use. ❊

. . . .

Avocado Sauce

In Guatemala, this is the specialty sauce used to top hot dogs, whether they're served up in a bun (page 153) or wrapped in tortillas (page 89). It also makes a fun topping for tacos, quesadillas, and tostones (page 186). The addition of sour cream has a dual purpose. First, it keeps the avocado green and fresh for a long period of time. Vendors compete for business, and the better the food looks the more customers will want to buy it. Second, it's cheaper to produce than if it were made with only avocados, and this allows street vendors to charge customers a bit less. Covered well, the sauce will keep in the refrigerator for up to 12 hours.

Makes 1 ¾–2 cups (enough for 8 hot dogs or 12 mixtas)

2 Hass avocados
½ cup finely grated white onion
1 large garlic clove, minced
¼ teaspoon oregano
2 tablespoons sour cream
Lime juice, to taste
Salt and freshly ground black pepper, to taste

Slice the avocados in half. Remove and discard the pits and remove the flesh to a small bowl. Mash together the avocados, onions, garlic, and oregano. Stir in the sour cream; season with lime juice, salt, and pepper. Cover with plastic wrap and chill until ready to use. ✳

Raw Tomatillo Salsa

This salsa is tart and refreshing, and since its sour undertones lend a sharp contrast to the creaminess of cheese, I often use it to top quesadillas. Tomatillos resemble miniature green tomatoes but are members of the gooseberry family and, as such, are wrapped in a papery husk. I rub off the husks under cold running water, and then give the tomatillos a gentle rub with my fingers to remove the sticky residue. There is no need to peel tomatillos because their skins are thin and edible. Try to get the smallest possible tomatillos since they begin to turn bitter if allowed to grow too much. This raw salsa is also delicious as a condiment for tacos, huaraches, sopes, and tostadas. It'll keep in the refrigerator for up to three days.

Makes approximately 1 ½ cups

10 medium tomatillos, husks removed, and rinsed and quartered
3 large garlic cloves, roughly chopped
2 jalapeño peppers, roughly chopped (do not seed)
1 cup packed cilantro (leaves and tender stems), chopped
¼ cup cold water
Salt and freshly ground black pepper, to taste

In a blender, combine the tomatillos, garlic, jalapeños, cilantro, and water; blend until smooth (if needed to get the motor running, add a bit more water, one tablespoon at a time). Transfer the sauce to a bowl and season with salt and pepper. Chill until ready to serve. ✳

Avocado-Tomatillo Taco Truck Sauce

This is perhaps the most popular avocado sauce used by taco truck vendors in Mexico. A little sour and very creamy, it's used to top everything from *totopos* (fried tortilla chips) to tacos and chilaquiles. The acidity of the tomatillos keeps the avocado fresh and vibrantly green for up to three days, if properly refrigerated. You can put it in a squirt bottle or spoon it directly onto your food. This recipe has a spicy kick, so if you desire a milder flavor, seed and devein the chiles. My daughter Nikki, who doesn't care much for avocados, eats this sauce by the spoonful. Try saying the name of this sauce quickly and you'll see how catchy it is.

Makes 2 ½ cups

> 4–5 medium tomatillos, husks removed, rinsed and chopped
>   (you should have 1 cup)
> 2 serrano chiles, stems removed (seeded and deveined
>   if less heat is desired)
> 1 cup packed cilantro (leaves and tender stems), chopped
> ¼ cup minced white onion
> ¼ cup water
> 1 Hass avocado
> Lime juice, to taste
> Salt and freshly ground black pepper, to taste

In a blender, combine the tomatillos, chiles, cilantro, onions, and water; blend until smooth. Slice the avocado in half and remove and discard the pit. Scoop out the flesh of the avocado and add it to the blender; blend until smooth. Transfer the sauce to a large bowl; season with lime juice, salt, and pepper. ✳

Assorted condiments: (1) Avocado-Tomatillo Taco Truck Sauce, (2) Colombian Hot Sauce (Ají Colombiano) (page 279), (3) Classic Chimichurri (page 183), (4) Francisco's Chimichurri (page 272), (5) Red Garlic Sauce (page 274), (6) Corn and Avocado Salsa (page 277), (7) Peruvian Spicy Onion Salsa (Salsa Criolla) (page 275)

Francisco's Chimichurri

There are many versions of this Argentinean condiment, but this one developed by my friend Francisco Fumagalli is one of the best I've ever had. Although most recipes for chimichurri call for parsley as the main component, here it shares center stage with the other ingredients. This chimichurri is speckled with carrots for a hint of sweetness, garlic for a surge of pungency, pepper flakes for a whisper of heat, and vinegar for a kiss of acidity. Francisco, who was born and raised in Argentina, descends from a line of restaurant owners and is a magnificent cook. This is a slight adaptation of his recipe, which was handed down to him by his family. He recommends using a food processor, but the ingredients can also be minced finely with a sharp knife. Chimichurri is the traditional accoutrement for *asados* (grilled meats), and it makes a great topping for sausage in buns called choripanes (page 154). Best of all, it tastes even better a day or two after it's made, and keeps for up to one week in the refrigerator; before serving, bring it to room temperature. For another rendition of this herb sauce, see the recipe for Yuca Fries with Classic Chimichurri (page 183).

Makes 2 cups

> 1 cup firmly packed flat-leaf or Italian parsley
>   (leaves and tender stems)
> 1 cup thinly sliced celery
> 1 cup minced carrots
> 3–4 large garlic cloves, minced
> ¼ cup apple cider vinegar
> 1 teaspoon salt, or to taste
> ½ teaspoon red pepper flakes
> ¾ cup canola or grape seed oil

In the bowl of a food processor fitted with a metal blade, combine the parsley, celery, carrots, and garlic. Pulse for 10–12 one-second intervals (stopping to scrape the sides of the bowl as needed) or until the mixture is very finely chopped (being careful not to turn it into a paste). Transfer to a bowl and stir in the vinegar, salt, and red pepper flakes. Whisk in the oil; cover and chill until ready to serve. ❖

Ecuadorian Peanut Sauce (Salsa de Maní)

This peanut sauce is used to dress several kinds of the street food in Ecuador, particularly those made with yuca or potatoes, including the potato pancakes called llapingachos (page 282). It's also used as an all-purpose sauce and is often spooned over grilled kabobs. Try it with Chicken on a Stick (page 208). This sauce is meant to be served warm and is easily reheated on the stove or in the microwave.

Makes 1 ¼ cups

2 tablespoons extra-virgin olive oil
½ cup minced white onion
1 teaspoon annatto (achiote) powder
½ teaspoon ground cumin
½ cup unsalted smooth peanut butter
¾ cup whole milk
Salt, to taste

In a small saucepan, heat the oil over medium heat; add the onions, annatto, and cumin and cook until the onions are soft, about 1–2 minutes. In a small bowl, whisk together the peanut butter and the milk until smooth and add it to the onion mixture. Reduce the heat to medium-low and cook for 2–3 minutes or until heated through; season with salt and serve.

❊⟩ NOTE: I like my sauce on the thick side, but if you prefer it thinner, add a bit more milk at the end of the recipe and warm it through.

Red Garlic Sauce

Peruvians use this ultra garlicky sauce liberally on everything from French fries to their famous rotisserie chicken. In Peru and Panama, it's often served over boiled meat stews called *sancochos* (see page 124). This sauce is traditionally prepared in an oval-shaped stone mortar and pestle called a *batán*, but it turns out beautifully in a food processor. It's vital that you peel the tomatoes before processing the sauce (see note) or the texture will be ruined. The sauce is also delicious spooned over poached chicken, fried eggs, or baked potatoes. It even makes a great salsa to eat with tortilla chips or fried plantain chips (pages 182 and 186). Rocotos are large, spicy red peppers with black seeds and are native to Peru. You can find them frozen whole or preserved in jars or cans in most Latin stores. If you can't find them, substitute two hot chiles of your choice. It won't be the same without the rocotos, but it will still be delicious.

Makes 1 ½ cups

5 large plum tomatoes, peeled and roughly chopped (see note)
2 rocoto peppers, seeded and roughly chopped
5 large garlic cloves, minced
½ teaspoon salt, or to taste

Place the tomatoes, peppers, garlic, and salt in the bowl of a food processor; process until smooth.

NOTE: To peel tomatoes, bring 2 cups of water to a rolling boil in a small pot. Fill a medium bowl with iced water. Cut a small X with a sharp knife in the bottom of each tomato. Working in batches, place the tomatoes in the boiling water for 1 minute; immediately remove them with a slotted spoon and place them in the iced water for 1 minute. Their skin should peel off easily.

Peruvian Spicy Onion Salsa (Salsa Criolla)

The month our daughter Alessandra was born was one of the hottest on record, and I remember having very little time to cook and even less energy. Back then, I made many ceviches because they took no time to put together. While the baby napped, Luis and I would sit and enjoy a refreshing and healthy lunch. We ate ceviches so often that the only other person we saw more than our child was our fishmonger. Here, pungent onions are pickled and spiced up in this ubiquitous accoutrement on Peruvian streets. It's used to flavor my Fried Squid Ceviche (page 52), but it also goes on top of sandwiches like the butifarras on page 140 and Peruvian Tamales (page 249). It's also great spooned over poached or grilled seafood or on steaks. Beware! It's highly addictive.

Serves 4–6

> 3 cups very thinly sliced red onion (sliced on the bias)
> 1–2 ají amarillo peppers, seeded, deveined, and very thinly sliced
> ⅓ cup fresh lime juice
> 1 teaspoon red wine vinegar
> Salt and freshly ground black pepper, to taste
> 2 tablespoons extra-virgin olive oil
> ¼ cup chopped cilantro (leaves and tender stems) (optional)

Place the onions in a medium bowl, cover with cold water, and let them soak for 20 minutes. Drain the onions and return them to the bowl; stir in the ají, lime juice, and vinegar; season with salt and pepper. Stir in the olive oil and let it sit at room temperature for at least 10 minutes (up to 3 hours) before serving. Store the salsa in the refrigerator for up to 5 days. Stir in the cilantro (if using) just before serving. ❊

Golf Sauce (Salsa Golf)

Similar to a thousand island dressing but without the lumps, this sweet and savory sauce became a popular condiment at many golf clubs in Latin America in the mid-1900s. Later on, it trickled onto the streets, where it's now used as a topping for items like Costa Rican Tacos Ticos (page 93) and Sausage and French Fry Toss (page 179). Latin Americans put it on hot dogs, French fries, and simple salads called *ensaladas mixtas*. I use it in my recipe for Shrimp Cocktail (page 56). Street vendors often provide this sauce in squirt bottles so that customers can add it liberally to their food. Since I was a little girl, I've found it creamy and addictive. Kept well covered, this sauce will last for up to one week in your refrigerator.

Makes 1 ⅓ cups

> ¾ cup mayonnaise
> ½ cup ketchup
> 2 teaspoons Worcestershire sauce
> 2 teaspoons yellow mustard
> Salt and freshly ground black pepper, to taste

In a small bowl, whisk together the mayonnaise, ketchup, Worcestershire sauce, and mustard; season liberally with salt and pepper. Cover and chill until ready to use. ❄

Spicy Mayonnaise

Street carts in Peru often feature this mayonnaise in squirt bottles to drizzle over French fries (page 175), salchipapas (page 179), and the beef kabobs known as *anticuchos* (page 206). It also happens to make an unorthodox but delicious addition to sandwiches like my "Goat" Sandwich (page 139). If properly covered, it will keep in your refrigerator for up to one week. Ají panca is a long, reddish-brown pepper from Peru. It can be found in paste form in most Latin stores; if you can't find it, use Sriracha sauce instead.

Makes 1 ½ cups

1 cup mayonnaise

½ cup plain yogurt

1 teaspoon Dijon mustard

½ teaspoon ají panca paste or Sriracha sauce, or to taste

½ teaspoon Worcestershire sauce

½ teaspoon minced garlic

Fresh lime juice, to taste

Salt and freshly ground black pepper, to taste

In a medium bowl, combine the mayonnaise, yogurt, mustard, ají, Worcestershire sauce and garlic; season with lime juice, salt, and pepper; chill until ready to serve. ✻

Corn and Avocado Salsa

This is a very pretty salsa filled with colors that remind me of the paper wreaths that adorned Guatemalan streets during the fairs I would go to as a child. Buttery avocado meets crispy onion, and the sweetness of the corn plays off the spicy hint of smoky chiles. This is a great salsa to top tacos, empanadas, and tortas. Try it with Shrimp and Masa Empanadas (page 230), as a topping for sopes, or with chips.

Makes about 3 ½ cups

3 Hass avocados

¾ cup sour cream

½ cup minced red onion

½ cup fresh (or frozen and thawed) corn kernels

1 chipotle chile in adobo, puréed to a paste

1 teaspoon adobo sauce (from the canned chipotles)

½ cup minced cilantro (leaves and tender stems)

Fresh lime juice, to taste

Salt and freshly ground black pepper, to taste

Slice the avocados in half, remove and discard the pits, and scoop out the flesh into a medium bowl; mash the avocados. Add the sour cream, onions, corn, chipotle, adobo sauce, and cilantro; season with lime juice, salt, and pepper. ✻

Sweet Dried Chile Sauce

Toppings are meant to be fun, vibrant, and delicious—just like this sauce. A little bit of this mild and subtly sweet condiment is enough to kick any recipe up a notch. Like many Latin American kids, I started eating chiles almost as soon as I could tie my own shoelaces. However, I wasn't exposed to the variety of dried chiles with chocolate- and raisinlike nuances until I was in my teens and had become interested in cooking. I loved to grind them until they were a fine powder that I could sprinkle on everything. Use this sauce to top huaraches, tacos, sopes, and tostadas. I'll even drizzle it on grilled chicken breasts or fish and use it in place of mayonnaise for many of my sandwiches. This sauce is so delicious that you'll want to eat it with a spoon.

Makes about 2 ½ cups

    2 ancho chiles
    2 guajillo chiles
    2 cups chicken broth, hot
    2 teaspoons extra-virgin olive oil
    1 cup minced onion
    2 large garlic cloves, roughly chopped
    1 teaspoon dried thyme
    ½ teaspoon ground cumin
    ½ teaspoon ground coriander
    ½ teaspoon ground cinnamon
    2 tablespoons brown sugar
    ¼ cup honey
    ½ cup whipping cream
    1 teaspoon salt, or to taste
    ¼ teaspoon freshly ground black pepper, or to taste

Place the chiles in a large bowl and cover with the chicken broth. Let them stand for 10 minutes to reconstitute (use a plate to keep them submerged). Drain the chiles, reserving the broth; seed and devein the chiles and set aside.

In a large skillet with high sides, heat the olive oil over medium-high heat; add the onions and cook until softened, about 2–3 minutes; add the garlic, thyme, cumin, coriander, and cinnamon and cook until fragrant, about 30 seconds. Add the chiles along with the broth and bring the liquid to a boil over high heat; reduce the heat, cover, and simmer for 10 minutes. Cool slightly and transfer to a blender; add the brown sugar, honey, whipping cream, salt and pepper and blend until smooth. Keep warm until ready to use or cover and refrigerate for up to 2 days. Freeze for up to 2 months. ❋

Colombian Hot Sauce (Ají Colombiano)

This is the typical hot sauce served all over Colombia, where it's known as ají. At first sight, it may remind you of Mexican pico de gallo, but the addition of green onions and a hefty splash of vinegar give it a completely different flavor. Some cooks like their ají chunky; others like it smooth. I like mine somewhere in the middle, so I make sure to chop everything very finely. Ají is served on everything from arepitas to empanadas, like my Beef and Potato Empanadas (page 228). It's also great with stews, like my Potato, Chicken, and Corn Stew (page 126); and kabobs, like my Beef Kabobs in Beer Marinade (page 203) and Chicken on a Stick (page 208). I make it often and put it on everything I can. It keeps well in the refrigerator for up to one week. Although I prefer not to, some cooks add chopped hard-boiled eggs to this sauce. If you add them, make sure to eat the sauce within a day.

Makes 2 cups

1½ cups seeded and minced plum tomatoes
⅓ cup minced white onion
⅓ cup thinly sliced green onions
¼ cup minced flat-leaf or Italian parsley (leaves and tender stems)
¼ cup minced cilantro (leaves and tender stems)
¼ cup minced serrano chiles or jalapeños (with seeds), or to taste
¼ cup white wine vinegar
¼ cup fresh lime juice
Salt, to taste

In a nonreactive bowl, combine the tomatoes, white and green onions, parsley, cilantro, chiles, vinegar, and lime juice; season with salt. Let it sit at room temperature for 1 hour in order for the flavors to blend. Refrigerate until ready to serve. ❋

Colombian Rolls (Pandebono)

Dense, sweet, and savory rolls like these are sold street-side in most Colombian cities. They're popular at breakfast time when they're enjoyed with coffee or hot chocolate. The name *pandebono* is said to have originated many years ago when an Italian baker visiting the Valle del Cauca discovered bread so delicious he called it "pan del bono" or "good bread." You'll need two different kinds of flours to make the dough, a yuca starch called *almidón de yuca*, yuca harina, or tapioca starch and the same precooked cornmeal used to make arepas. The two flours combined produce a chewy roll. Pandebono dough is sometimes shaped into wreaths, but it's easier to slather sweet butter on rolls. I like to serve them with soups or stews, like the ones in this book.

Makes 12 rolls

> 1 cup yuca flour
> 1 cup harina pan or masarepa (precooked cornmeal)
> 2 tablespoons sugar
> ½ teaspoon salt
> 3 cups queso fresco or queso blanco
> 2 large eggs, well beaten
> ½ cup milk

Preheat the oven to 425°F and line a baking sheet with parchment paper. In the bowl of a food processor fitted with a metal blade, combine the yuca flour, harina pan, sugar, and salt; pulse for 10 seconds, just to combine. Add the cheese, eggs, and milk and pulse until the dough comes together (because brands of precooked cornmeal may vary slightly, you may have to add a bit more milk to make this hold together. In this case, add it one tablespoon at a time).

Turn the dough out onto a clean surface and knead it just until it forms a ball, about 30 seconds. Transfer the dough to a bowl, cover it with a towel, and let it rest for 10 minutes.

Turn the dough onto a lightly floured surface and form it into a 12 × 1½-inch log. Slice the log into 12 pieces (each roughly 1 inch thick). Roll each piece of dough into a ball (you may have to press it together a bit to help the dough hold its shape). Place the balls 3 inches apart on the prepared baking sheet and flatten them slightly with your hand (they'll

Condiments, Toppings, & Side Dishes

still be round but the tops will be tapered a bit). Bake them for approximately 20–25 minutes or until slightly golden and cooked through (the bottoms should be crispy and slightly browned). Serve immediately.

❋} NOTE: You can make the dough and shape the rolls up to 2 hours before they're baked. After placing them on the prepared baking sheets, cover lightly with plastic wrap, and refrigerate; add about 5–8 minutes to the baking time. Serve immediately.

Yucatán Pickled Onions (Cebollas Encurtidas Yucatecas)

This is the refreshing accoutrement of choice for spicy chicken, called tinga (page 76), and *cochinita pibil*, a slow-roasted pork dish. The sour intonations of the onions counteract the heat in any dish. This is a very pretty condiment because the onions become a light lilac color as they macerate. When refrigerated, it keeps for up to a week, but since you can use it as a topping for sopes, tacos, or tostadas or spicy grilled chicken, shrimp, or scallops, you'll find that it won't last that long.

Makes 2 cups

3 cups very thinly sliced red onion
1 large garlic clove, peeled and left whole
½ cup fresh orange juice
⅓ cup apple cider vinegar
¼ cup fresh lemon juice
1 teaspoon salt
2 sprigs fresh thyme (or ½ teaspoon dried)
¼ teaspoon allspice berries
¼ teaspoon black peppercorns

Fill a large bowl with iced water. Place the onions in a bowl and cover them with boiling water. Let them sit for 1 minute; drain. Plunge them into the iced water; let them sit for 3 minutes; drain. In a medium bowl, combine the onions, garlic, orange juice, vinegar, lemon juice, salt, thyme, allspice, and peppercorns; cover well and chill for at least 8 hours or overnight. ❋

Ecuadorian Potato, Annatto, and Cheese Cakes (Llapingachos) with Onion Relish

Molten cheese oozes from the centers of these potato cakes like hot lava. Sold at marketplaces and from roadside eateries in Ecuador, they're traditionally served with an onion relish and a peanut sauce. The result is a striking collision of contrasts—soft and crisp and savory, sweet, and sour—that land deliciously on the palate. Llapingachos are often part of a main course platter that includes avocados, tomatoes, fried eggs, and sausages. They pair very nicely with grilled meats and with my Beef Skewers Bathed in Orange and Annatto (page 202). These delicate cakes must be sautéed in very little oil; if you use too much, they'll fall apart. Chilling them before cooking helps them hold their shape.

Makes 10

- 2 tablespoons plus 2 teaspoons vegetable oil, divided
- ½ cup minced white onion
- 1 teaspoon annatto (achiote) powder
- 2 pounds russet potatoes, boiled until tender, peeled and mashed until smooth
- 1 teaspoon salt, or more to taste
- 4 ounces grated Muenster cheese
- 2 cups very thinly sliced red onion
- 4 plum tomatoes, seeded and cut lengthwise into thin strips (about 1 cup)
- 2 tablespoons minced cilantro (leaves and tender stems)
- Fresh lemon juice, to taste
- 2 Hass avocados
- Ecuadorian Peanut Sauce (page 273)

Line a baking sheet with parchment paper. In a small skillet, heat 2 tablespoons of the oil over medium heat; add the onions and the annatto powder and cook, stirring, until the onions are softened, about 3 minutes; set aside to cool.

In a large bowl, combine the onions, salt, and potatoes and knead until the potatoes have a uniform, golden color. Divide the mixture into 10 equal pieces (a bit over ⅓ cup each); roll each into a ball. Working with one ball at a time, make an indentation in the center of the ball with your thumb and place about 1 tablespoon of the cheese in it; roll the potatoes back into a ball and flatten it into a patty roughly 2½ inches wide by ½ inch tall, making sure the cheese is secure in the middle (or it will seep and burn as the potatoes cook); place it on the prepared baking sheet. Repeat with the remaining ingredients and chill, uncovered in the refrigerator for at least 1 hour (but no more than 2).

In the meantime, make the onion relish: in a medium bowl, combine the red onion, tomatoes, cilantro, and lemon juice; season with salt, to taste and chill until ready to use.

Heat a nonstick pan over medium to medium-high heat and brush it very lightly with some of the remaining oil. Working in batches, add the patties and cook on each side for 2–3 minutes or until golden (flip them carefully; they can break easily); transfer to a serving platter. Brush the pan with another light coating of oil and cook the rest of the patties, as directed above.

Slice the avocados in half and remove and discard the pits. Scoop out the flesh, chop it up, and stir it into the relish. Serve immediately or keep them warm in a 250°F oven for up to 30 minutes before serving. Top with the relish. Serve with the peanut sauce on the side. ❊

Refried Black Beans
(Frijoles Negros y Volteados)

While at college in Massachusetts, I introduced my friends to this Central American version of refried beans, in which black bean purée is first strained to remove the skins of the beans, and then cooked until thickened. I would spread the beans on baguette slices with a little bit of cream cheese, and they'd gobble them up. Unlike the Traditional Mexican Refried Beans on page 286, these are always lump free. They're used to stuff pupusas, baleadas, quesadillas, and the Plantain and Bean Fritters on page 178. In Guatemala, *volteados* means "tossed," and it refers to the fact that if allowed to thicken even further, the beans become a paste that can be tossed easily into a pan to form a loaf, called a *maleta*. I've provide instructions on how to make the loaf below. You can always use canned refried beans for any of the recipes that call for beans in this book, but these are truly worth the time and effort that goes into making them.

Makes 3 ½ cups (serves 6–8)

> 1 pound black beans, soaked for at least 8 hours or overnight
>   (or use the quick-soaking method on page 22)
> 3 large garlic cloves, peeled and left whole
> 1 medium white onion, peeled and halved
> 1 bay leaf
> 2 teaspoons salt, or to taste
> ¼ cup lard or vegetable oil (plus 1 tablespoon if making
>   frijoles volteados)

Drain the presoaked beans and combine them with the garlic, onion, and bay leaf in a large pot. Add cold water to cover the beans by 2 inches (about 8 cups—but the size of your pot will dictate how much water you need). Bring the beans to a boil over medium-high heat; cover, reduce the heat to low, and simmer very slowly for 1–1½ hours or until the beans are fork-tender, adding more water as needed. Add the salt and allow the beans to cool slightly, about 20 minutes; drain the beans, reserve the cooking liquid, and discard the bay leaf.

Working in batches, purée the beans, garlic, and onion in a blender until smooth, adding as much of the reserved cooking liquid as needed to help the motor run (the texture will be like that of a thick soup or very loose mashed potatoes). Strain the beans through a sieve into a bowl pressing them down, and discard the solids.

Heat the ¼ cup of lard in a large nonstick pan over medium heat; add the puréed bean mixture all at once(careful, it will spatter) and cook, stirring, until they come to a boil, about 3–4 minutes. Reduce the heat and simmer (the beans should bubble gently), stirring occasionally, until they thicken into a paste with the consistency of thick mashed potatoes (anywhere from 30 to 40 minutes, depending on how much liquid you added during the blending process). Cool, cover, and chill until you're ready to use (they'll keep for up to 3 days in the refrigerator). Reheat them before using.

To make frijoles volteados: Place the remaining tablespoon of the lard into a large nonstick pan (see note) set over medium heat. Add the refried beans and cook, stirring, until they are very thick (like playdough) and slide easily from the bottom of the pan (anywhere from 5 to 10 minutes). Hold the pan by the handle with both hands. Flip the beans over a few times in the frying pan—much in the same manner that you would flip a pancake without a spatula—until the beans form an oblong loaf (you can also divide the beans into portions and flip them into smaller mounds). Slide the bean loaf onto a plate and serve. If you're not comfortable flipping the beans in the pan, press the beans together with a rubber spatula against the side of the pan until you form an oblong loaf.

*} NOTE: Don't attempt to make volteados in other than a nonstick pan or they'll stick and burn.

Traditional Mexican Refried Beans

These are classic refried beans: simple, comforting, absolutely delicious, and the accoutrement of choice for many Mexican street foods. I like mine on the thicker side, in a spreadable consistency that lends itself to be slathered with crema on steaming-hot tortillas. If desired, thin them by adding a bit more liquid. If you've only ever had canned refried beans or those served in chain restaurants, you'll be pleasantly surprised by the intense flavor and deep succulence that the real version has to offer. Beans can be bland if not seasoned properly, so be sure to season the beans with a generous amount of salt while they're frying. Use these beans to top tostadas and sopes and to fill quesadillas. I love to top these beans with cheese, crema, cilantro, and Jalapeños, Onions, and Carrots in Escabeche (page 266) and eat them with tortilla chips.

Serves 8

> 1 pound pinto beans, picked over for stones or other debris
> ¼ large white onion plus ½ cup minced onion
> 1 bay leaf
> 1 large garlic clove, peeled and left whole
> ¼ cup lard or vegetable oil
> 1½ teaspoons salt, or to taste

Place the beans in a large bowl; cover with cold water. Soak them for 8 hours or overnight (or use the quick-soaking method on page 22). Drain the beans and place them in a large Dutch oven. Add the onion quarter, bay leaf, and garlic; cover with cold water by 2½ inches (about 8 cups, but it will depend on the size of your pot). Bring the beans to a boil over medium-high heat; cover, reduce the heat, and simmer for 1–1½ hours or until beans are tender (adding more water if needed). Remove from the heat; reserve 2 cups of the cooking liquid and drain the beans (see note). Discard the bay leaf and reserve the onions and garlic.

In a large skillet, heat the lard over medium-high heat. Add the minced onions and cook until they begin to turn a golden color, about 2 minutes. Add the beans, the reserved onions and garlic, and the salt; using a potato masher, mash the beans to a consistency of lumpy mashed potatoes, adding the reserved liquid a little bit at a time as needed to help you mash them. Heat well and serve.

❋} NOTE: If you're making the beans ahead of time, reserve an additional cup of cooking liquid to thin them out when you reheat them (or add water).

Beef Picadillo

Picadillo means "minced mixture," and versions of this ground beef mélange are found all over Latin America. This one is similar to one I learned to make as a newlywed, and it features sweet and spicy undertones. It's what I use to fill my Beef Taquitos (page 97), but you can also use it to stuff Chiles Rellenos (page 165) and Stuffed Potato Balls (page 168), or to top sopes (page 65). The ingredient list is long but the recipe is easy. Resist the urge to drain the fat from the ground beef here; it solidifies when chilled and when used as a filling for tortillas or chiles will prevent the filling from falling apart during frying. (Also, if you drain the fat, you'll drain off the spices with it.) Be sure to prepare the ground beef at least two hours before you plan to use it. It can be frozen for up to two months. Thaw it in the refrigerator overnight and reheat it on the stove or in the microwave on HIGH until it's hot. Leftovers are delicious over steamed rice or simply wrapped in warm tortillas.

Makes 3 cups

2 tablespoons extra-virgin olive oil
2 tablespoons unsalted butter
1 pound ground chuck
1 cup minced yellow onion
1 cup minced cabbage
½ cup minced carrot
½ cup minced green beans
½ cup minced red bell pepper
2 bay leaves
2 teaspoons dried thyme
1½ teaspoons salt
¼ teaspoon freshly ground black pepper
½ cup minced plum tomatoes
¼ cup ketchup
¼ cup tomato paste

In a large skillet, heat the oil and butter over medium-high heat; add the beef, onions, cabbage, carrot, green beans, and bell pepper; cook for 2 minutes, stirring to combine and breaking down the beef with a spoon. Add the bay leaves, thyme, salt, and pepper; cook until the beef is no longer pink, about 2–3 minutes. Add the tomatoes, ketchup, and tomato paste; stir well and bring to a boil; cover, reduce the heat to a simmer, and cook for 15–20 minutes or until all of the vegetables are tender. Uncover and cook until the liquid has reduced and thickened, about 2–3 minutes (the mixture will appear almost dry). Discard the bay leaves. Serve hot if you're eating it immediately; or if you're using it as part of another recipe, chill it for at least 2 hours or up to overnight. ❊

Central American Red Beans
and Rice (Gallo Pinto)

Central American Red Beans and Rice (Gallo Pinto)

Gallo pinto, a popular side dish sold on Nicaraguan and Costa Rican streets, means "red rooster." Tey, my Nicaraguan sister-in-law, taught me to sauté the beans until they begin to pop and get slightly toasted, giving the dish a nutty flavor. Worcestershire sauce is a very popular ingredient in Latin America, but it's so difficult to pronounce that it's simply called *salsa inglesa*, or English sauce. Here, it's used to provide a tangy sweetness, a piquant touch, and a burst of color. This is a great dish to make with leftover white rice from previous meals.

Serves 6–8

- 2½ tablespoons vegetable oil
- ½ cup minced white onion
- ½ cup minced red bell pepper
- 2 large garlic cloves, minced
- 3 cups cooked dark red kidney beans (or two 16-ounce cans, drained)
- 3½ cups cooked white rice
- ⅓ cup plus 2 tablespoons Worcestershire Sauce
- ½ cup chicken broth or water
- Salt and freshly ground black pepper, to taste

In a large skillet with high sides, heat the oil over medium-high heat; add the onions and bell peppers and sauté until soft, about 2–3 minutes. Stir in the garlic and cook until fragrant, about 30 seconds. Reduce the heat to medium and add the beans, tossing them as they cook for 5–6 minutes—the beans will split open. Add the rice, Worcestershire sauce, and broth; stir to coat the rice well until it's uniformly colored (you shouldn't have any white grains remaining). Season with salt and pepper; reduce the heat and cook for 2–3 minutes. Serve hot. ❈

Mexican Rice (Sopa Seca de Arroz)

This is perhaps the most recognizable Latin American side dish in the United States, and it's a favorite way to make rice throughout Mexico. Truth be told, it's name in Spanish, literally translates into "dry soup" and it's so given because it's flavored with exactly the same ingredients as rice soup would be, but here, the grains are allowed to absorb all of the liquid. This is a very easy recipe to follow and one of my favorites to pair with most of the food in this book. Recipes for pilaf-style rice dishes were brought over by the Spaniards, who learned the technique from the Persians. Today, rice pilafs abound in Latin America. To make a pilaf, the rice is always sautéed in some kind of fat before any liquid is added. The end result is a tasty, fluffy rice. I use lard, but feel free to use butter or vegetable oil if you prefer. Here the rice should turn a golden color, which adds a toasty flavor to the finished dish. But watch it carefully so it doesn't burn during this stage. The liquid used here is a mixture of broth and spicy sofrito that adds flavor and spiciness to the finished dish. I like this so much that I often make a whole meal of it by serving it in bowls with slightly runny fried eggs on top. It can be prepared ahead of time and reheated easily in the microwave.

Serves 6–8

- 1 (14.5-ounce) can whole fire-roasted tomatoes
- 2 large garlic cloves, peeled and left whole
- ½ teaspoon ground coriander
- ½ teaspoon ground cumin
- 1 serrano chile (seeded and deveined, if less heat is desired), roughly chopped
- 1 teaspoon salt
- ¼ teaspoon freshly ground black pepper
- 2 tablespoons melted lard (or vegetable oil)
- 1 cup minced yellow onion
- 1 cup minced celery
- 1½ cups converted long-grain rice
- 2 roasted poblano peppers, peeled, seeded, deveined, and chopped into ½-inch pieces
- 1½ cups chicken broth
- ¼ cup sliced green onions

In a blender, combine the tomatoes, garlic, coriander, cumin, serrano chile, salt, and pepper; blend for 1 minute or until smooth.

In a medium skillet with high sides and a tight-fitting lid, melt the lard over medium-high heat; add the onions and celery and cook, stirring often, until soft, about 2–3 minutes. Add the rice and stir to coat with the lard; continue stirring and toasting until the rice turns golden, about 2–3 minutes. Add the poblanos and the blended vegetables (the mixture will splatter a little bit) and continue stirring for 2 minutes. Add the chicken broth and stir briefly. Bring the liquid to a boil; cover, reduce the heat to low, and simmer until all the liquid has been absorbed, about 20 minutes. Fluff the rice with a fork, transfer to a platter, and garnish with green onions; serve immediately. ✳

SWEETS, CANDY, & ICE CREAM

My husband and I were high school sweethearts, and for several years while we were in college we dated long distance. I've heard it said that absence makes the heart grow fonder, and in our case, distance certainly made the time we spent together much sweeter. That and the myriad desserts we would share every time we got together.

One day when he was visiting me at my parent's home, we heard a man outside on the street chanting, "Vendo corbatas!" ("I sell ties!") I turned to my then boyfriend and asked him if he had a couple of dollars to spare, that I was going to go buy two ties. He looked perplexed, but he just handed me a few bills without asking me a single question. When I walked back into my house carrying my goodies, he burst out laughing. What I had purchased were two giant pieces of fried dough, each tied into a knot, just like a man's necktie. They were flaky, warm, and covered in gooey honey. He, of course, had imagined that I had rushed out to get him a fashion accessory, and later he confessed that he thought it very strange that I would get so excited about ties that only cost a dollar a piece. That day I fell in love with him all over again.

If you've never chewed on a piece of sugarcane, you've missed out on an unforgettable experience. In coastal areas of Latin America, for instance, where sugarcane abounds, it's sold for a few cents apiece. As you gnaw at the woody fibers, little bursts of sweet juice explode in your mouth. In Latin America, dessert can mean something different depending on whether you're strolling by in a city park or walking along the beach. On the streets, sweet desserts range from fried dough coated in white grains of sugar, to cookies of all different kinds, to a virtual rainbow of colorful frozen treats. Latin America is like a giant Sugarland, where the sweet tooth is satiated only one dessert at a time.

Lollipops are a huge deal there as they are anywhere where children abound, from the multicolored, cone-shaped *pirulís*, to the giant, round *chupetes* that tint your whole mouth red when you lick them. There are also the miniature anise-flavored candies called *anicillos* that you can purchase by the bagful. I expressly remember eating *coloricos*, balls made of different layers of colored candy, that made curious kids' fingers sticky every time they'd pull them out of their mouths to see what color the candies turned into next. You'll also find street vendors selling candies made out of coffee, caramels that taste like watermelon, and sweet lollipops spiked with chile. Of course, Latin America is the land of the gum tree, and bubble gum often finds its way into the pockets of children. Fruits are transformed into *ates* or *dulces de fruta*—enormous blocks of

An ice cream and cotton candy cart in Buenos Aires, Argentina.

fruit-flavored fudge that can be cut into smaller squares so that they can be nibbled on as you walk. Coconut sweets, called *cocadas*, are plentiful as well; some are soft and chewy, while others are granular and dense.

Sticky, gooey milk caramel, called dulce de leche, cajeta, or *arequipe* depending on where you are, is sometimes sold in wooden boxes so you can eat it just as it is with a spoon; other times it's stuffed between two giant rice paper wafers so you can nibble on them and enjoy them melting slowly on your tongue. Dulce de leche is also sandwiched between cookies called *alfajores*, which are so tender that they disintegrate in your mouth as soon as you bite into them, coating your palate with a mixture of sweet pulverized crumbs and sticky goodness.

Custards and puddings are extremely popular on the streets as well. Some are made with sweet milk and cornstarch, others are thickened with rice or tapioca pearls, and yet others are tinted yellow with the oils of egg yolks and perfumed with the fragrance of rum.

Icy desserts are always a welcome sight, especially on the hot days of summer when shady corners are scarce and the wind has gone to sleep. *Granizadas*, shaved ice that street vendors flavor to order with sweetened syrups, turning it a multiplicity of colors, are very popular. In places like Costa Rica and Colombia, shaved ice is topped with sweetened condensed milk and cocoa or ground coffee and eaten with wooden spoons.

Meringues or *turrones* are found throughout the Latin continent, sometimes made to be soft and shiny so that you can eat them out of a cup, or baked into beautiful clouds of sugary goodness that can be bitten off in pieces. I still remember eating chocolate-dipped, meringue-filled ice cream cones that tasted like s'mores.

Ice cream is in a category all of its own. Whether it's called *nieve*, *mantecado*, or *helado*, you'll find the usual flavors—chocolate, vanilla, and strawberry—but there are also tropical fruit flavors, like pineapple, *mamey*, tamarind, banana, mango, guava, passion fruit, and coconut. Other tempting flavors include coffee, rice milk, rum and raisins, dulce de leche, and Mexican chocolate—and that's just the tip of the iceberg. Among my favorite flavors are *zapote*, soursop, corn, and avocado. If it can be churned, you can bet that it's an ice cream flavor somewhere in Latin America.

Life's not always a treat, but on the streets, you can sweeten almost any day. On Latin American streets, desserts are popular around the clock. I've put together a selection of some of the most famous offerings you'll find there. Whether you are in Mexico City or São Paulo, you can experience moments of sweet surrender. Here's hoping that these recipes will make your life sweeter, one dessert at a time.

Coconut Macaroons (Cocadas)

These chewy candies are sold on the streets of virtually every country in Latin America. The classic, easy mix, drop, and bake recipe is popular with kids of all ages. These macaroons are drizzled with white chocolate; but slivered almonds, lime zest, or raisins make excellent additions. Serve them with tropical fruit sorbets. (For extra fun, grownups may want to add a splash of rum!) Yum!

Makes 20–22 macaroons

> 2⅔ cups lightly packed shredded sweetened coconut
> ¾ cup sweetened condensed milk
> 1 large egg, lightly beaten
> ¼ teaspoon almond extract
> 4 ounces white chocolate (optional)

Preheat the oven to 325°F and line 2 large cookie sheets with parchment paper. In a medium bowl, combine the coconut, condensed milk, egg, and almond extract. Let it rest for 5 minutes for the coconut to absorb the liquid. Drop the mixture by heaping tablespoonfuls onto the prepared cookie sheets and bake for 20–22 minutes or until they are dry and begin to brown on top. Remove them from the oven and cool for 5 minutes before transferring to a rack to cool completely.

If you're using the chocolate, place it in a double boiler over barely simmering water and stir until it's melted, about 2–3 minutes (or place the chocolate in a microwave-safe bowl and microwave on HIGH for 30-second intervals, stirring after each one, until melted). Drizzle the chocolate on the cookies; allow the chocolate to harden before serving. These will stay fresh in an airtight container (at room temperature) for several days. ❊

Brazilian Chocolate Candies (Brigadeiros)

Brazilian Chocolate Candies (Brigadeiros)

I don't know about you, but I go through days of intense chocolate cravings, and these sweet, sticky, and soft chocolate morsels always hit the spot. They're a bit chewy, very chocolaty, and completely luscious. Brigadeiros are the national candies of Brazil, and they're sold on streets and in fancy candy stores alike. My Brazilian friends tell me that they're the candy of choice for children's birthday parties, and I can see why: these pretty, miniature confections are always bound to make people happy— big or small. There are white chocolate variations made with nuts, like pistachios, or coconut, but this is the classic recipe. Rolling the candies in butter helps the sprinkles stick to the surface of the brigadeiros, creating the candies' signature look. Brigadeiros will stay soft and chewy for up to one week if kept in an airtight container, but they can be stored for up to three weeks. Keep in mind, though, that the longer they're stored, the grainier their texture will become.

Makes 32–34 candies

> 1 (14-ounce) can sweetened condensed milk
> ½ cup cocoa powder, spooned into cup, then leveled
> 3 tablespoons unsalted butter at room temperature, divided
> ¾–1 cup chocolate sprinkles (see note)
> Petit four paper cups (see note)

Place the condensed milk in a medium saucepan over low heat and stir to loosen, about 1 minute. Gradually sift the cocoa powder into the condensed milk, stirring well between additions (it will take about 5 minutes to incorporate it all); add 1 tablespoon of the butter, stirring until smooth. Increase the heat to medium; continue cooking, stirring constantly and making sure to scrape the bottom and sides of the pan, until the mixture comes to a boil, about 1–2 minutes (be careful not to burn it). Immediately reduce the heat to low and cook, stirring, until the mixture thickens to the consistency of fudge and begins to pull away from the sides and the bottom of the pan, about 4 minutes.

Working quickly, pour the chocolate mixture onto an ungreased baking sheet or into a large bowl and cool completely, about 45 minutes (the mixture will thicken into a chewy consistency). Using your hands, roll the cooled chocolate into balls by the teaspoonful (it helps to coat the spoon with cooking spray so that the candy doesn't stick to it). Rub some butter between the palms of your hands and roll the balls again to coat them with the butter. Roll the brigadeiros into the sprinkles to coat and place each in a paper cup. Let sit at room temperature for 1 hour before storing them in airtight containers.

❃} NOTE: Brigadeiros may also be rolled in chopped pistachios, sugar, or cocoa.
Petit fours paper cups are smaller than cupcake baking paper cups. If you can't find them, store the brigadeiros between layers of parchment paper (so they won't stick to each other).

Rice Pudding (Arroz con Leche)

Sweet, thick, and gooey rice pudding is scented with *canela de Celaya* (Ceylon cinnamon)—colloquially known as Mexican cinnamon—in one of the most comforting desserts on the Latin street food scene. Whether it's sold in tiny plastic cups with disposable spoons to go or served warm in ceramic mugs, rice pudding always hits the spot. I make mine with short-grain rice because it yields the creamiest consistency. I always find it hard to resist when it's still warm; the sweet aroma is so enticing that it makes waiting for it to cool feel like an eternity. Some cooks add raisins, but when it comes to this dessert, I'm a purist. I like mine on the thick side, but feel free to add a splash of milk or two if you prefer it thinner.

Serves 6

1 cup short-grain rice (such as Arborio or Bomba)
3½ cups whole milk, or more, to taste
1 stick Mexican cinnamon (canela)
½ cup sugar, or to taste

In a medium pot over medium heat, combine the rice, 3 cups of the milk, and the cinnamon. Cook for 4–5 minutes or until it comes to a simmer (being careful not to let it boil or it will boil over). Reduce the heat to low and cook, stirring constantly, until the pudding has thickened and the rice has softened, about 15 minutes. Remove from the heat. Add the sugar and the rest of the milk, stirring to combine. Let it cool for 20 minutes; discard the cinnamon stick. Cover and chill for at least 1 hour (up to 2 days) before serving. ❃

Candied Yams (Camotes Enmielados)

You'll find different interpretations of these sweet and sticky sweet potatoes all over the continent, but in Mexico, they're covered in syrup and drenched in cream. Although people often confuse sweet potatoes and yams, they are not the same thing. Popular in Latin America, true yams (*camotes* or *batatas*) are not cultivated in the United States, but sweet potatoes make a delicious substitute in this recipe. This dessert is sweetened with *piloncillo* or *panela*, unrefined cane sugar that is molded into cones. It's easy to find in any Latin grocery store, but in a pinch use dark brown sugar instead.

Serves 8

> 2 pounds piloncillo or panela
> 5 cups water
> 2 sticks Mexican cinnamon (canela)
> 5 whole cloves
> 6 large sweet potatoes or yams (about 3½ pounds),
>   peeled and cut into large chunks
> 1 cup Mexican crema or crème fraîche (optional)

In a large Dutch oven over medium-high heat, combine the piloncillo and water, stirring and breaking up the piloncillo until it's dissolved; stir in the cinnamon and cloves. Bring the syrup to a boil; reduce the heat to medium and cook until it is reduced by one-third, about 15–20 minutes. Add the sweet potatoes and cook until tender and the syrup has thickened and coats them well, about 25–28 minutes. Discard the cinnamon. Cool the potatoes for 30 minutes. Serve warm, drizzled with crema (if using). Refrigerate any leftovers and eat within 2 weeks, reheated. ❊

Dulce de Leche Sandwich Cookies (Alfajores)

Dulce de Leche Sandwich Cookies (Alfajores)

My late uncle Mirko had the sweetest tooth of anyone I've ever known and a boisterous laugh that I miss to this day. Back in the seventies, he was a frequent visitor to my parents' house. I simply adored him. He would often arrive carrying a bag of these dainty, sweet Argentinean cookies known as alfajores: two cookies stuffed with gooey milk caramel called dulce de leche. These pretty cookies are sold on the streets of many South American cities. In recent years, alfajores have become very trendy, moving from the streets into city cafés that specialize in this kind of cookie. You'll find endless varieties: some are stuffed with jams and gourmet jellies; others are coated in white, milk, or dark chocolate. However, my favorite is still this classic version. A hefty addition of cornstarch to the shortbread pastry produces a tender texture. When you bite into them, the pastry melts in your mouth and the caramel coats your palate. For me, eating an *alfajor* is like a religious experience because it always lifts my spirit to new heights. Prepared dulce de leche is available in most supermarkets and gourmet stores. Buy an extra jar because you'll want to eat it up with a spoon when nobody's watching.

Makes 16 cookies

- 1 cup all-purpose flour
- 1 cup cornstarch
- 1 teaspoon baking powder
- ⅛ teaspoon salt
- ½ cup (1 stick) unsalted butter, at room temperature
- ¾ cup sugar
- 1 large egg
- 1 large egg yolk
- 1 tablespoon cognac or brandy
- 1 teaspoon vanilla
- 2¼ cups prepared dulce de leche
- 1 cup grated coconut

Sift the flour, cornstarch, baking powder, and salt into a large bowl; set aside. Using an electric mixer, beat the butter and the sugar on high speed until creamy, about 2 minutes. With the mixer on low speed, add

To assemble the alfajores: Spread the dulce de leche evenly on the bottom of a cookie.

Place another cookie, bottom side down, on top, and spread a bit of the dulce de leche along the edge of the cookie.

Roll the edge in the grated coconut.

the egg, egg yolk, cognac, and vanilla; beat just until combined, about 1 minute (stopping once or twice to scrape the sides of the bowl). Add the flour mixture in batches, mixing at low speed, just until the dough comes together (stopping to scrape the sides of the bowl as needed). Do not overmix. Wrap the dough in plastic wrap and chill it for at least 4 hours (or overnight).

Line two baking sheets with parchment paper. Preheat the oven to 350°F. Remove the dough from the refrigerator and let it sit at room temperature until soft enough to roll out, about 10 minutes. On a lightly floured surface, roll out the dough to ⅛-inch thickness. With a 2½-inch round cookie cutter, cut out 32 rounds (rerolling the dough as needed) (see note). Transfer the rounds to the prepared baking sheets and bake for 15–18 minutes or until the edges turn lightly golden. Cool the cookies for 1 minute on the sheets before transferring to cooling racks; cool completely.

Spread out the coconut on a shallow plate; set aside. Evenly spread 1 tablespoon of the dulce de leche onto the bottom of a cookie; top with another cookie and press gently to join. Repeat until all the cookies are filled. Using a spatula spread a bit of dulce de leche along the outer edges of the cookies and roll the edges into the grated coconut. Eat the alfajores within 2 days or freeze for up to 2 months; thaw, uncovered, at room temperature before serving.

⁂} NOTE: You can make these any size you wish. Adjust the baking time accordingly.

Sweets, Candy, & Ice Cream

Sesame Seed Cookies (Champurradas)

These buttery cookies are sold on the streets of Guatemala, where they often become breakfast along with a cup of coffee. They are traditionally made with lard, but I find them to be even more delicate when prepared with fresh butter. You'll find these sold in a variety of sizes, but I prefer them small. Guatemalans eat these cookies alone, smothered in jam, or as a sweet complement to Refried Black Beans (page 284). This is one of my husband's favorite recipes because they remind him of leisurely childhood *meriendas* (snack times) and bring back happy memories.

Makes 12 cookies

> 4 cups all-purpose flour, plus more for shaping the dough
> 1 tablespoon baking powder
> Pinch salt
> 13 tablespoons butter, at room temperature, or lard
> ¾ cup sugar
> 2 large eggs
> 2 teaspoons sesame seeds

Sift the flour, baking powder, and salt into a large bowl; set aside. Using an electric mixer, cream the butter and the sugar until light and fluffy, about 2 minutes, stopping occasionally to scrape the sides of the bowl. Add the eggs, beating until they are fully incorporated, about 2 minutes, stopping halfway through to scrape the side of the bowl. With the mixer on low speed, gradually add the dry ingredients. Increase the speed to medium and beat just until the dough holds together, about 20–30 seconds. Turn the dough out onto a clean surface and gather it into a ball; place it back in the bowl; cover and chill for 30 minutes.

Preheat the oven to 350°F. Place the oven racks at the upper and lower middle positions. Line two large baking sheets with parchment paper. Divide the dough into 12 equal parts (not quite ¼ cup each) and shape them into balls. Place them 4 inches apart on the prepared sheets. Using your hands or a large plate dipped in flour lightly press down each ball until it's 5 inches wide and ⅙ inch thick. Sprinkle the tops with sesame seeds and bake, reversing the position of the baking sheets midway through, for 20–22 minutes or until they turn lightly golden. Cool the cookies on the baking sheet for 1 minute before transferring to a cooling rack. Cool them completely. ❋

Orange-Scented Fried Dough (Nuégados)

My favorite place in the world is the colonial city of Antigua, Guatemala, where pebbled streets, ancient ruins, old churches, and houses with brightly colored walls welcome hordes of tourists each year. It's a short ride away from Guatemala City, and in my youth I often went there to have lunch and to visit old church ruins. On our way out of the city, we would always stop in a little shop called Casa de Doña María Gordillo. The family business was founded in 1872 by a cloistered nun and a friend. It specializes in *dulces típicos* (typical candies) such as these sweet fried dough balls (like doughnut holes) perfumed with the essence of oranges. There was nowhere to sit down and eat them; you simply stopped, bought a box of candies, and ate them on the road. For many years, the original recipe was a well-guarded secret kept behind convent walls. Today, it is still closely guarded. This is my lose interpretation of their recipe, based on how I remember them. For a lighter taste, fry the nuégados in oil instead of the traditional lard. Like all fried dough, these are best enjoyed the day they're made.

Makes 45–50 nuégados

3¾ cups all-purpose flour (plus more for dusting surface
    during kneading)
1 teaspoon baking powder
½ teaspoon salt
4 large eggs
8 large egg yolks
¼ cup fresh orange juice
Vegetable oil for frying
12 cups sifted confectioners' sugar
⅔ cup water
⅔ cup light corn syrup
1 teaspoon vanilla extract
¼ teaspoon orange extract

Sweets, Candy, & Ice Cream

Fit two large baking pans with metal cooling racks; set aside. Place the flour directly on a clean counter; whisk in the baking powder and salt until combined. With your fingers, make a large well in the center. In a medium bowl, whisk together the eggs, egg yolks, and orange juice and pour this into the middle of the well. Using a fork, start incorporating the flour into the wet ingredients (as if to make pasta) by bringing the flour from the inner walls of the well into the center without breaking the well. When the dough begins to come together, knead it gently with your fingers, incorporating all of the flour until it forms a soft, smooth ball; knead an additional 1–2 minutes (adding more flour, if needed, to prevent the dough from sticking to the work surface; see note). Cover the dough with a clean towel and let it rest for 15 minutes.

With floured hands, roll the dough into ¾-inch balls. In a large skillet with high sides, heat 2–3 inches of oil to 360°F (or if using a deep fryer, follow manufacturer's instructions). Working in batches, drop the balls of dough into the oil and fry them, turning often, until they are lightly golden, about 2–3 minutes. Transfer them to the prepared racks to drain. When they are all fried, set them aside and make the glaze.

In a large heat-proof bowl, combine the confectioners' sugar, water, corn syrup, vanilla, and orange extract; set the bowl over a pan of barely simmering water and, using a wooden spoon, stir the glaze until smooth; remove from the heat and cool for 2–3 minutes or until the glaze is thick enough to coat the balls.

Working in batches, drop the balls in the glaze, turning to coat them well; using a spoon, place them back on the racks (if the glaze begins to harden, place the bowl over the warm water to soften). Allow them to dry for 1 hour before storing them in airtight containers.

❊⟩ NOTE: If the day is humid or rainy, the dough may need more flour; add only enough to produce smooth dough.

Giant Meringues (Espumillas)

Giant Meringues (Espumillas)

Have you ever wanted to eat a cloud? As a child, I'd find myself looking at the shapes of pillowy white clouds against the indigo Guatemalan skies and wondering if they tasted like these sweet morsels. Meringues are extremely popular throughout Latin America, and you'll find them sold in a variety of sizes and colors. Recipes for meringues were brought to the New World by the Spaniards during the colonial period, at a time when nuns in convents were in charge of producing most of the sweets and sugar was one of the few indulgences allowed them. These are large ones—crispy on the outside, a bit chewy in the middle. The addition of cream of tartar is crucial, particularly in Latin countries where high humidity makes meringues weep. Cream of tartar also stabilizes the egg whites, allowing them to whip properly. In Guatemala and El Salvador these are sometimes filled with whipped cream. Adding one or two drops of food coloring gives them a pastel hue. For a great dessert, serve these with ice cream and berries.

Makes 10–12 meringues

> 4 large egg whites, at room temperature (see note)
> 1 teaspoon cream of tartar
> 1½ cups granulated sugar

Preheat the oven to 225°F. Line two large baking sheets with parchment paper. In a large, clean glass or copper bowl, place the egg whites and the cream of tartar; using an electric mixer, beat on high speed until frothy (about 30 seconds). With the mixer on high speed, gradually add the sugar, beating until all of the sugar has been incorporated and the meringue forms stiff, shiny peaks, about 4 minutes total.

Drop the mixture by heaping ⅓–½ cupfuls on the prepared sheets. Bake on the middle rack of the oven for 20 minutes; turn the oven off and leave the meringues in the oven for 1 hour or until dry. Remove them from the oven and cool completely on the baking sheets before transferring to tins. They'll keep for about 1 week in a dry place.

❧ NOTE: Egg whites beat best and reach their optimal volume when they're at room temperature. Do not substitute pasteurized egg whites or prepackaged egg whites, as these will not whip up the same as fresh egg whites. Clean the bowl and beaters you'll use to whip egg whites with a mixture of 1 tablespoon salt and 2 tablespoons vinegar (or lemon juice) to ensure that all fat remnants from past recipes have been removed (fat residue will prevent the egg whites from grabbing on to the sides of the bowl, which will cause them to deflate). Rinse well with water and dry.

For daintier meringues, place the mixture in a piping bag fitted with a large rose tip and pipe them onto the prepared sheets; decrease the baking time, and after turning the oven off, check them occasionally, removing them only when they look dry.

Butternut Squash and Sweet Potato Doughnuts (Picarones)

These crispy pillows of anise-scented dough called *picarones* are a cross between funnel cakes and doughnuts. They're draped in luscious syrup called *miel de chancaca*, made with unrefined sugar. Fried dough is always good, but the warm syrup makes these totally irresistible. Peruvians and Chileans eat them on the streets leisurely, particularly during winter months when they offer a warm and comforting respite from the cold. These are meant to be unevenly shaped and are usually fried to order. Make the dough ahead of time in order to give it enough time to rise.

Makes 24–28 picarones

½ pound panela, piloncillo, or dark brown sugar, grated
1 stick Mexican cinnamon (canela)
1 orange, quartered
6 whole cloves
2 packets active dry yeast (¼-ounce each) (see note)
1 cup warm (110°–120°F) water
¼ cup sugar
7 cups all-purpose flour, sifted (plus more for kneading and shaping)
1 pound sweet potatoes, peeled, cooked, and mashed
1 pound butternut squash peeled, seeded, cooked, and mashed
1 teaspoon anise seeds
Vegetable oil for frying

In a medium pot over medium heat, combine the piloncillo, cinnamon, orange, cloves, and 1 cup of water. Stir until the sugar is dissolved; bring to a simmer and cook until the mixture has thickened, about 15 minutes. Cool, cover, and refrigerate it until ready to use.

In a large bowl, combine the yeast, water, and sugar and let it sit for 10 minutes (it should be frothy). Add 5 cups of the flour and the butternut squash, sweet potato, and anise and using a sturdy spatula, mix until well incorporated. Cover with a clean kitchen towel; place it in a draft-free part of your kitchen and allow it to rise for 1 hour (it should double in volume). Punch down the dough and add 1 cup of the flour, stirring until combined. Turn the dough onto a floured surface and knead in the remaining flour until the dough is smooth, about 3 minutes (flouring the surface as needed to prevent the dough from sticking). Cover and let it rest for 10 minutes.

On a floured surface, roll out the dough to ½-inch thickness and using a 3-inch round cutter, cut out rounds. Use a 1-inch round cutter to cut a hole in the center of each. Reroll the scraps (and the holes) and repeat with the rest of the dough. If you don't have round cutters, with floured hands, shape ⅓-cup portions of the dough into 7-inch logs; join the ends and press them together to form circles.

Fit a large baking pan with a metal cooling rack; set aside. In a large skillet with high sides, heat 2–3 inches of oil to 350°F (or use a deep fryer according to the manufacturer's directions). Carefully slide the dough rounds, four at a time, in the oil (they should float immediately in the oil). Fry for 2 minutes on the first side; turn and fry for 1–2 minutes on the other side, or until they're a dark, golden color. Using a slotted spoon (or tongs), transfer them to the prepared rack to drain. See note.

Place them on a large platter and drizzle with the syrup; serve immediately with extra syrup on the side.

⁑ NOTE: If you're not sure if your yeast is still alive, you'll want to test it before you use it. To proof the yeast, stir a packet of yeast and 1 teaspoon sugar into 1 cup of warm (110°–120°F) water. If the mixture froths, the yeast is alive. If it does nothing, then the yeast is old. Toss it away and purchase new yeast.

Picarones are best eaten fresh, but you can freeze leftovers (without the syrup) for up to 1 month; reheat them on a baking pan in a 250°F oven for 10–12 minutes. Make a new batch of the syrup to drizzle over them.

Churros con Chocolate

Churros con Chocolate

This is classic crunchy, crispy, creamy, and sweet fried dough at its best. Churros arrived in Latin America with the Spaniards in the fifteenth century. Today, they are among the most popular street foods. To make your own superfine sugar, whir granulated sugar in a food processor for about a minute. You'll need a good-quality cookie press or a large pastry bag fitted with a large star tip to make these. Every year during the twelve days before Christmas, many Catholics across Latin America celebrate with *posadas*, where participants reenact the plight of Mary and Joseph as they looked for a place to stay on their way to Bethlehem. A group of celebrants stands outside the door singing, asking to be let in; another group inside denies them three times. After the third time, they're invited in and a party ensues. In Guatemala, these celebrations always include serving churros with chocolate.

Serves 12

FOR THE CHURROS
2 cups all-purpose flour
¾ teaspoon salt
1 tablespoon ground cinnamon, divided (see note)
2 cups water
¼ cup canola or vegetable oil plus more for frying the churros
4 large eggs, at room temperature
2 cups superfine sugar

FOR THE SAUCE
1 cup heavy cream
12 ounces semisweet chocolate, chopped
1 tablespoon unsalted butter, at room temperature

In a mixing bowl, whisk together the flour, salt, and 1½ teaspoons of the cinnamon. Sift the mixture into another bowl 3 times.

In a medium pot, bring the water to a boil over medium-high heat; add the ¼ cup of oil and the flour mixture, stirring quickly with a wooden spoon until the dough is smooth. Transfer the dough to an electric mixer with a paddle attachment and beat on high speed for 2 minutes to cool slightly. Add the eggs one at a time, beating well after each addition, adding the next egg only when the first one has been absorbed (each time you add an egg, the dough will appear to fall apart but then will come back together again). After the last egg is added and the dough is mixed well, cover with plastic wrap; let it sit at room temperature for 10–15 minutes or until cool enough to handle.

Meanwhile, make the sauce: In a heavy saucepan, bring the cream to a simmer over medium heat. Turn off the heat, add the chocolate, and let the mixture rest for about 1 minute. Use a rubber spatula to stir the mixture until all of the chocolate has melted; add the butter and stir until incorporated. Keep warm over a water bath until ready to serve.

Combine the superfine sugar and the remaining cinnamon on a large baking sheet; set aside. Fit a large baking pan with a metal cooling rack. In a large pot, heat 2–3 inches of oil to 360°F (or use a deep fryer according to the manufacturer's instructions). Transfer the dough to a cookie press or pastry bag fitted with a large star tip; pipe 5- to 6-inch strips of dough directly into the oil. Fry them, turning once or twice until lightly browned, about 2–3 minutes (see note). Remove them carefully from the oil and drain on the prepared racks for 1 minute. While still warm, roll them in the sugar and cinnamon mixture. Place the finished churros back on the rack and keep warm for up to 1 hour in a 200°F oven, or place them in paper bags to keep crispy at room temperature for up to 2 hours. Serve with the chocolate sauce for dipping.

❊⟩ NOTE: Use Mexican cinnamon (canela) if you can find it and grind it in a spice grinder.

The churros will brown too quickly and remain raw in the center if the oil gets too hot. In this case, remove the pan from the heat and let the oil cool slightly before proceeding with the recipe.

· ·

Coffee Ice Cream
(Helado de Café con Leche)

Coffee-infused custard creates a creamy, smooth, and absolutely divine ice cream. Ice cream goes by many names in Latin America: *nieves*, *helados*, and *mantecados*, among others. It comes in as many flavors and colors as you can imagine. Like many Latin Americans, I was introduced to coffee when I was quite small in the form of sweetened *café con leche* (coffee-flavored milk). I remember swirling the warm liquid in my mouth, sa-

Sweets, Candy, & Ice Cream

voring each sip, and feeling very much like a grownup. This is my cold version of that childhood drink. In Guatemala, the coffee flavor would have come from *esencia*, a concentrated form of coffee extracted from roasted coffee beans. The extraction process is arduous, though, so I prefer to use good-quality espresso powder instead. Making ice cream is very easy: simply create egg-based custard, flavor it, and churn it in an ice cream maker.

Makes 1 quart

  8 large egg yolks
  1½ cups sugar
  2 cups milk
  1½ cups heavy cream
  1 tablespoon instant espresso coffee granules
  1½ teaspoons vanilla extract

Fill a bowl with iced water; set aside. In a large bowl, whisk together the egg yolks and sugar until they are a pale lemony color, about 2 minutes; set aside. In a large saucepan over medium heat, combine the milk and cream. Bring them to a low simmer, stir in the coffee until it is dissolved, and remove from the heat. Slowly add ½ cup of the warm mixture to the egg yolks, whisking vigorously. Add another ½ cup of the warm mixture and whisk again. Add 1 more cup of the cream mixture and whisk to combine. Pour the egg yolk mixture into the saucepan and whisk well with the remaining cream mixture. Return the pan to the heat and cook the custard over medium-low heat, stirring constantly, until it begins to thicken and coats the back of a spoon, about 10–12 minutes (don't let it boil or it will curdle).

Remove the custard from the heat and pass it through a sieve into a large bowl. Set the bowl directly over the iced water and stir until cool to the touch, about 3 minutes; stir in the vanilla. Cover the surface of the custard with a piece of parchment paper to prevent a skin from forming, and cover the bowl with plastic wrap; refrigerate for at least 2 hours (up to 6 hours). Freeze in an ice cream maker according to the manufacturer's instructions until it's of a soft-serve consistency. Transfer to a clean container and freeze for at least 2 hours before serving. ❊

Avocado Ice Cream

Avocado Ice Cream

Avocado ice cream is a common offering in the coastal towns of Brazil, and its smooth and luxurious texture with a deliciously buttery mouth-feel seduces the senses. Most people in the United States are accustomed to using avocados in savory dishes, such as guacamole, but in Latin America it's used in desserts as well. Its high fat content (the monoun-saturated kind that is good for us), helps this ice cream achieve a custardy consistency unlike any other. I've served this to skeptical friends who've become fans. This ice cream is good on its own or topped with slivered, toasted almonds. It's very rich, so serve it at the end of a light meal. Try it and discover what Latin Americans have known for centuries: avocados are good from appetizer to dessert!

Makes 1 quart

> 2 Hass avocados
> 2 tablespoons fresh lemon juice
> 5 large egg yolks
> ¾ cup sugar
> 1½ cups heavy cream
> 1 cup milk
> 1 (14-ounce) can sweetened condensed milk

Slice the avocados lengthwise, discard the pits, and remove the flesh with a spoon to a medium bowl. Add the lemon juice and mash until smooth (you should have anywhere from 1 to 1¼ cups). Cover the bowl with plastic wrap and set aside.

In a large bowl, whisk together the egg yolks and sugar until they are a pale lemony color, about 2 minutes; set aside. In a large saucepan over medium heat, whisk together the cream, milk, and condensed milk; bring the mixture to a low simmer and cook for about 8–10 minutes. Remove from the heat. Slowly add ½ cup of the cream mixture to the egg yolks, whisking vigorously. Add another ½ cup of the cream mixture and whisk again. Add 1 more cup of the cream mixture and whisk to combine. Pour the egg yolk mixture into the saucepan and whisk well with the remaining cream mixture. Return the pan to the heat and cook the custard over medium-low heat, stirring constantly, until it begins to thicken and coats the back of a spoon, about 2–4 minutes (do not let it boil or it will curdle).

Remove the custard from the heat and cool slightly (about 3–5 minutes). Fill a large bowl with iced water; set aside. Add the avocados to the custard and stir until combined. Pass the mixture through a sieve into a large bowl; set the bowl in the iced water and stir until cool to the touch, about 3–5 minutes. Cover the surface of the custard with a piece of parchment paper to prevent a skin from forming, cover the bowl with plastic wrap, and refrigerate for at least 2 hours (up to 6 hours). Freeze it in an ice cream maker according to the manufacturer's instructions until it has a soft-serve consistency. Transfer to a clean container and freeze for at least 2 hours before serving. ❊

Coconut Ice Cream

Coconuts grow abundantly in the coastal areas of Latin America, from Mexico all the way to Brazil, and you'll find plenty of vendors offering similar renditions of this ice cream. This one is sweet and creamy and features a few bits of coconut that give it texture. You'll need an ice cream maker to make this and the other ice creams in this chapter, but it's well worth the investment. I always keep the tub of my machine frozen and ready to go so that I can whip up ice cream on a whim. Serve this one in ice cream cones or in fancy crystal goblets. For a truly decadent dessert, make the chocolate sauce for the churros on page 313 and spoon it generously on top.

Makes 1 quart

    8 large egg yolks
    ¾ cup sugar
    1 cup milk
    1 (14-ounce) can light coconut milk
    1 (14-ounce) can sweetened condensed milk
    1 cup heavy cream
    ½ teaspoon vanilla extract
    ½ cup desiccated coconut (sweetened or unsweetened)

Sweets, Candy, & Ice Cream

Fill a bowl with iced water; set aside. In a large bowl, whisk together the egg yolks and sugar until they are a pale lemony color, about 2 minutes; set aside. In a large saucepan over medium to medium-high heat, whisk together the coconut milk, condensed milk, and cream; bring the mixture to a low simmer and immediately remove the pan from the heat. Slowly add ½ cup of the cream mixture to the egg yolks, whisking vigorously. Add another ½ cup of the cream mixture and whisk again. Add 1 more cup of the cream mixture and whisk to combine. Pour the egg yolk mixture into the saucepan and whisk well with the remaining cream mixture. Return the pan to the heat and cook the custard over medium-low heat, stirring constantly, until it begins to thicken and coats the back of a spoon, about 2–4 minutes (do not let it boil or it will curdle).

Remove the custard from the heat and pass it through a sieve into a large bowl. Set the bowl in the iced water and stir the custard for 3 minutes or until cool to the touch; stir in the vanilla. Cover the surface of the custard with a piece of parchment paper to prevent a skin from forming, cover the bowl with plastic wrap, and refrigerate for at least 2 hours (up to 6 hours). When ready, stir in the coconut and freeze in an ice cream maker according to the manufacturer's instructions until it has a soft-serve consistency. Transfer to a clean container and freeze for at least 2 hours before serving. ❉

THE BEVERAGE CART

You can be eating the most fabulous sandwich or enjoying the most authentic taco, but they won't do you any good if you don't have something equally as delicious to drink with them. You won't run out of options when you walk the streets of Latin America in search of a refreshing beverage. Sure, icy cold margaritas and beer served in glasses with salted rims may be the first things to come to mind, but the drinks you'll find on the streets are typically nonalcoholic. Instead, they're thirst-quenching, colorful drinks made with natural ingredients. Here is a short primer.

On hot summer days, few things are as refreshing as a glass of icy-cold *horchata*. There are many versions of this sweet, milky-white rice drink found in Latin America. It originated in Spain, but it has been part of the beverage compendium on this continent for centuries. In El Salvador, it's made with a tree nut called *morro*, but in most countries, the flavor of the rice milk is always enhanced with almonds and cinnamon. Horchata, although it's sweet, never cloys the palate. It's the ideal beverage to tame the spiciness of any dish.

A short riddle I learned as a child went something like this: "Sky above and sky below and the ocean in the middle. What is it?" The answer is: a coconut. Nothing brings you closer to nature—other than drinking a glass of water, of course—than imbibing the cooling juice of a freshly cut coconut. Whether you are strolling along the beaches of Belize, touring a Brazilian city, or running errands through the streets of Nicaragua, you'll often see coconut vendors with their machetes in hand slicing off just

(opposite, from top) Street ingenuity: a moveable fruit juice bar in Chiapas, Mexico.

Coconut water is nature's most refreshing offering on a hot summer day.

Aguas frescas come in all the colors of the rainbow in Mexico.

320

enough of the tops of the green globes, to leave a thin film of white flesh. When you purchase a coconut, you use a straw to puncture the white veil and drink the nectarous liquid directly from its source. Sweet but not too sweet, a bit tangy but not sour, coconut water is amazingly refreshing. I always make a point of drinking it whenever I can.

The most common beverages you'll find on the streets, however, are those made with fresh fruit. From the *maracuyá* (passion fruit juice) found in Venezuela to the *jugo de marañón* (cashew fruit juice) you'll find in Guatemala, juices are ubiquitous. Mango, tamarind, cantaloupe, watermelon, and even cucumbers are transformed into fresh and natural beverages. Add a bit of milk to the equation and the drinks become *merengadas*.

Within the same family of beverages, you'll find *batidos*, which are smoothies made with fruit, sugar, and ice, and *frescos* or *aguas*, which are fruit juices stirred into sweetened water. If you've ever visited a Mexican market, you've probably seen the colorful spectrum of delicious *aguas* all lined up in giant glass jars. They range from the deep purple *agua de betabel*, made with beets, apples, and oranges, to the yellow *agua de piña*, made with pineapple rinds. In Peru, if the fruits are previously frozen, they're puréed with lots of ice until they develop a texture similar to sorbet, but can be sipped through a straw. These are called *cremoladas*, which when poured over ice become *raspaduras*.

In Central America, limeades—there are no yellow lemons south of the border, instead you'll find key limes or Persian limes—are often mixed with other flavorings like anise seeds or vanilla. *Limonadas*, as they're known in Latin America, abound on the streets as well, and in places like Mexico, they're thickened with chia seeds—yes, the same ones that can be bought to grow as ornamental plants—that swell, become gloppy, and add texture to otherwise smooth drinks. In Venezuela, you can buy *papelón*, limeade sweetened with panela (unrefined sugar).

Latin Americans have been drinking iced herbal teas and floral concoctions for centuries. The most famous is *agua de flor de Jamaica*, the tangy, garnet-red tea made with hibiscus flowers and sweetened with unrefined sugar. In Paraguay, you'll find a cold herbal tea called *tereré*, and in Guatemala, children are often introduced to iced teas with *agua de canela*, made with sweet cinnamon.

Chichas are iced teas made with boiled corn. In Peru, *chicha morada* and *mazamorra* are made with purple corn and pineapple and are always sweetened with unrefined sugar. They taste a bit spicy—like punch. Others made with peanuts and different herbs are thicker.

Latin Americans drink all kinds of warm concoctions on a daily basis, and most of them are served in their own traditional-style mugs. In Mexico and Guatemala, you'll find *atoles*, thick drinks made with corn, plantains, oatmeal, chocolate, or cornstarch, to name just a few options, that are served in thick glasses or in mugs called *pocillos*. In Argentina, Uruguay, and Paraguay, you can get *yerba mate*, a thick and powerful tea lauded for its curative powers; it's steeped in kettles called *pavas* and imbibed with silver straws from bulbous cups called *bombillas*.

A street vendor in Lima, Peru, sells sweets, snacks, and beverages.

Hot chocolate drinks are beloved in Latin America, from the Mexican hot chocolate whipped until frothy, to the Nicaraguan or Costa Rican *pinolillo*, made with ground toasted white corn, cacao, spices, and water. Most famous of all is coffee in all of its permutations, from the *cortaditos* (espresso and steamed milk) of Venezuela and the *café con leche* (coffee with milk) beloved by both children and adults, to the thick *cubanos* drunk from thimble-sized cups with enough power to keep you awake all day.

You won't go thirsty on the streets of Latin America. Why bother drinking sodas when you have such an assortment of natural drinks to choose from? I selected a few of the drinks that pair best with most of the dishes in this book.

Salud, my friends! Here's to your health!

The Beverage Cart

Rice and Almond Milk Smoothie (Horchata de Arroz)

Across Latin America during the summer months, you'll find this refreshing, milky-white drink that has a smooth, sweet taste embellished with a whisper of cinnamon. Since the rice needs to soak, you'll have to start this drink a few hours before you intend to serve it. Don't use converted white rice; it lacks body and will not work in this recipe. Always stir horchata well before serving it with lots of ice. For your next party, serve it spiked with a bit of dark rum. It's delicioso.

Serves 6

> 1 cup long-grain white rice
> ½ cup slivered almonds
> 1½ cups sugar, or to taste, divided
> 1 stick Mexican cinnamon (canela), broken into small pieces
> 7 cups water, divided
> Ice cubes

Place the rice in a medium bowl; cover it with cold water and let it sit at room temperature for at least 5 hours (but no more than 12 hours). Drain the rice and transfer it to a blender; add the almonds, ½ cup of the sugar, and the cinnamon. Add 4 cups of the water; blend on high speed for 2 minutes. Pour the mixture through a very fine sieve into a large bowl. Return the solids in the sieve to the blender; add the remaining water and blend on high speed for 1 minute; pour the mixture through the sieve into the bowl and discard the solids. Line the sieve with a piece of cheesecloth and pour the liquid through the sieve into a large pitcher (this will remove most of the rice solids that may have escaped, although some will always remain and descend to the bottom of the horchata as it sits). Stir in the remaining sugar until dissolved; chill for at least 1 hour before serving. ✳

Mexican Hot Chocolate

In Latin America, rich, thick chocolate is whisked with a special wooden gadget called a *molinillo* until it becomes frothy and totally irresistible. Latin American children learn at an early age to recognize the clicking sound of molinillos rhythmically announcing the comforting flavors to come. Mexican chocolate, which can be found in most grocery stores, is a blend of cacao, sugar, and cinnamon. Some versions are prepared with a bit of vanilla or ground almonds. Oaxacan nuns are credited with being the first to add cinnamon and vanilla to cacao. Milk, believe it or not, is actually a recent addition to this hot drink, which used to be made strictly with water. In fact, in Mexico, when someone is angry, they say they're "boiling like water for chocolate" (estoy como agua para chocolate). Use a whisk to beat the chocolate in this recipe; it won't be as frothy as the chocolate prepared with a *molinillo*, but it will taste just as good. You can use skim or low-fat milk here if you wish, but whole milk yields a much frothier and thicker drink.

Serves 4–6

> 6 ounces Mexican chocolate, coarsely chopped
> 4 cups whole milk, or more, to taste
> ⅛ teaspoon vanilla extract

In a medium pot, heat the chocolate and milk over medium-high heat, stirring with a wooden spatula, until all of the chocolate has melted, about for 4–5 minutes. Let it come to a simmer; reduce the heat to low and whisk until frothy, about 2 minutes. Stir in the vanilla. Serve immediately. ❋

Mexican Hot Chocolate with Cornmeal and Milk Pudding Empanadas (Empanadas de Manjar Blanco) (page 238)

Pineapple Smoothie (Batido de Piña),
Hibiscus Iced Tea (Agua de Rosa de Jamaica)
(page 331), and Rice and Almond Milk
Smoothie (Horchata de Arroz) (page 323)

Pineapple Smoothie (Batido de Piña)

Along the coastal areas of Latin America, you'll find plenty of fruit stands to purchase cool and refreshing fruit drinks called batidos. They're very easy to make and a great way to get kids to consume their daily fruit requirement. Because the acidity of pineapples varies greatly, it's best to taste a piece of the fruit and assess how sweet it is before adding any sugar. This smoothie makes amazing popsicles or paletas; simply pour it into popsicle containers and freeze until solid. Whether you serve it chilled with a straw or frozen on a stick, this tropical drink will undoubtedly refresh your palate.

Serves 4

1 medium pineapple, peeled, cored, and chopped coarsely
1½ cups cold water
¾ cup sugar, or to taste
2 teaspoons fresh lime juice

In a blender, combine the pineapple, water, sugar, and lime juice; blend for 1–2 minutes or until it's smooth and frothy. Taste and adjust the sugar to your liking. Transfer it to a pitcher and serve immediately over ice or chill for up to 2 hours before serving. Stir just before serving. ❋

Banana Smoothie (Batido de Banano)

This is the creamiest smoothie you'll probably ever have. When I was little, my great-grandfather's wife, Gladys, used to make delicious banana smoothies for my brothers and me, just like the ones sold at the Mercado Central in Guatemala City. She claimed hers were much cheaper to make and better than any other. Who was I to argue? And why would I, when we loved her smooth and velvety concoction so much? To make us feel like we were having it on the street, she'd serve it in plastic cups with straws. Sometimes, she'd even splurge and add a red cherry on the top. My great-grandfather—my *abuelito* Alec—was my favorite person in the whole wide world when I was little; his white beard and blue eyes reminded me of Santa Claus. But, I have to say, whenever I had this smoothie, he had a little competition. Here is her recipe to the best of my recollection.

Serves 2

2 ripe bananas, peeled and cut into large chunks
1–1½ cups whole milk
1–2 tablespoons honey, or to taste
½ teaspoon vanilla extract
¾ cup crushed ice

Place all of the ingredients in a blender and blend on high speed until smooth. Serve immediately. ❉

Anise-Scented Limeade
(Limonada con Anís)

Limeade is another favorite *agua fresca*, made with the juice of fresh limes. I will never forget the first time I was invited to my future in-laws' home for an elegant dinner. For dessert, I was presented with a bowl of fluffy seven-minute icing, called *turrón*, and a glass of limeade. As you can imagine, the sugary dessert made me very thirsty, so I immediately reached for the glass in hopes of clearing the sweet taste in my mouth. To my surprise, it was the sourest limeade I had ever had, and it did nothing to help me in my predicament. With this experience in mind, I made a point of sparing others the pain and created this smooth drink. It's one of my husband's favorites. *Limonadas* like this one are found all over the Latin American continent. Since plain water absorbs sugar best without the acid, always sweeten the water first before you add the lime juice. Anise is a frequent addition to sweets in Latin America. Here, the essence of licorice kicks this familiar drink up a notch. Serve it over plenty of ice.

Serves 4–6

> 4 cups water, at room temperature (see note)
> 1½ cups sugar
> 1 cup fresh lime juice
> ¼ teaspoon anise extract

In a one-quart pitcher, combine the water and the sugar and stir with a spatula until the sugar has dissolved. Add the lime juice and anise extract and stir to combine. Chill until it's very cold; serve over ice.

❉⟩ NOTE: It's important that you start with water that is at room temperature so it will absorb all of the sugar. Cold water impedes absorption. If you've ever tried to stir sugar into iced tea, you've probably experienced the frustration of having to add large amounts of sugar before any sweetening occurs.

Cinnamon Iced Tea (Agua de Canela)

Sweet cinnamon and sugar enhance this Latin American iced tea. You'll find it sold at festivals and fairs, and it's often served at children's birthday parties. Mexican cinnamon (canela), also known as Ceylon cinnamon, is sweeter than the kind we generally use in the United States (which comes from the Cassia tree) and has a flavor reminiscent of red hots candy. It's also brittle and easy to break up into pieces, which makes it ideal for grinding into powders. Canela is widely available in Latin stores.

Serves 6–8

> 4 sticks Mexican cinnamon (canela), broken into pieces
> 8 ounces piloncillo (or dark brown sugar)
> 8 cups water

Place the canela and four cups of water in a large pot over high heat. Bring the water to a rolling boil and turn the heat off. Cover and steep for 30 minutes; set aside.

In the meantime, place the piloncillo and the remaining water in a medium pot over medium heat. Using a wooden spoon, break up the piloncillo and stir until it dissolves completely (about 8–10 minutes, depending on how hard the piloncillo is).

Stir the hot sugar syrup into the tea; bring to room temperature. Strain the tea through a sieve into a large pitcher; discard the cinnamon sticks and stir well. Chill and serve over ice. ❈

Hibiscus Iced Tea
(Agua de Rosa de Jamaica)

This garnet-red tea made with dried hibiscus flowers has a tart flavor reminiscent of cranberries and molasses. It's very easy to make and very popular in Mexico and in Guatemala, where it's sold from enormous glass jars that shimmer in the sunlight. Few drinks are as refreshing as this one. Traditionally, it's sweetened with unrefined sugar (called piloncillo, panela, or *raspadura*) that has been shaped into disks or cones. In a pinch, you can substitute dark brown or granulated (white) sugar. I love to serve it over crushed ice.

Serves 6–8

> 2 cups dried hibiscus flowers (also known as Jamaica)
> 8 ounces piloncillo (or dark brown sugar)
> 8 cups water
> Ice

In a medium pot over high heat, combine the hibiscus flowers and 4 cups of the water. When the water reaches a rolling boil, turn off the heat, cover the pot, and let the mixture steep for 15 minutes (the water will turn a bright garnet color; see note). Strain the liquid into a large heat-resistant pitcher or bowl; discard the flowers and let the drink cool.

In the meantime, make a sugar syrup: place the piloncillo and the remaining water in a medium pot over medium heat and stir, breaking up the piloncillo with a wooden spoon until it dissolves completely (about 8–10 minutes, depending on how hard the piloncillo is). Add the sugar syrup to the red liquid and stir to combine; chill until very cold (at least 2 hours). Serve over ice.

✳} NOTE: Hibiscus will stain your clothes, so be careful.

Orangeade (Naranjada)

This is one of the simplest *aguas frescas* (fruit-infused waters) to make. On the streets, you'll see large glass jars filled with these brightly colored flavored waters. This sweet drink is akin to lemonade but less acidic, and it's more refreshing than plain orange juice. This is one of my daughters' favorite drinks on hot summer days. Serve this very well chilled over crushed ice.

Serves 4–6

> 4 cups water
> 1¼ cups sugar
> 1½ cups fresh orange juice
> Mint leaves
> 4 maraschino cherries (optional)

In a one-quart pitcher, combine the water and the sugar; stir with a spatula until the sugar has dissolved. Add the orange juice and stir to combine. Chill until it's very cold; serve over ice, garnished with mint leaves and cherries (if using). ❊

Sources for Ingredients

The following are some excellent sources for items that you may not be able to find in your local grocery store or Latin American tienda.

Cuban Food Market
www.cubanfoodmarket.com
This is *the* mail order source for Cuban ingredients, including bread to make Cuban sandwiches.

Dean & DeLuca
www.deandeluca.com
With many locations around the country, find plenty of herbs and spices, including chile powders, dried Mexican oregano, and annatto seeds.

Frieda's
4465 Corporate Center Drive
Los Alamitos, CA 90720
(800) 241-1771
www.friedas.com
Find dried chiles (guajillo, ancho, pasilla, etc.), plantains, pepitas (raw pumpkin seeds), banana leaves, corn husks, Mexican canela, and piloncillo (or panela).

Goya Foods
www.goya.com
Find Mexican and Central and South American ingredients like precooked corn flour for arepas, canned and frozen yuca, chiltepines and rocoto peppers, ají amarillo (whole and paste), refried beans, hominy, capers, olives, annatto seeds and powder, piloncillo, chipotle chiles in adobo, tortillas, and guava jelly.

La Fe
www.lafe.com
A great source for empanada disks, crema, frozen yuca, and fruit pulps (mango, soursop, etc.).

La Tienda
Williamsburg, Virginia
(800) 710-4304
www.tienda.com
Although it specializes in products from Spain, it has a great line of what it calls "New World products" that include ají amarillo (whole and paste), rocoto peppers (paste), ají panca (paste), quinoa, and smoked paprika.

Melissa's Produce
www.melissas.com
A great source for dried chiles (ancho, guajillo, chipotle, etc.), Mexican cinnamon (canela), banana leaves, corn husks, pepitas (raw pumpkin seeds), piloncillo (or panela), and yuca.

Penzey's Spices
www.penzeys.com
A fantastic source for spices, including ancho chiles (whole and ground), anise seeds, annatto, Mexican canela (called Ceylon soft-stick cinnamon on the website), chipotle, guajillo peppers, coriander, and cumin.

Roland Foods
http://rolandfood.elsstore.com
www.mexgrocer.com/brand-roland.html
A great source for dulce de leche, chiles, hearts of palm, oil, olives, capers, etc.

Selected Reading

Brooks, Shirley Lomax. *Argentina Cooks! Treasured Recipes from the Nine Regions of Argentina*. New York: Hippocrene Books, 2001.

Kennedy, Diana. *The Art of Mexican Cooking: Traditional Mexican Cooking for Aficionados*. New York: Bantam, 1989.

———. *The Essential Cuisines of Mexico*. New York: Clarkson Potter, 2000.

———. *From My Mexican Kitchen: Techniques and Ingredients*. New York: Clarkson Potter, 2003.

Kijac, Maria Baez. *The South American Table: The Flavor and Soul of Authentic Home Cooking from Patagonia to Rio de Janeiro, with 450 Recipes*. New York: Harvard Common Press, 2003.

Laurd, Elisabeth. *The Latin American Kitchen: A Book of Essential Ingredients with over 200 Authentic Recipes*. New York: Kyle Books, 2006.

Lovera, José Rafael. *Food Culture in South America (Food Culture around the World)*. New York: Greenwood Press, 2005.

Ortiz, Elisabeth Lambert, and Nick Caistor. *A Taste of Latin America: Recipes and Stories*. New York: Interlink, 1999.

Palma, Ricardo. *Tradiciones Peruanas*. Sevilla: Editorial Doble, 2007.

Santa María, Francisco de. *Diccionario de Mejicanismos Razonado, Comprobado con Citas de Autoridades Comparado con El De Americanismos Y con Los Vocabularios Provinciales De Los Más Distinguidos Diccionaristas Hispanoamericanos*. Mexico: Ed. Purrua, 1992.

Tannahill, Reay. *Food in History*. London: Penguin, 1988.

Toussaint-Samat, Maguelonne. *The History of Food*. Cambridge, Mass.: Blackwell Publishers Inc., 1994.

Photograph Credits

Index

Italic page numbers refer to photographs.

Ingredients
  basic ingredients, 19–22
  pantry, 18
  preparation of, 16–17, 18, 25
  quality of, 15, 16, 29
  sources for, 333
  substitutions for, 17–18
Italian influences
  in Argentina, 8, 84, 209
  in Peru, 46
Italianos, 132

J
Jalapeños
  Jalapeños, Onions, and Carrots in
    Escabeche, 266, *267*
Jamones del país, 140
Jicama Salad, 34–35
Jocotes, 29
Jugo de marañón, 321

K
Kabobs. *See* Food on a stick
Kennedy, Diana, 159
Kick-in-the-Pants-Spicy Shrimp in
  Chile-Lime Dressing (Aguachile de
  Camarones), 55–56

L
Laguas, 111
Lard, as basic ingredient, 19
Latin American Popsicles (Paletas), 9, 26,
  195, 198, *199*, 327
Latin bowls. *See* Soups and stews
Latin Slaw (Curtido), 41, 69
Layered Potato, Crab, and Avocado Salad
  (Causa Limeña de Cangrejo), 58–59
Lebanese influences
  in Brazil, 8, 173
  in Dominican Republic, 173
  in Mexico, 8, 173
Limonadas
  Limonada con Anís (Anise-Scented
    Limeade), 329
  varieties of, 321
Llapingachos (Ecuadorian Potato,
  Annatto, and Cheese Cakes) with
  Onion Relish, 264, 273, 282–83

Locros, 111
Lomo saltado, 210

M
Macedonia (Tropical Fruit Salad), 35
Maíz, 240
Malanga, 240
Mangos
  Green Mango Salad (Ensalada de Mango
    con Limón, Pepitoria y Chile), 36
Manjar blanco, 238
Mantecados, 296, 314
Maracuyá, 321
Mariquitas (Fried Plantain Chips), 163, 182
Masa, for tamales, 243
Masa harina
  as basic ingredient, 19
  Handmade Corn Tortillas, 63–64
  Shrimp and Masa Empanadas
    (Empanadas de Camarón), 230–32
  for tortillas, 60–62
Masarepa, as basic ingredient, 19
Masitas, 235
Master Dough for South American
  Empanadas, 212–13
Mayan traditions, 89, 119
Mayonnaise
  Corn Stew with Mayonnaise, Cheese
    and Chile Serrano (Esquites), *128*,
    129–30
  Spicy Mayonnaise, *181*, 276–77
Mazamorra, 322
Measuring cups and spoons, 23
Meat. *See* Beef; Chicken; Pork; Sausage;
  Veal
Medianoche, 143
Membrillo con Limón y Sal (Quince
  Salad), 37
Merengadas, 321
Meringues
  Giant Meringues (Espumillas), *308*,
    309–10
  varieties of, 296
Metal cooling racks, 22
Mexico
  aguas frescas, 321, *321*
  atoles, 322
  caldos, 111

Ecuadorian Potato, Annatto, and
Cheese Cakes (Llapingachos) with
Onion Relish, 264, 273, 282–83
French Fries (Papitas Fritas), 175
Layered Potato, Crab, and Avocado
Salad (Causa Limeña de Cangrejo),
58–59
Potato, Chicken, and Corn Stew (Ajíaco
Bogotano), 111, 126–27
Potato and Chorizo Masa Boats (Sopes
de Papa y Chorizo), 65, 66, 67
Sausage and French Fry Toss
(Salchipapas), 179–80, 181
Stuffed Potato Balls (Papas Rellenas),
168–69
tamales made with, 240
Pots and pans
baking pans, 22
Dutch oven, 24
high-sided skillet or enamel-coated
pot, 22
nonstick skillet or griddle, 24
quality of, 24
Pozoles
Green Pozole, 118, 119–20
in Mexico, 112, 116
Red Pozole, 116–17
Presilla, Maricel, 54
Pucheros, 111, 113
Pudding
Cornmeal and Milk Pudding
Empanadas (Empanadas de Manjar
Blanco), 238–39, 325
Rice Pudding (Arroz con Leche), 300
Puerto Rico
Citrus and Garlic–Infused Plantain and
Pork Rinds (Mofongo), 26, 163, 190–91
cuchifritos, 162
fried foods, 163
Fried Plantain Chips (Mariquitas,
Plataninas, or Chifles), 163, 182
pasteles, 240
puestos, 5
Punta Del Este, Uruguay, 139
Pupusas
Bean-Stuffed Masa Cakes (Pupusas de
Frijol Negro), 68, 69, 70
Cheese Pupusas, 71–72
shaping and filling, 70

Q

Quesadillas de Rajas (Poblano and Cheese
Quesadillas), 158, 159–60
Quibes (Bulgur, Beef, and Pine Nut
Fritters), 172, 173–74
Quinces
Miniature Quince Empanadas
(Empanaditas de Membrillo), 235
Quince Salad (Membrillo con Limón y
Sal), 37

R

Radishes
Beef and Radish Soft Tacos (Tacos de
Salpicón), 94–95
Radish Slaw with Pork Rinds (Chojín),
38, 39
Raisins
Corn and Cinnamon Tamales with
Raisins and Cheese (Humintas or
Tamalitos de Elote), 260–61
Ranchos, 5
Raspaduras, 321
Raw foods. See also Ceviches; Salads;
Slaws varieties of, 29–31
Raw Tomatillo Salsa, 269
Recado, 246
Red Chilaquiles, 107–8, 109
Red Pozole, 116–17
Refried Black Beans (Frijoles Negros y
Volteados), 284–85
Reina Pepiadas (Arepas with Chicken and
Avocado Salad), 134, 136–37
Religious festivals, 5–6, 202
Rellenitos (Plantain and Bean Fritters),
163, 178–79
Repulgue method, 211, 218
Rice
Central American Red Beans and Rice
(Gallo Pinto), 290, 291
Mexican Rice (Sopa Seca de Arroz),
292–93
Rice and Almond Milk Smoothie
(Horchata de Arroz), 198, 320, 323,
326
Rice Pudding (Arroz con Leche), 300
as side dish, 264
tamales made with, 240
Rio de Janeiro, Brazil, 173

Ríos, Luisa Fernanda, 228–29
Rocoto peppers, 249
Roasted Tomato Sauce, 265
Ropa vieja, 112, 123
Ruler, 23
Ruz, Elenita, 132

S

Salads. *See also* Slaws
  Arepas with Chicken and Avocado
    Salad (Reina Pepiadas), *134*, 136–37
  Beet Salad Tostadas (Guatemalan
    Enchilada), *80*, 81–82
  Brazilian Hearts of Palm Salad (Salada
    de Palmito), 40
  Green Mango Salad (Ensalada de Mango
    con Limón, Pepitoria y Chile), 36
  Jicama Salad, 34–35
  Layered Potato, Crab, and Avocado
    Salad (Causa Limeña de Cangrejo),
    58–59
  Orange, Onion, and Pepita Salad, 32, *33*
  Quince Salad (Membrillo con Limón y
    Sal), 37
  raw foods, 31
  Tropical Fruit Salad (Macedonia), 35
  Yuca, Cabbage, and Pork Rind Salad
    (Vigorón), *42*, 43–44
Salchipapas (Sausage and French Fry Toss),
  179–80, *181*
Salsas. *See* Sauces
Salteñas
  Pastry Dough for Salteñas, 213–14
  Salteñas de Pollo Bolivianas (Bolivian
    Chicken Empanadas), 220, 221–22
Salvador de Bahia, Brazil, 176
San Andrés, Colombia, 126
Sancocho Panameño (Chicken and Root
  Vegetable Stew), 111, *111*, 124–25, 274
Sandal-Shaped Stuffed Tortillas with
  Assorted Toppings (Huaraches),
  72–74
Sandúches, 132
Sanduiches, 132
Sandwiches
  Arepa Sandwiches with Tomato-
    Enhanced Scrambled Eggs (Arepas
    con Huevos Perico), 156
  Arepas con Queso, *134*, 135–36

Arepas with Chicken and Avocado Salad
  (Reina Pepiadas), *134*, 136–37
Brazilian Roast Beef Sandwich (Bauru),
  157
Chilean Steak and Cheese Sandwich
  (Barros Luco), 144–45
The Cuban Sandwich (Cubano), *142*,
  143–44
"Goat" Sandwich (Chivito Uruguayo),
  138, 139–40
Hot Dogs with Sauerkraut and Avocado
  (Shucos), *152*, 153
Plantain Sandwich with Shredded Beef
  in Annatto Sauce (Patacón Pisao con
  Carne Mechada), 150–51
Poblano and Cheese Quesadillas
  (Quesadillas de Rajas), *158*, 159–60
Pork Burgers with Cabbage Slaw
  (Chimichurris), 145–46, *147*
Sandwiches with Breaded Veal Cutlets
  (Pan con Milanesa or Carlitos),
  148–49
Sausage in a Bun (Choripán) with
  Francisco's Chimichurri, 154, *155*, 272
Sliced Pork Sandwiches with Salsa
  Criolla (Butifarras), 11, 140–41
varieties of, 131–33
Sanguches, 132
Sangüiches, 132
San Salvador, El Salvador, 68
Santamaría, Francisco, 86
Santiago, Chile, 144
São Paulo, Brazil, 157, 173, 296
Sauces
  All-Purpose Tomato Sauce (Salsa
    Casera), *69*, 268
  Avocado Sauce, 268–69
  Avocado-Tomatillo Taco Truck Sauce,
    270, *271*
  Colombian Hot Sauce (Ají
    Colombiano), *205*, *271*, 279
  Corn and Avocado Salsa, *271*, 277
  Ecuadorian Peanut Sauce (Salsa de
    Maní), 273
  "frying," 119
  Golf Sauce (Salsa Golf), 276
  Peruvian Spicy Onion Salsa (Salsa
    Criolla), 140, 249, *251*, *271*, 275
  Raw Tomatillo Salsa, 269

Red Garlic Sauce, *271*, 274
Roasted Tomato Sauce, 265
Sweet Dried Chile Sauce, 278–79
Tomato Sauce, 71–72, 97–98
Sauerkraut
    Hot Dogs with Sauerkraut and Avocado
        (Shucos), *152, 153*
Sausage. *See also* Hot dogs
    Sausage and French Fry Toss
        (Salchipapas), 179–80, *181*
    Sausage in a Bun (Choripán) with
        Francisco's Chimichurri, 154, *155*, 272
Scallops with Creamy Yellow Ají Sauce
    (Tiradito), 46–47
Seafood
    Cod Croquettes (Bacalaítos), 188–89
    Crab Ceviche (Ceviche de Cangrejo), 45
    Flounder Ceviche with Corn Nuts
        (Ceviche de Lenguado), 47–48, *49*
    Fried Squid Ceviche (Ceviche Frito),
        52–53
    Kick-in-the-Pants-Spicy Shrimp in
        Chile-Lime Dressing (Aguachile de
        Camarones), 55–56
    Layered Potato, Crab, and Avocado
        Salad (Causa Limeña de Cangrejo),
        58–59
    raw foods, 30
    Scallops with Creamy Yellow Ají Sauce
        (Tiradito), 46–47
    Seafood and Coconut Stew (Tapado de
        Mariscos), 120–21
    Shrimp and Masa Empanadas
        (Empanadas de Camarón), 230–32
    Shrimp Ceviche, 54–55
    Shrimp Cocktail (Coctel de
        Camarones), 56, *57*
    Tuna Ceviche, 50, *51*
    Tuna Ceviche with Soy Sauce and
        Seaweed (Ceviche Nikkei), 52
    Tuna Empanadas (Empanadas de Atún),
        223–24
Seaweed
    Tuna Ceviche with Soy Sauce and
        Seaweed (Ceviche Nikkei), 52
Serrano chiles
    Corn Stew with Mayonnaise, Cheese,
        and Chile Serrano (Esquites), *128*,
        129–30

Sesame Seed Cookies (Champurradas), 305
Shepherd's-Style Pork and Pineapple
    Tacos (Tacos al Pastor), *104, 105–6*
Shrimp
    Kick-in-the-Pants-Spicy Shrimp in
        Chile-Lime Dressing (Aguachile de
        Camarones), 55–56
    Shrimp and Masa Empanadas
        (Empanadas de Camarón), 230–32
    Shrimp Ceviche, 54–55
    Shrimp Cocktail (Coctel de
        Camarones), 56, *57*
Shucos (Hot Dogs with Sauerkraut and
    Avocado), *152, 153*
Side dishes
    Beef Picadillo, 288–89
    Central American Red Beans and Rice
        (Gallo Pinto), 290, *291*
    Colombian Rolls (Pandebono), 280–81
    Ecuadorian Potato, Annatto, and
        Cheese Cakes (Llapingachos) with
        Onion Relish, 264, 273, 282–83
    Mexican Rice (Sopa Seca de Arroz),
        292–93
    Refried Black Beans (Frijoles Negros y
        Volteados), 284–85
    Traditional Mexican Refried Beans,
        286–87
    varieties of, 9, 13, 111, 262, *263*–64
Skillets
    large, high-sided, 22
    nonstick or griddle, 24
Slaws
    Latin Slaw (Curtido), 41
    Pork Burgers with Cabbage Slaw
        (Chimichurris), 145–46, *147*
    Radish Slaw with Pork Rinds (Chojín),
        38, 39
    raw foods, 31
Sliced Pork Sandwiches with Salsa Criolla
    (Butifarras), 11, 140–41
Sofrito, 156, 168, 223, 292
Sopa Seca de Arroz (Mexican Rice),
    292–93
Sopes
    as flatbread, 62
    Potato and Chorizo Masa Boats (Sopes
        de Papa y Chorizo), 65, *66, 67*
    shaping and frying, 67

Honduran Breakfast Wraps with
Homemade Flour Tortillas (Baleadas),
90–91
Red Chilaquiles, 107–8, *109*
Shepherd's-Style Pork and Pineapple
Tacos (Tacos al Pastor), *104*, 105–6
Tacos with Pork Carnitas, 102–3
varieties of, 86–88
Taíno people, 193
Tamales
assembling in corn husks, *256–57*
banana leaf preparation, 242
Chipilín Tamales, 258–59
Corn and Cinnamon Tamales with
Raisins and Cheese (Humintas *or*
Tamalitos de Elote), 260–61
corn husk preparation, 241–42
Green Chicken Tamales (Tamales
Verdes), *252*, 255–57
Guatemalan Christmas Tamales
(Tamales Colorados), 246–48, *252*
Peruvian Tamales, 249–50, *251*
Pork and Roasted Tomato Tamales
(Chuchitos), 240, *252*, 253–54, 265
varieties of, 240–41
Venezuelan Tamales (Hallacas), 244–45
working with masa, 243
Tamalitos de Elote (Corn and Cinnamon
Tamales with Raisins and Cheese),
260–61
Tamarind, as basic ingredient, 21
Tapado de Mariscos (Seafood and
Coconut Stew), 120–21
Teas
Cinnamon Iced Tea (Agua de Canela),
330
Hibiscus Iced Tea (Agua de Rosa de
Jamaica), *326*, 331
yerba mate, 322
Tentenpiés, 79
Tereré, 322
Tinga, 281
Tiradito (Scallops with Creamy Yellow
Ají Sauce), 46–47
Tomatillos
Avocado-Tomatillo Taco Truck Sauce,
270, *271*
as basic ingredient, 20–21
Raw Tomatillo Salsa, 269

Tomatoes
All-Purpose Tomato Sauce (Salsa
Casera), 69, 268
Arepa Sandwiches with Tomato-
Enhanced Scrambled Eggs (Arepas
con Huevos Perico), 156
Beef Taquitos with Tomato Sauce, *96*,
97–98
Fried Tomato, Basil, and Mozzarella
Empanadas (Empanadas Caprese),
227–28
Grilled Beef (Carne Asada) Tacos with
Roasted Tomato Salsa, 101–2
Pork and Roasted Tomato Tamales
(Chuchitos), 240, *252*, 253–54, 265
Roasted Tomato Sauce, 265
Tomato and Basil Pizza, 84–85
Tomato Sauce, 71–72, 97–98
Toppings. *See* Condiments and
toppings
Tortas, 132
Tortilla press, 23
Tortillas. *See also* Huaraches; Pupusas;
Sopes; Tacos; Tostadas
Guatemalan Hot Dog Wraps (Mixtas),
89
Handmade Corn Tortillas, 63–64
Honduran Breakfast Wraps with
Homemade Flour Tortillas
(Baleadas), 90–91
masa harina for, 60–62
Tortilleras, 6
Tostadas
Beet Salad Tostadas (Guatemalan
Enchilada), *80*, 81–82
tortillas for, 61
Tostadas with Spicy Chicken (Tostadas
de Tinga), 76–77
Tricolor Tostadas (Tostadas de Feria),
78, 79
Tostones (Fried Plantains) with
Guacamole, *142*, 186–87
Totopos, 270
Traditional Mexican Refried Beans,
286–87
Tricolor Tostadas (Tostadas de Feria),
78, 79
Trinidad, Cuba, *6*, *7*
Tropical Fruit Salad (Macedonia), 35